Rethinking Childhood

The Rutgers Series in Childhood Studies

Edited by Myra Bluebond-Langner

Advisory Board

    Joan Jacobs Brumberg

    Perri Klass

    Jill Korbin

    Bambi Schiefflin

    Enid Schildkraut

Rethinking Childhood

EDITED BY
PETER B. PUFALL
RICHARD P. UNSWORTH

RUTGERS UNIVERSITY PRESS
New Brunswick, New Jersey, and London

Library of Congress Cataloging-in-Publication Data

Rethinking childhood / edited by Peter B. Pufall and Richard P. Unsworth.
    p. cm.—(The Rutgers series in childhood studies)
    Includes bibliographical references and index.
    ISBN 0-8135-3364-3 (cloth: alk. paper)—ISBN 0-8135-3365-1 (pbk. : alk. paper)
    1. Children. 2. Children—Social conditions. I. Pufall, Peter B. II. Unsworth,
Richard P. III. Series.

HQ767. 9 .R46 2004
305.23—dc21

2003009389

British Cataloging-in-Publication data for this book is available from the British Library

The publication program of Rutgers University Press is supported by the Board of
Governors of Rutgers, The State University of New Jersey.

Manufactured in the United States of America

The editors dedicate this book to their children and grandchildren,
Abigail, Bill, Eleanor, Elizabeth, Hannah, John, Lewis, Lucy,
Matthew, Matilda, Miles, Molly, Sarah, Teresa, and Thomas,
who might have seen more of us had we not been
Rethinking Childhood

Contents

Preface

This book has had an interesting history. The seed for the undertaking was planted by school psychologist Joy Unsworth, who named the issue for us, pointing to the rapidly growing triad of abuse, neglect, and poverty afflicting children in our society. That concern was reinforced in conversations with Marian Wright Edelman, the founder of the Children's Defense Fund. At Smith College, the concern took root when a group of student leaders, faculty members, and others formed a Coalition for Children, with the purpose of focusing community attention on the welfare of children. The Coalition articulated an agenda and developed a program of education and service around that purpose.

About the same time, two other events occurred. A paper entitled "A Proposal for Responding to the National Childhood Crisis" was presented to members of the Smith faculty by Lester Little, then a professor of history and now director of the American Academy in Rome, Lella Gandini of the School of Education at the University of Massachusetts, and Cathy Weisman Topal, a teacher of visual arts at the Smith College Day School. Their paper called for a sustained and interdisciplinary faculty discussion to determine what resources Smith College might muster to help meet the growing list of conditions adversely affecting the welfare of children in our society.

The second event was the creation of the Kahn Institute for Liberal Studies at Smith, funded by the estate of Smith alumna Louise Kahn, 1931, and her husband, Edmund. The Institute was founded to support "collaborative research among faculty, students and visiting scholars without regard to the traditional boundaries of departments, programs, and academic divisions." Such a purpose was tailor made for a study dealing with children's issues, issues that require the shared concern and common attention of people from many disciplines.

Members of the Coalition for Children then submitted a proposal to the Kahn Institute, asking that the first Kahn Institute project be a year-long study entitled "Exploring Ecologies of Children." The proposal was endorsed and the project was undertaken in 1998–1999. The study began in earnest when a cross-disciplinary group of twenty Kahn Fellows was brought together, ten faculty members and ten senior students. They gathered for weekly seminars and invited visiting Fellows to meet with them and to make public presentations designed to spark widening awareness and attention to the issues outlined in the Little-Gandini-Topal paper. At the end of the year's work, a series of papers by Kahn Fellows summed up the discussions undertaken, the issues addressed, and the progress made in getting an interdisciplinary handle on them.

Then early in the academic year 1999–2000, four of those Kahn Fellows gathered a team of twelve scholars from the United States and the United Kingdom to devise the frame and outline the content of a publication. The planning group placed much of its attention on trying to understand the reason so many of the problems we identify as plagues of our youngest seem unresolvable. Those discussions reinforced our awareness that academic disciplines nominally dedicated to the study of children tended to organize their empirical and practical work around ill-examined assumptions about children. More critically, they tended to study childhood by segmenting its facets and putting them under the methodological glass of each particular academic discipline, rather than seeing children first as persons and only then looking at the behaviors, social settings, and problems of their subjects.

At the end of the planning group's first round of discussions, Stephen Graubard, then the editor of *Daedalus*, the journal of the American Academy of Arts and Sciences, made this clarifying observation: "America's children are scarcely known, . . . [their] voices too rarely heard, their resources rarely acknowledged. . . . Are [we] unwilling to see them as agents, able in many ways to make their own destinies and anxious to do so? Do we take sufficient account of their skills? Do we know what they think?" He suggested that the aim of our publication should be "to contribute to a re-thinking of childhood, . . . to listen to children, to hear them, to see them as having agency, and to understand the restraints under which they live their lives."

This book picks up those themes. Its organization reflects its focus on voice and agency as the writers return to those two themes throughout the chapters that follow. They speak from the variety of perspectives represented by their academic disciplines and professional experience. The twenty writers come from the United States, the United Kingdom, and New Zealand. They represent eleven different fields in the humanities and social sciences and several professional fields. This team of writers has approached its task with a commitment to transparent language in an effort to share as widely as possible a body of inquiry about and observations of children that challenges conventional assumptions.

An important part of the development of the book was the Writers' Conference, which drew the writers together from around the United States and from abroad. In preparation for the conference, the authors wrote chapter drafts and circulated them to their colleagues. They then came to the conference having read the full collection of material drafted for the book. There ensued a vigorous exchange of critiques and ideas, all of which contributed to the quality and direction of the writing, but equally to the emerging sense of what an interdisciplinary project involved. As a result of the Writers' Conference we became not only partners in a common pursuit but beneficiaries of each other's training, experience, and insight. That process required each of us to listen for insight from unfamiliar quarters and to speak and write in accessible terms, forgoing the convenience of academic jargon.

In due course, Rutgers University's Center for Children and Childhood Studies took an interest in this project. The Center's purposes include the development of a series of publications on childhood issues. This book is one of the first of that series. Rutgers University Press described its publishing program thus: "The series will reflect the new view of children and approaches to the study of childhood. . . . Authors will come from a variety of fields including anthropology, criminal justice, history, literature, psychology, religion and sociology. Books will be addressed not only to a scholarly audience, but also to those directly responsible for ministering to children's needs and formulating policies affecting their lives and futures." It is a principal purpose of this book to serve the mission and the audience envisioned by the Center.

Who children are, what they can do, and how they negotiate their relationships with one another, with their parents, and with the larger world around them—these are questions viewed much differently now than they were three or four decades ago. Understanding those changes is of vital importance to a diverse range of institutions and professions, to say nothing of their importance to those who do the parenting in our society. The contemporary field of childhood studies demonstrates unmistakably that children not only have minds of their own but also have values, aspirations, and societies of their own. Some of them overlap significantly with the minds, values, aspirations, and societies of the grownups; but others are original and will become the raw material of their self-determining future. Their victories and defeats, their treasures and dreams are not always the ones adults know or wish for; but they are no less real for all that.

The authors who together have written this book have no illusions that this or any other single work will transform the social equations that inhibit or diminish the well-being of our youngest citizens. The authors have made their contributions, however, with the shared hope that their writing will reveal new insights into the nature of these social equations and will suggest ways in which they can be reformulated. The study reported in this book must be regarded as a work in progress. It is intended to add to those forces—scholarly, political, religious, and educational—already at work to affirm the rights and protect the human dignity of our children.

Acknowledgments

The editors are indebted to the many participants in and contributors to this project. Some have been mentioned already in the Preface, but others deserve special note. Among those who labored consistently to generate the work of the Coalition for Children were Professor Raymond Ducharme and the two principal student leaders in the Coalition, Jane Palmer and Susan Bentsi-Enchill. The book itself would not have come to fruition without the help of the Kahn Institute and its director, Marjorie Senechal, at every step on the way. The editors remain as Senior Fellows of the Institute. The writers have given generously of their time and talent over a period of nearly two years. Six of them (Etheredge, Hearst, Allen, Singer, and the editors) served as Kahn Fellows during the original year of study; and three others (James, Matthews, and Woodhouse) were members of the Advisory Committee. We also owe much to the interest, guidance, and encouragement of Smith College President Ruth Simmons and later to the generous support offered by Acting President John Connelly and Provost Susan Bourque.

Rethinking Childhood

The Imperative and the Process for Rethinking Childhood

Introduction

PETER B. PUFALL
RICHARD P. UNSWORTH

Oᴜʀ ᴀᴛᴛᴇᴍᴘᴛ ɪɴ this book to rethink childhood is based on assumptions about why such a project is necessary at this point in history and about how such a project can be carried out. Once our purpose and methodology were determined, we could find the common underlying themes of our work, could decide on the kinds of questions that need to be asked, and could reflect on what exactly we are looking at when we study children and childhood.

Why Rethink Childhood?

The need for rethinking childhood grows out of both our social ambivalence about children and the particular problems children face in society today.

SOCIAL AMBIVALENCE ABOUT CHILDHOOD

The year is 1912; the setting is Scene 3 of *The Music Man*. Professor Harold Hill is warning the citizens of River City, Iowa, that their children are headed toward a decadent and unpromising future. He tells them, in his best apocalyptic voice, that they fail their children when they refuse to recognize the moral bomb ticking in their midst: a *pool table* has just been installed in the local café. Professor Hill is a traveling salesman. He knows the way to make his living as a total stranger in town: "First you shake them up, then you shake them down."[1]

Adults perennially get shaken up—feeling something between anxiety and despair—when they confront disturbing trends in the present and contemplate the uncertain futures of their children. Sadly, their troubled thoughts are often fully warranted. Violence happens to children, whether imposed by strangers, acquaintances, friends, or family members. Children become the innocent victims of other persons' HIV infections. Advertisers focus on children as a market and persuade them to buy the goods and accompanying life-style that are pitched to them. In some nations, children are drafted into the military, handed guns, then frightened into using them. And everywhere, being sure of their invulnerability, children themselves frequently abandon good sense in favor of testing the limits, only to discover that living beyond limits can exact a high price.

Yet in the face of these vulnerabilities, the human race continues to set great store by its children's potential, counting on them to restore a measure of the justice and civility that has been eroded from society by their parents' generation. When the prophet Isaiah speaks his memorable vision of the "Peaceable Kingdom," where the lion lies down with the lamb, his recitation ends with the epigram "and a little child shall lead them." That view of the child has a certain power to stir hope. In the process, however, it has led some to romanticize children by portraying them as embodiments of innocence, as did the American painter Edward Hicks in his *Peaceable Kingdom* series. In his *Discourse on the Origin of Inequality*, Jean Jacques Rousseau (1755) viewed children as "noble savages" whose inherent sense of morality could be either enhanced or corrupted. But Isaiah's insight still has power. It resists the idealization of children as innocent exemplars of a return to well-being by the whole natural world.

Rethinking childhood makes sense only when it is not driven either by our fears or by our idealizing visions. It is not a call to a romantic view of children that equates respect and active listening with handing over the keys to the kingdom. Rethinking requires a thorough examination of the validity of both sides of this apparent ambivalence in society's estimation of its children—patronizing on the one hand and idealizing on the other. It is a challenge to understand children as they are and where they are by listening to them and understanding the ways in which they act to create their own futures.

This vacillation between darker and lighter estimates of children and childhood has been around from time immemorial. So rethinking childhood is hardly new; it is a perpetual experience and a perpetual challenge. Why then write a book with such a title? The reason is both simple and complex. The simple part is the fact that our puzzlement about childhood never quite subsides. It begins anew whenever the child grows up and has a child. As Erikson (1963) observed, when family works, infant and parent form a healthy attachment. The child has the first experience of trust, and the parent experiences a rebound of hope. But the family never works perfectly, so the trust can be injured and the hope can fade; and we can be driven back to the drawing board to redesign our thinking. The complex part of the process is the fact that, this time around, we may be faced with a challenge and an opportunity that are truly new, at least if we compare the present with recent centuries in Western societies. We may be on the cusp of a paradigm shift in thinking about childhood.

Over many centuries, most of these societies have been more deeply indebted than they know to the ancient Greeks for their understanding of childhood and of the care and regard that should be given children. In Chapter 2 Gareth Matthews points out the durable, indeed intractable, influence of Aristotle's picture of children as a class of humans that has the potential to become, but is never yet fully, human. Being fully human, in the Aristotelian view, assumes some standard of maturity, a standard presumably realized by the already mature and used by them as a measure of the child. This notion of maturity refers to an ephemeral quality of spiritual, intellectual, and moral "finish" that most aspire to but only some achieve.

When we set out to rethink childhood against the backdrop of present knowledge and continuing research about children, we are bound to take into account a number of realities of childhood that require post-Aristotelian and post-Rousseauistic consideration. Present research leads us, time and again, to see children differently than we have in the recent past: as fully human beings, quite apart from any measure we might use to determine their progress toward maturity. Seeing children as fully human means that we see their full humanity in the here and now, not only in a near or distant future. When violence happens to a child, it is not the potential but the actual humanity of a person that is violated. When love is given to or received from children, the reciprocal gift involves actual, not potential, persons. The patronizing habits of mind that adults often display in their interactions with children, particularly those regarded as "disadvantaged," are increasingly understood as inappropriate to the people who face each other across the divide between adult and child.

THE CURRENT PROBLEMATIC NATURE OF CHILDHOOD

Childhood has become particularly problematic in our time. Even within the United States, the most prosperous nation in the world, an estimated 20 percent or more of children are living in poverty. Social institutions that we look to as an immediate source of nurturance for children are failing them. Families dissolve as divorce rates continue to be high; schools fail to meet the educational needs of children, especially minority children.

Childhood is problematic also for reasons beyond those presented by family, school, and neighborhood. Mass media now reach into children's lives in unanticipated ways. As Enola Aird demonstrates in Chapter 8, an entire segment of the advertising industry is aimed specifically at them, with dubious consequences. Many believe that the terrorist acts of September 11, 2001, transformed children's sense of personal safety and whom they might see as a threat to that safety. This public tragedy has alerted us all—scholars, parents, public policymakers, and politicians alike—to the reality that the lives of children are no longer bounded by their homes, schools, or neighborhoods.

A child-centered perspective on these problems can shed light on our understanding of children's present lives and provide insights into the policies and practices that might improve the quality of their lives. By listening to what children say, for example, about poverty, divorce, neighborhood, and schools, contributors to this book are able to offer some new insights into children's experience in each of those circumstances. In their chapter conclusions, many of these authors suggest the kinds of public policy and practice that are in the best interest of children.

How Can We Rethink Childhood?

The social ambivalence about and the problematic nature of childhood are critical reasons for the writing of this book, but we have a further purpose: to frame a new interdisciplinary approach to child study and a new conceptualization of child development. This goal arises from problems with the way we currently study childhood and specifically with the way our academic disciplines approach the study of children.

THE EMERGING PARADIGM

In recent decades, it has dawned on us again that the fundamental human relationship between adults and children needs rethinking, but this time with the benefit of a new paradigm—a new conceptual model or template against which we can test the appropriateness of our thought about any child, about children as a class within our common humanity, and about childhood as an estate, not just a moment, in which fully human transactions occur; Allison James describes the need for such a model more fully in Chapter 1.

Many events have expanded the array of questions we ask about childhood. Not least is the instant availability of knowledge about the state of children's lives the world over. In 2002, an Internet search for childhood-studies centers produced 755,000 related websites in universities and organizations the world over. Most of these were less than ten years old, and many were probably a good deal newer. The sheer mass of thought and inquiry, of available data and interviews, has advanced the knowledge about children at great speed, as Raymond Ducharme's listing of Internet sites makes clear in the Resources for Further Research at the end of the book.

If there is any problem with that phenomenon, it is the fact that the many clusters of scholars addressing these questions too often do their work in isolation from, or at best in parallel with, each other. Each cluster thinks and speaks in the language of its own academic discipline, and communication among these centers is rare. As long as their dialogue continues to be bounded by the conventional academic fences, their separate advances will not cross-pollinate their common thinking. The hard fact is that basic research in the humanities, sciences, and social sciences has not yet spawned the needed working principles for effective interchange among the many disciplines involved in childhood studies. But awareness is rising that those concerned with the well-being of children need to act collectively to develop and use a new paradigm for understanding childhood.

A paradigm is a linguistic or conceptual mold designed to shape thinking. Like a clam's shell, it is the exoskeleton of an idea. And like the shell on a lobster, it can be discarded periodically whenever knowledge outgrows the mold. As we increase our understanding of anything as complex and mysterious as childhood, any paradigm that helps such an understanding come about may itself, in time, have to be shifted.

It will be useful to the reader to keep in mind two levels of meaning ascribed to the term *paradigm*. One classical meaning of paradigm is a set of rules that gives structure or order to a domain of thought or analysis. Once upon a time, when almost every schoolchild recited "amo, amas, amat, amamus, amatis, amant," the recitation of these forms provided a list of paradigms, or examples, for managing to write properly a whole class of Latin verbs. But who conjugates verbs or declines nouns these days? A few schoolchildren and even fewer scholars.

The more common current use of paradigm retains the meaning of model or example, but it relies less on abstract principles of observation alone and more on the messy chaos of actual experience. It connotes the use of examples and metaphors drawn from experience, as well as the use of strictly logical models, to carry out the interpretive work of scholarship. This meaning of paradigm involves a revolution in thinking; and it is fair to ask what happens when, as in any revolution, the establishment is overthrown and the renegades don't yet agree on what the new order should look like. Surely if Charles Dickens were alive, he would be uncomprehending of the way we talk in this book about childhood. A Victorian Englishman's notion of childhood is worlds apart from our descriptions. Equally surely, the scholar or the parent of the late twenty-first century will wonder what we could have been thinking when we identified the constructs of childhood that appear here.

A useful paradigm, then, is one that brings coherence to a field of study in its time and that in the process sets out some intellectual boundaries of the field. But its use imposes a burden because those boundaries can also confine our system of inquiry. So a new paradigm for childhood is ambitious and modest at the same time. It is willing to challenge or break those boundaries that are erected by the scholar's disciplinary "native language," but it is modest in both its tenor and its ambition. Disciplinary distinctiveness is not utterly abandoned for the simple reason that it cannot be. Even when there is a common umbrella term, such as *childhood studies*, we may gather under it a group of scholars who talk about the same topic in quite different terms, terms that may not stand on common axioms.

Nevertheless, the search for a new paradigm is one that can be satisfied only by a model of interpretation that both embraces and then reaches beyond the distinctive conceptual apparatus of these different disciplines. Thinking in terms of a new paradigm requires an intellectually self-transcending effort. For those of us participating in this project, that was one of its principal values. Our religious or social scientific or philosophical or scientific or educational or historical or legal languages had to be used as means of communicating across disciplinary boundaries because children's lives cannot be fully captured inside any one of them.

ASPECTS OF A NEW METHODOLOGY

Right now, a new paradigm of childhood is actively being constructed by the scholars, lawyers, physicians, and teachers (to name but a few) who are willing to share ideas with one another to get a grip on childhood, the better to serve those who are in it and the better to understand what those children could bring to the table of human wisdom and experience at which we all sit, whatever our age. Critical to a new paradigm is a new methodology, a new way of mounting the inquiry and conducting the analysis. We can offer insight into some methodological issues in constructing a new paradigm on two levels. One is more mundane, more recycled than revolutionary. The other flirts with being revolutionary.

RECYCLED METHODOLOGY.   The interview is still the method of choice when seeking to understand children's experiences. In this context recycling an old method achieves a new purpose, particularly if the interview content is examined sharply. How interview questions are framed will have a decisive effect on the responses obtained. So one mode of recycling is to take a hard look at the form of the questions, asking—for instance—whether they are sufficiently open-ended to elicit responses from the personal experiences and the candid attitudes of those interviewed. Children need as much to tell as we need to learn from their telling. As Eileen Lindner points out in Chapter 3, it is not enough to interview children in and about the abstract, as has been the conventional method in the study of children's attitudes about morality. Instead, we have to find ways that are ethically appropriate to find out how children experience the issues of moral choice and decision. Posing questions about hypothetical persons facing hypothetical choices in their hypothetical lives addresses the ethical issue and provides useful information about how children who are emotionally removed from the reality think about it. But we need to construct other methodologies that situate children more immediately within the realities of their lives.

Of course we are not limited to interviews of individual children. Justine Cassell (Chapter 7), Susan Etheredge (Chapter 5), and Matthews (Chapter 2) apply variations on ethnographic research. They enter children's lives to see how they live them as social problem solvers, students, and philosophers. As we take more seriously the challenge of how children understand themselves, their social reality, and the larger world within which their immediate lives are nested, we will discover new methodologies that will put us in a better position to create public policy and practice that are well informed by children's takes on their experience.

RADICAL METHODOLOGY: INTERDISCIPLINARY DISCUSSION. From the outset, the contributors to this book understood the great temptation to stretch or squeeze childhood to fit the Procrustean bed of our own theoretical constructs; and we all reckoned with the fact that our own academic disciplines probably leave out as much as they address by virtue of their own implicit selectivity and prejudice. That reckoning led to spending substantial time discussing the approach we would take to understanding childhood. We dubbed the approach *interdisciplinary*, then took care to say what we meant by the term and to differentiate it from another academic descriptor, *multidisciplinary*. A multidisciplinary publication brings together writings by authors in differing fields who can shed light on the topic at hand. It does not ask the writers to engage with one another, only with the topic. A discussion can be called interdisciplinary in more than a perfunctory fashion when it has certain methodological as well as psychological attributes. It consciously uses a certain interpenetrating language, it is characterized by an abandonment of territoriality, and it engages its participants in active listening.

Using *interpenetrating language* comes down to employing terms that an intelligent inquirer can understand without knowing the shorthand that every academic discipline develops for itself. Those shorthand terms can be as obscure to the outsider as they are illuminating to the insider. Too often they arise from having read the same books, listened to the same lecturers, and been credentialed by the same mentors. To leave behind the safety of one's shorthand means taking the risk that others may regard one as well-meaning but unsophisticated, the academy's ultimate damnation by faint praise. An interpenetrating language has a second characteristic as well. It capitalizes on shared insights and uses them as building blocks for a deeper common inquiry. Interpenetrating language sharpens a question or firms up a construct, especially when it does not arise from one's own field.

Henry Kissinger is credited with saying that academic politics are so vicious because there is so little at stake. He was mistaken. Academic politics become vicious when the wrong things are at stake. Academic territoriality is a matter of claiming sole prospecting rights to a mother lode of insights in one's field. Although it might be loathe to admit it, the average academic department tends to defend its territory as much to protect its budget as to pursue its Truth. Good interdisciplinary discussion emerges when the mental habits of territoriality are dropped and the vulnerability of one's argument is recognized. The *absence of territoriality* is a liberating condition of interdisciplinary conversation. It permits the participants to let down their guard and muster the courage to explore unknown ground with unfamiliar tools.

Active listening is a simple enough concept; it just is not as common as it might be among scholars. It is a sine qua non of interdisciplinary discussion. To listen actively is to focus intently on what the other is saying and to do so without silently framing the reply that will be offered at the earliest opportunity. It involves figuring out the question that needs to be asked next, not in order to nail the error but simply to advance the inquiry. Because active listening is a transaction between persons, it requires listening for the personal as well as the intellectual experience that lies behind an assertion. Finally, active listening involves a measure of self-transcendence, a spiritual commodity not easily come by in intellectually zealous communities.

HOWEVER, RETHINKING CHILDHOOD implies not only the cooperation of disciplines but also a change in the way theorists and practitioners engage each other. For many the current model of engagement is linear. Researchers are the ones who provide basic knowledge about children, and practitioners are the ones who apply that knowledge. This model presumes that the agenda of theorists is the same as that of practitioners. However, they are not always the same, and when this is the case, theorists have nothing to say to practitioners. A shift to an interactive model will do much to dislodge that obstacle. Study and practice share twin purposes, purposes that may not be identical but that are mutually important— one to increase understanding, the other to enable the application of understanding. The study of childhood produces ideas and insights that help practitioners create a valid agenda for serving the best interests of the child.

The Centrality of Voice and Agency

As the contributors to this book went about our work together, *voice* and *agency* became the two foci of our inquiry. These terms were commandeered from our disciplines, not invented by us. They became the most useful tools for weaving the fabric of our general argument. By voice we refer to that cluster of intentions, hopes, grievances, and expectations that children guard as their own. This voice surfaces only when the adult has learned to ask and get out of the way. By agency we refer to the fact that children are much more self-determining actors than we generally think. They measure issues against their own interests and values, they make up their own minds, they take action as a function of their own wills—that is, if the more powerful class, the adults, allows them to do so. Together, the concepts of voice and agency kept us grounded. They also helped us get through the thicket of each other's academic linguistics to understand better what was really being talked about.

The many overlapping dialogues that were part of the creation of this book repeatedly pointed us toward the generative aspects of children's own capabilities, and therefore toward realities that were quite independent of our own ideation. The terms of discussion that emerged made it increasingly clear that the next level of inquiry into childhood will have to predicate that independence and look at children themselves as serious contributors to any further dialogue about them.

Agency and voice serve development in complementary ways. Children act as agents in various ways at any one time in the course of their development; and certainly the range and sophistication of their agency changes over time. In all its varieties, agency means that children's actions affect their worlds and especially their social worlds. Paradoxically, children's agency can go unnoticed by adults until the children are recognized as exercising that agency appropriately in situations that students of children's development have neglected completely. Matthews's study of the child as philosopher (Chapter 2) and Lindner's reflections on the child as theologian (Chapter 3) both reveal the agentive work of children as they grapple with serious questions. This way of understanding agency emphasizes children's quest to make sense of their world and to construct a good fit with it. Voice is an expression of agency. It puts the focus on children's commitment to make known their ability to act on their own behalf, whether to ensure their own interests or to modify the world that surrounds them. The naturally complementary quality of voice and agency drives us to see them as coupled together. It is also the reason we see them as equally necessary components of being fully human.

As social beings, children are inherently agentive, and they voice their views in order to be heard, to persuade, to move others to action. As children act and ask to be heard, they are both building and experiencing their social reality and constructing their identity in the process. Neither their social reality nor their identity are elements in isolation from their social world. They are both parts of a mutual and ongoing construction. Our study of children hinges on understanding that mutuality between voice and agency; and that understanding, in turn, puts us in a more confident position to build on developmental theory and introduce public policy.

New and Recycled Questions

A new paradigm does not simply bring coherence to a field, it identifies questions that need to be asked. Some of them will be newly minted, but others will be old ones that have been newly polished, honed, and put into circulation.

We are unlikely to ask children to bear witness to any serious matter if we do not believe they can discriminate fact from fantasy, right from wrong, or resist the interpretations of authority. However, if a central assumption of our paradigm is that children have both voice and agency, then we want to know also when children's testimony is to be trusted and when it might not be. By emphasizing children's voice and agency we do not enshrine those characteristics. We mean to respect and validate those qualities of childhood, but our respect or validation does not make them infallible or beyond critique. Those who will elaborate a new paradigm for childhood will have a first challenge in the need to formulate those questions that will test the concepts of voice and agency as well as validate them. On the surface this question of when to trust and when not to trust the testimony of another person is the same one we ask of adults, even though, when asked of children, it may entail special subsidiary questions that are unique to their experience, their linguistic competence, and the level of their objectivity.

Although we are not in a position to identify all the primary questions of childhood study, we can note that the source of those questions will necessarily involve more than the customary perspective of the behavioral sciences. The emerging field of applied developmental science has begun this quest (Lerner, Fisher, and Weinberg 2000). The existing disciplinary boundaries now under attack from applied developmental science are those that have distinguished basic and applied developmental study. The first critical move called for by the applied developmentalists is to abandon the notion that scientific research questions are constructed exclusively from existing social and behavioral theory. Those questions can be and often are situated in social realities, not only in the laboratory, the library, or the field study. Natural experiments in many developmental, educational, and behavioral fields are aimed at finding what works well and what does not. The aim is the same for both: we want to know why, and we want to know why not. For example, we want to know what accounts for the fact that some schools work better than most others. What explains the resilience of many youngsters who thrive in schools, neighborhoods, and families that are identified as "high risk" (Robbins and Rutter 1990)? What accounts for the resilience of schools within which African American children thrive academically and culturally, as described by Wade Boykin and Brenda Allen in Chapter 6?

Applied developmental science has been construed broadly as "out-reach research" (Jensen, Hoagwood, and Trickett 1999). Those working within this perspective look to communities for developmental issues that need to be better understood, or they evaluate programs intended to meet the needs and enhance the well-being of children. Applied developmental science has the potential to contribute to experimental and theoretical developmental science, but its first impulse is to be pragmatic. So it tends to ask, "What works that is also palatable, feasible, durable, affordable and sustainable in real world settings?" (Lerner, Fisher, and Weinberg 2000, 14). This emphasis on what works is hardly new. The philosopher John Dewey built much of his pragmatic approach to educational and social questions on this same foundation. Those who would bring together more closely the interests of research and practice should find an intellectual common ground in the approaches to truth questions taken by Dewey and his fellow pragmatists.

In many cases, the questions that emerge from an analysis of children's lives are recycled. The fact that they are not novel should not devalue them. As distinguished an American psychologist and philosopher as William James set out many of his definitive ideas a century ago in *Pragmatism: A New Name for Some Old Ways of Thinking* (1907). It is not surprising that some of the old questions have dropped from sight, but they are still asked in classrooms, homes, doctors' offices, and anywhere children are the focus of our attention and, in particular, anytime we are observing them in their niches. The issue is whether we can refresh and refine those questions to fit the circumstances and experiences of the children of this generation. Many questions that seek to understand children's experience are simply newer versions of familiar ones.

On visiting the website of the United Way of America (www.unitedway.org), one is gratified to see that United Way has an agenda for the needs of children. That gratification is tempered, however, by the absence of questions asked of or by children about their experiences in their schools, families, or neighborhoods, or about being poor. The United Way agenda is driven by concerns with outcomes that adults find reassuring, and is not necessarily about outcomes that children find fulfilling. To be sure, it is important to know whether children are mastering a curriculum; it is also important to know whether they have any idea about what that mastery will mean to their lives beyond the next report card.

The practical and theoretical value of asking children to comment on their lives is simple: it opens an avenue for discovery to those who study childhood in order to serve the best interest of the child. Here are two clear cases: Rhonda Singer (Chapter 12) asked members of youth basketball teams some searching but open-ended questions about what it meant to them to play the game. The answers she got challenged the coaches, most of whom had an agenda that was an imperfect match for the players' agenda. Jan Pryor and Robert Emery (Chapter 10) ferreted out a surprising series of responses from children about their experiences as children of divorced parents. Although some responses were of the sort one might expect, many were not.

These new or recycled questions emerge throughout this book. In many cases, they were the ones posed to children as part of a research inquiry. The fact that the children's responses were neither predictable nor always agreeable is enough to make the point that no substantial gains will be made in understanding what children regard as important about their own circumstance unless their voice is heard by adults who are willing to listen without imposing any implied acceptable responses.

Studying Children and Childhood

If we are to study and understand children in the context of their childhoods, we need to ask "what" is a child and "when" is a child, even though the first question seems too obvious to need asking and the second seems too obscure to elicit an answer.

WHAT IS A CHILD?

The fundamental answer to the question of what is a child is contained in the United Nations Convention on the Rights of Children (CRC). Within the preamble of that document we are asked to bear in mind that "the peoples of the United Nations have, in the Charter, reaffirmed their faith in fundamental human rights and in the dignity and worth of the human person" and "in the Universal Declaration of Human Rights the United Nations has proclaimed that childhood is entitled to special care and assistance." More directly, children are humans who because of their developmental status require special protection. Given that all but two nations ratified the CRC within two years of its endorsement by the United Nations General Assembly, it is clear that, at this time in history, the proposition that children are human beings with rights and dignity is not controversial. Even the United States, one of the two nations that have not ratified the CRC, agrees with the claim that all children are human. Children have not always been viewed as full human beings with rights and dignity; and, in all likelihood, the degree to which signatory nations support the Convention's practical intent depends on what each one perceives to be granted by this claim and what the social cost of those grants will be.

As a legal document, the CRC identifies the rights that flow from being human as "inherent . . . equal . . . and inalienable." In Chapter 13, Barbara Woodhouse partitions these rights into "dignity-based" and "need-based" rights. Dignity-based rights include life, identity (which is realized in name, family, citizenship), expression (the right to form and voice views), association, and privacy. These rights are not granted provisionally; nevertheless, the CRC recognizes that children only gradually gain the necessary competencies to exercise these rights as adults do. The CRC recognizes, as well, that children do not always have the physical, personal, and social power to protect their rights. Hence, children are accorded need-based, or protective, rights, such as the rights to be nurtured, sheltered, educated, and protected from exploitation.

Two dignity-based rights, identity (discussed by Alice Hearst in Chapter 14) and expression (discussed by Woodhouse in Chapter 13), thread their way through every chapter of this book. The implication of having dignity-based rights is that they protect qualities or competencies that are fundamental to being human. Within this book two competencies are examined: agency and voice. The realization of need-based rights is examined explicitly with respect to family (by Pryor and Emery in Chapter 10) and education (by Etheredge in Chapter 5) and again in the discussions of neighborhood (by James Spilsbury and Jill Korbin in Chapter 11) and the marketplace (by Aird in Chapter 8).

From a behavioral perspective, identity is much more than the information contained on a birth certificate or passport; it is expressed in the way we act and the views we put forward. Acknowledging identity as a right granted all humans independent of age means, by extension, that agency and voice are human qualities that exist in some form from infancy. Our biological (Plomin 1989) and psychological uniqueness (Chess and Thomas 1999; Kagan 1984) are well documented. By and large, infants are alike in the repertoire of qualities and actions by which they invite and maintain interactions with others and, in particular with their caregivers. Infants vary temperamentally (Chess and Thomas 1999). Some (referred to as "easy" children) quickly adopt regular sleep and eating patterns, tolerate frustration with little fuss, and respond with smiles and affection when approached; but others (referred to as "difficult" children) do the opposite.

The fact that we refer to these temperamental styles as easy and difficult indicates their social importance. The way an infant behaves is part of a dynamic process of constructing social realities. Chess and Thomas (1999) point out that temperament alone does not determine social relationships; those relationships are also determined by the fit "between the expectations and demands (of an organism's social world) and the organism's own capacities, characteristics, and style of behaving" (3). The key insight is that temperament emerges from the interactions of infants and adults. To extend this point over human development in general, we see childhood as situated within society, and we seek to understand children as they develop through numerous life transitions that are determined by a collective and shared process of change (Corsaro, Molinari, and Rosier 2002).

Two points need to be emphasized at this juncture. One is developed by Jack Meacham in Chapter 4. The perspective we are advocating entails a tripartite set of forces that regulate development. Biology and environment or nature and nurture constitute the more familiar dyad. It has become rather popular to state that neither one nor the other nor the one added to the other explains child development. It is the interaction of both. Curiously the child is missing in all these accounts, or, if present, the child somehow emerges out of the joint action of nature and nurture. Neither of these perspectives offers a satisfactory account of the child; and Meacham takes that lack of an explanation on squarely. He points out that we cannot understand development without including the child as an actor, as a third force in our effort to understand why children develop as they do. That stance means that we are obliged to focus our attention both on the qualities of agency and on the ways these qualities make children participants in their own development.

The second point that needs emphasis is Dewey's long-standing challenge to put the experiencing person at the center of our inquiry. We have not always done well in answering this challenge. Our knowledge of children's experience of poverty, divorce, and many other situations is significantly impoverished when compared with the statistical information we have about children's lives. For example, we have reasonably accurate estimates of the number of children living in poverty, how long they are likely to live there, and their likelihood of continuing to live in poverty when they are adults; but we do not know much of their experience of poverty. How do they perceive themselves, their family, and their social status while living in poverty? How do those perceptions affect whether they feel comfortable or embarrassed when they bring a classmate home from school? How does poverty affect their perceptions of their mothers or fathers as caring parents and providers? Karen Gray's interviews with children (Chapter 9) make it amply clear that there is no single answer to these questions. However, children's descriptions of their lives in poverty reveal more than their awareness of having to do without material things. They reveal the children's sense of the ways in which their own personal lives and their parents' personal lives, typically their mothers' lives, were shaped by poverty.

In seeking to understand children's experience we are setting a very different agenda than the one the United States is currently following. It is common to claim that education is failing our children. The accumulated facts leave little doubt that this claim is true to a greater extent than we can tolerate. If we are to be part of the process of transforming education, however, we need to know more than the facts of children's performance on standardized tests; and we need to do more than focus our energies on teaching children how to pass the new high-stakes tests. We need to know what the shared and collective process of education is. How are the culture of the classroom and the value of education constructed within the classroom? What are we conveying to our children about the value of education?

When we think how poorly the schools are doing, we often focus attention on how poorly our minority children are doing and, in particular, our African American children. Consider African American children's views of the educational process. Many of them would prefer to learn facts and solve problems through communal efforts just as they might prefer to work cooperatively on a task at home. In most schools, however, they are told that learning is an individual and even a competitive task. Moreover, the message they take away is not only that schools are emphasizing a style of learning different from the one deeply rooted in their culture but also that the majority culture disparages the value of learning through communal activity. In Chapter 6 Boykin and Allen review educational research that reinforces this analysis of children's experience and shows that it is not unrelated to educational outcomes. When communal values are honored within the learning process, African American children perform better than when those values are not supported. In fact, where there is acceptance of communal-learning styles, any differences in performance outcomes between African American and other ethnic groups tend to diminish or disappear.

Our answer to the first question—What is a child?—therefore is not limited to characterizing the idealized child as many child-centered perspectives do. We start with the assumption that children are agents and that they have voice even before they have words. These qualities thrust them immediately into the construction of their social reality and make them participants in the continued reconstruction of their agency. Though adults are the principal partners of children as they transform their way of thinking about and acting within their social worlds (Rogoff 1993), even a casual analysis of their social lives indicates that there is more to this transformation than hanging out with adults. They create society with their peers; and they create special social worlds with their friends (Furth 1992; Youniss and Damon 1992). These peer societies are more than places of retreat from the demands of adult society.

Children seem to establish peer relationships with ease and zest. By their preteen years, they do not even have to share the same space in order to have significant peer relationships, as is evident in their constructive participation in the Internet world of Junior Summit (as described by Cassell in Chapter 7). As Cassell shows, when children share a commitment to work for social change, they remain engaged through a long process of identifying a common social problem and a plan of action. Their own society has an integrity-marked resistance to adult intervention, as is illustrated by their ability to create a common bond even though they do not share the same television programs, follow the same sports, and struggle with the same teachers and coursework. They are able to establish forms of trust that can overcome the cultural resentments their adult political leaders refuse to relinquish.

Agency and voice are general qualities of persons that change over the course of development and must be understood within the contexts in which they take place. Children are philosophers, at least when we ask philosophical questions. Their commentaries on poverty, divorce, the purpose of sport, and social capital indicate that as they try to make sense of their own lives, they are also folk sociologists, moralists, cultural anthropologists, psychologists, and theologians, particularly when they seek a spiritual explanation of life while being confronted by their own or another's death. As Matthews points out in Chapter 2, when they speak as philosophers, they do not echo the rather uninspiring philosophical adult formulations about justice, time, and person. As philosophers and theologians, their mental life goes beyond specific experiences of justice meted out at home or school; it goes beyond learning the conventions for telling time; and it probes beyond the vocational roles of mother, teacher, coach that we often use to capture the person's identity.

It would be incorrect to assume that because children have gifts of voice and agency, the goal of childhood study should be to characterize the cognitive characteristics of a developing child. We see that task as the goal of cognitive science and related fields. It would be imprudent to lose sight of what cognitive scientists know about mental life, but the goal of childhood study is broader and always socially situated. Our goal is to listen to children's voices and observe their social actions so that we can understand whether they are experiencing a "good" or "poor" fit within the myriad of their social realties (being a sibling, living with a family, playing a sport, learning an instrument, making sense out of tragedy). Achieving that goal helps us understand how children participate in the construction of these experiences.

WHEN IS A CHILD?

It is common to give a time-normative reading to a "when" question. We often ask, "At what age will a child walk, talk, differentiate fantasy from reality, or know the difference between right and wrong?" Answers to these questions have practical value. They inform us when to expect children to master competencies that are critical to their effective functioning within society. Answers to these questions have empirical value as well. Developmental scientists include time-normative statements in their theories primarily as a measure by which to predict change over time. If their predictions are inaccurate, the validity of their theories is in doubt.

Ideally, theory and practice should be equal partners in childhood study. They share the common goal of wanting to predict when children typically reach behavioral and psychological benchmarks. Together they should be able to offer answers to typical developmental questions of when it is appropriate for children to enter group infant care or start primary school or drive a car or make decisions about living arrangements with divorced parents or become sexually active.

Unfortunately, the ideal of theorists and practitioners working cooperatively toward a common goal is, too often, only an ideal. In some cases, developmental theory has not been in place to guide social practice. In other cases, developmental scientists and practitioners have been looking in different directions. Most societies have not been troubled greatly by this disjunction. We often feel confident that our folk theories and shared intuitions about children provide sufficient guides to our normative decisions. When these decisions are used as general guidelines rather than specific predictions, we can feel reasonably confident that the designated norm will probably do no harm or, at least, little harm when applied in social practice.

For example, the CRC sets eighteen years of age as the upper limit of childhood unless the law of a country grants majority status at an earlier age (Article 1). Clearly, those who drafted the CRC were not convinced that all children make the transition from childhood to adulthood at the same age. Nevertheless they were compelled to designate a terminal age for childhood when dealing with what Woodhouse in Chapter 13 refers to as the paradox of children's rights. Dignity-based rights (life, identity, expression, association, and privacy) are the rights of all human beings independent of age; yet children are thought not to be sufficiently competent to act responsibly with respect to their rights. When do we expect our children to be competent enough to exercise their dignity-based rights autonomously and responsibly? And when is a society free of its obligation to honor children's particular need-based rights?

This paradox cannot be left without one further comment. The CRC describes human rights as "inherent." That description has been taken by some to mean that rights are not socially situated. It is true that an appeal to "inherent" rights can be used to deny that rights are socially created, but it is a logical mistake to equate "situated" with "created." It remains the case that societies differ widely in their views of the exercise of "inherent" rights, some stressing the autonomy of individual persons and others stressing the exercise of rights as a community matter. In both instances, it is reasonable to see human rights as socially situated.

The manner in which the CRC handles the question When is a child? indicates that the "when" is not so much a call for age-normative responses as it is a call to reflect on the meaning of childhood in contrast to both majority and maturity. In Chapter 1 James makes the compelling point that although time-normative answers may appear to be conceptually and in practice trouble free, they are neither. They are theoretically troublesome because of our tendency to associate age with biological growth. Maturation is understood as a biological process more than a developmental process. Hence change is attributed to a biological time clock rather than to children acting within society. An age-induced biological bias may interrupt a search for personal-social transactions as part of the explanation for why our children typically mature when they do.

Some will argue that our fear is overstated that age-normative determinants of childhood make us susceptible to biological explanations and, at the same time, less sensitive than we need be to the ways in which development is socially constructed. That argument is instructive, for biological bias is diminished considerably as we compare cultures and especially as we compare societies that differ vividly in social traditions, the definition of gender roles, and the demands on children to take on community responsibilities. In those cases, we willingly acknowledge that there are many childhoods and that they are socially constructed (for example, Morelli and Tronick 1991). We are less sensitive to cultural variation within the same community, especially when there is a presumed common quest for identity—for example, to be Americans. In this circumstance, we often fail to look carefully to see the ways cultures vary within a pluralistic society. It follows that we do not see that children within different cultures are experiencing different childhoods. Moreover, if we are not seeking out cultural variation, we are not going to identify cultural integrity. And, in turn, we are not likely to discover the particular personal and social resources that are cultivated within each culture.

Seeking to understand the implications of asking When is a child? necessarily reflects back on our effort to answer the question What is a child? In this book, the "when" question is asked less frequently than the "what" question. This is not to diminish its importance. None of the contributing authors doubts that children experience in different ways as they develop, and those differences are germane to our understanding of why children engage their worlds so differently at different points in their lives. As childhood study matures, studies dedicated to such questions of developmental differences will, we presume, become more commonplace.

EXAMINING CHILDREN AS A CLASS

When we study children we are looking at those whose experience is formed in part because they are members of a class. Studies of children in poverty versus children who are not living in poverty or studies of children of divorced parents versus children whose parents are not divorced or studies of girls versus studies of boys are founded on the expectation that children within one group of each pair share experiences that are not shared within the other group of that pair. Singer's interviews of girls and boys in Chapter 12 make it amply clear that they have a different view of the fun of playing youth basketball—not simply because they are girls or boys but because girls and boys bring different values and expectations to recreational sports. Among other differences are their experiences with competition and their views about whether being competitive is appropriate. The childhood of girls is different from the childhood of boys, and much of that difference is based in the experiences that differentiate girl from boy children. If all we can say as students of childhood is that "girls will be girls and boys will be boys," we have done little to advance our understanding of why differences exist. We will not be in a position to recommend changes in public policy if we believe it is in the best interest of girls and boys to be children rather than to be girl or boy children.

We have the potential of constructing more comprehensive theory and more effective policy if we examine the childhoods of children. We need to be able to describe the childhoods of children who are raised in poverty, of those in divorced homes, and as girls or boys. We need to know the social expectations, opportunities, and values that shape the childhoods of each group of children. In what ways are they different? And, just as important, in what ways are they the same? We cannot understand these differences by looking only at statistics about health, school completion, those living in poverty, or those within divorced homes. We need to know how their childhoods differed, and we need to know how they experienced those differences. One of the ways to gain an insight into their experiences is by listening to their voices as they describe their childhoods.

Listening is a simple process. Parents listen to their children in different ways than their teachers do. Sociologists listen to them differently than psychologists do. When we compare notes, we often wonder if we were listening to the same children. In our opinion, this discrepancy is not grounds for despair; this variety of views is the foundation for a textured picture of childhood. Within childhood studies, the construct of childhood is more valid when viewed through the lenses of several disciplines.

The Children of This Book

The children we describe in this book are primarily between three and twelve years of age. The choice is not arbitrary, but neither is it exclusive. As we have seen, the term *childhood* is affixed to a moving target, and it changes as definitions of maturity and dependence change, both historically and sociologically. We took this age range because in common speech it refers to persons no longer infants and not yet adolescents. It also applies conveniently to the group served in early education and in primary and middle schools.

Our focus is also limited in that we give primary attention to children in the United States. But commonalities cut across the experience of childhood in cultures around the world. That comes into view most sharply in Chapter 7, where Cassell describes how children from 139 different countries communicated with each other through the Internet. This chapter gives eloquent testimony to certain important instances of commonality, especially children's ability to cre-ate practical plans for social action.

Rethinking is a process done in time and within some social-historical con-text. Just as we easily grant that the childhoods in two distinctively different cultures are different, we should equally easily grant that childhoods within a culture change with time, sometimes slowly but sometimes quickly. Although we have not attempted to address all these many childhoods, we hope that a close examination of the central themes of this study will enable a better grasp of children's issues worldwide and offer a useful framework for addressing them. The rapid development of the personal computer and the Internet has altered the social worlds in which children act and speak. Traumatic events within com-munities and nations can also accelerate change in the social environments of childhood. We will gain the clearest insight into the experience of children when we know more about those changes and their impact on children and the social construction of childhood. Rethinking childhood is an imperative if we are to remain current in our understanding of children and their welfare.

Note

1. *The Music Man*, written by Meredith Willson and Franklin Lacey, produced by Morton DaCosta for Warner Brothers, 1962.

References

Chess, S., and A. Thomas. 1999. *Goodness of Fit: Clinical Applications from Infancy through Adult Life*. Philadelphia: Brunner/Mazel.

Corsaro, W. A., L. Molinari, and K. B. Rosier. 2002. "Sena and Carlotta: Transition Nar-ratives and Early Education in the United States and Italy." *Human Development* 45:323–348.

Erikson, E. H. 1963. *Childhood and Society*. 2d ed. New York: Norton.

Furth, H. 1992. "The Developmental Origin of Human Societies." In *Piaget's Theory: Pros-pects and Possibilities*, edited by H. Beilin and P. B. Pufall. Hillsdale, N.J.: Erlbaum.

Jensen, P., K. Hoagwood, and E. Trickett. 1999. "Ivory Towers or Earthen Trenches? Com-munity Collaborations to Foster 'Real World' Research." *Applied Developmental Sci-ence* 3 (4): 206–212.

Kagan, J. 1984. *The Nature of the Child*. New York: Basic Books.

Lerner, R. M., C. B. Fisher, and R. A. Weinberg. 2000. "Toward a Science of the People: Promoting Civil Society through the Application of Developmental Science." *De-velopmental Psychology* 71:11–20.

Morelli, G. A., and E. Z. Tronick. 1991. "Parenting and Child Development in the Efe Foragers and Lese Farmers of Zaire." In *Cultural Approaches to Parenting*, edited by M. Bornstein. Hillsdale, N.J.: Erlbaum.

Plomin, R. 1989. *Nature and Nurture: An Introduction to Human Behavioral Genetics*. Pa-cific Grove, Calif.: Brooks/Cole.

Robbins, L., and M. Rutter, eds. 1990. *Straight and Devious Pathways from Childhood to Adulthood*. Cambridge: Cambridge University Press.

Rogoff, B. 1993. "Children's Guided Participation and Participatory Appropriation in Sociocultural Activity." In *Development in Context: Acting and Thinking in Specific Environments*, edited by R. H. Wozniak and K. W. Fischer. Hillsdale, N.J.: Erlbaum.

Youniss, J., and W. Damon. 1992. "Social Construction in Piaget's Theory." In *Piaget's Theory: Prospects and Possibilities*, edited by H. Beilin and P. B. Pufall. Hillsdale, N.J.: Erlbaum.

Part I

Children's Voice and Agency

Understanding Childhood from an Interdisciplinary Perspective

Chapter 1

ALLISON JAMES

Problems and Potentials

Writing of his life growing up in Russia in the last quarter of the nineteenth century, the novelist Maxim Gorky ([1913] 1974) describes how, at the age of eleven, dispatched by his grandfather to go out into the world to make his own living, he became an apprentice shop-boy in the shoe trade. Elsewhere, describing everyday life in the French village of Montaillou in the fourteenth century, the historian Roy Ladurie reveals that at twelve years of age a young male peasant would become a "professional keeper of flocks," the responsibility of looking after flocks being "an age-old feature of rural education" (1980, 73). Similarly, in many parts of the developing world today children of comparable ages make an active contribution to household income and shoulder comparable familial responsibilities. Our current sense of *the child* is a strange figure within these accounts of childhood work. Contemporary children of similar ages in the United States or the United Kingdom are actively discouraged, and often legally forbidden, from participating in even quite elementary decision making about the shape and structure of their everyday lives at home and school (Christensen and James 2001). Thus, although the rights listed under the United Nations Convention on the Rights of the Child (CRC) might suggest that experiences of childhood are universal, the ways these rights come to be exercised and articulated by and for children in the course of their everyday lives vary extensively both within, as well as between, cultures.

The changing expectations of childhood and what children are capable of doing over the course of history and across cultures is only half the problem this chapter addresses. What childhood is and who children are depend not only on where one looks but also on the lens through which that gaze is directed. In this chapter, therefore, I explore a number of questions about ways of seeing childhood and the child and also of conceptualizing and understanding children's own experiences of their lives. In doing so, I consider the different conceptual and methodological insights that disciplinary traditions bring to the study of childhood and the extent to which there is benefit in drawing these insights together. In order to unravel the complexities of children's everyday lives and experiences, we need to develop a common understanding of what we simplify by using the generic term *childhood*. To that end, this chapter lays out the case for and agenda of a new interdisciplinary arena of childhood studies, one in which children's own voices may be heard making an active contribution. The questions central to this chapter are also recurrent themes throughout this book, which sets out to rethink and explore how children in the contemporary United States live in and across different social arenas and settings, where differences of ethnicity, age, gender, health, and economic status combine to produce diversities rather than commonalities in their lives.

The Birth of Childhood Studies

There is nothing new about childhood studies per se—children have long been the subject of academic interest and research. A wealth of literature on childhood—from psychology, sociology, anthropology, education, literature, medical science, law, and social policy—stretches back over the last century. But the claim made here is not that children are a novel focus for research; rather, the novelty lies in the ways the academy currently engages with children and the new directions that are thereby being opened up for further research under the interdisciplinary banner of childhood studies.

The seeds of this engagement were sown in the late 1970s, which saw the gradual emergence and coalescence of particular understandings into a new paradigm of children and childhood, with relevance for a variety of disciplines (Prout and James 1990). Now established as one of the central tenets of contemporary childhood studies, this paradigm has a sixfold agenda that, in large part, is pitched against the assumptions about children and childhood that were the mainstay of traditional developmental psychology and that had been transplanted, untheorized, into other disciplines. In brief, the elements of this paradigm framed the understanding of children and childhood with an evolutionary discourse in which "priority [was] accorded to biology in accounts of infant and early childhood development" (Burman 1994, 35) and to children's biological make-up as the overwhelmingly significant feature of the experience of childhood. In contrast, children's active social engagement with the world was traditionally underplayed and undertheorized, so that, for example, "the dyad of 'social' developmental research [was] almost always the mother-infant," with children's social relationships with other family members and friends accorded relatively little significance (Burman 1994, 43). As Burman pointedly remarks, the result has been "the permeation into research of particular ideological assumptions about the structure of families, about which relationship is the most important for a child, and how the social world is categorized into the domestic and the public" (Burman 1994, 43; see also Woodhead 1990).

Notwithstanding such problems, these ideas were embraced uncritically by other disciplines so that, for sociology at least, the study of children up until the 1970s was usually submerged within family sociology, and children's interests were taken as synonymous with those of their parents. Thus, as Qvortrup (1990, 87) has argued:

> All too often—in both research and policy—it is taken for granted that children and child families are more or less the same unit. . . . This problem arises not because of ill will, but is rather a problem of the sociology of knowledge in the sense that adults are often intoxicated with the view of children as dependents and themselves as fair representatives of children. Adults simply "forget" to raise other perspectives. It is more or less taken for granted that "what is good for the family is good for the child."

This problem was compounded when traditional socialization theory imported developmental psychology wholesale into its explanations, taking for granted the fact that children do come to learn about the social world and failing miserably to explain how exactly they accomplish it (Prout and James 1990). This importation, as Rafky (1973) wryly describes it, was a peculiar "psychologizing" of the social.

Elsewhere, in social work, John Bowlby's theory concerning children's needs and the impact of maternal deprivation on children's futures provided a baseline agenda for intervention in terms of their welfare despite, as Woodhead (1990) argues, there being a large question as to the extent to which such "needs" are innate and universal. As a consequence, in the practice of law and in social policy, children's needs were similarly universalized despite the accumulation of evidence about the importance of the cultural and social context for indicating significant variations in those needs (Woodhead 1990). In Chapter 14 Alice Hearst argues that within the United States this stance may be politically situated and self-serving insofar as meeting these needs is presumed to be the responsibility of the family and not the state.

Against this background, the new paradigm offered a way to break the study of children free from its traditional framing. This paradigm was originally stimulated by the work of the French historian Phillipe Aries (1962), who famously argued that the idea of childhood did not exist in medieval society; the ensuing debate over his ideas (de Mause 1976; Pollock 1983) led to the adoption of the more moderate view that childhood and children's experiences of being a child cannot be regarded as determined simply by their biological development. Instead, the new paradigm argued, children and young people's experiences of growing up are mediated significantly by culture, which produces a diversity, rather than a commonality, of childhoods both cross-culturally and through time (see also Kessen 1979). In the perspective created by this paradigm, the term *childhood* became used as a conceptual classification open to interpretation, and thus variation, rather than a simple and unproblematic description of a universal developmental phase. This shift away from seeing the term *childhood* as an unproblematic and simple descriptor of a material fact of life thus led to widespread recognition, across a range of disciplines, of the socially constructed character of the early phase of the life course. From the 1970s onward researchers began to pay closer attention to the processes and forms through which the construction of childhood takes place. In sum, the new paradigm begins from the social construction of childhood; it argues that the concept of childhood provides "an interpretative frame for contextualizing the early years of human life." This interpretive framework presents "childhood [as] a variable of social analysis . . . [that cannot be] divorced from other variables such as class, gender or ethnicity" (Prout and James 1990, 8).

The socially constructed character of childhood is most clearly demonstrated through examples of children's lives in societies where differing legal, social, and cultural expectations about children—ideas about their competencies, their needs, and their well-being—present radical contrasts with those deemed both normal and necessary for children in the United States. Briggs's (1982) work on Inuit childhood, for example, offers a picture of child rearing that in the United States or Europe would be thought highly inappropriate. Children as young as three years are encouraged by their parents and other family members to participate in conflictive and dangerous interpersonal games in which the child is teased, challenged, and frightened. Often contradictory, these games encourage both nurturant and aggressive values and are seen by Briggs as being integral to Inuit life. They teach children to cope with the real and often hidden dangers of living a hunting and gathering life. Games that tease a child about being abandoned, for example, are appropriate in a "nomadic society with flexible camp compositions, where a child not only can *see* the possibility of being left behind, but has actually experienced the departure—and sometimes the permanent loss—of people s/he is emotionally dependent on" (126). Childhood among the Inuit is in such ways socially and culturally constructed.

Another concern central to the growth of the new paradigm within childhood studies was the wish to explore children's own part in the shaping of childhood. If childhood does not take on a universal form and is not a common social experience determined by biology, then, it was argued, the part children themselves play in shaping their own social world and that of others must be taken into account alongside the socializing they receive in the family or the school. Thus, there is now an insistence within childhood studies that "children are not just the passive subjects of social structures and processes . . . [but] must be seen as active in the construction and determination of their own social lives" (Prout and James 1990, 8). In other words, the new paradigm argues for acknowledgment of the agency of children in shaping the form that "childhood" takes as a structural element within society, as an age-based stratification, and as the everyday social, political, and economic context within which children's lives unfold. And from within this concern grew the demand for children's rights and their advocacy.

By the turn of the century, therefore, the concerns about children being expressed in the academy were different from those that had been discussed prior to the 1970s, with rather different questions being asked across a range of disciplines about childhood and children's experiences of it. Dissenters from within developmental psychology were arguing for a radical de- and re-construction of the mainstream behaviorist and biologist strands of the discipline through placing increased emphasis on the problem of cultural bias. Such a project can, effectively, work to pathologize some childhoods if sufficient acknowledgment is not given to the variations that can arise from different cultural expectations of the behavior and experiences of children (see Richards and Light 1986; Ennew 1986; Woodhead 1990, 1996). Similarly, historians were arguing for the need to recognize the socially constructed character of past childhoods. As Hendrick (1990) persuasively showed, historians must learn to uncover in textual and documentary evidence the desired state of childhood that is on display and, by that means, to see historical commentaries about children as ideological, rather than factual, imperatives for particular kinds of contemporaneous social reform. And although sociology and anthropology began to engage with questions concerning children's own cultural worlds and ideas and their agency, role, and status in society, social-policy and legal specialists became focused on the possibilities for children's citizenship rights and new opportunities for their participation. This coming together of ideas from many different perspectives gave birth to the interdisciplinary character of childhood studies.

The Maturing of Childhood Studies

As with any birth, after the initial excitement and flurry of activity, a long process of maturation has begun for childhood studies. As part of this process, a number of concerns about children and childhood have come to dominate the discussion. Of particular significance now are two: a concern about children's rights and interests and a collective desire to make children's own voices and views audible and recognized within the adult world. Childhood studies pursues those concerns by using its new paradigm to explore and present a child's perspective on the social world. These developments can be contextualized within a wider public discourse both about rights and about child-protection issues.

That these particular concerns have become so central within childhood studies is, arguably, another reflection of the legacy bequeathed to it by developmental psychology—an insistence on the importance of biological age for our understanding of children's lives and behaviors. Of contemporary concern, for example, is the question of children's social status as citizens, their decision-making rights, and the extent to which adults will or will not permit their participation in the social world (James and James 2001; James and James forthcoming). Underlying all these issues is the questioning of age and its significance for children's lives and competence as social actors. Though clearly age is significant in regard to children's physical and mental development—children do grow up over time in a more or less predictable pattern—it is less clear how and in what ways and with what consequences this "fact of life" has been, or should be, incorporated into our understandings and conceptualizations of childhood.

Addressing this issue is of fundamental importance, not least because it can sharpen awareness of the cultural relativity of ideas of "the child" and raise questions about the extent to which "childhood" can be regarded as universal. How far does—or can—a particular child's age speak to his or her social maturity and competence or to the inherent "needs" he or she is supposed to have? What commonalities exist, for instance, in the lives of ten-year-old children worldwide or, indeed, among ten-year-old children living in different parts of the United States? Does the enormous diversity among them, once documented, begin to render "age" a less significant variable than we have traditionally been led to believe? When it comes to shaping social policy and justifying interventions in children's lives, should biological age take precedence over social experience? And, if so, at what stage might age be said to lose its deterministic grip on the shape that our lives take?

A first answer to such questions would appear to be offered by the CRC, which presumes that eighteen is the point when age no longer matters. Under the terms of the CRC, "the child" is defined as anyone under the age of eighteen years. However, even though setting a universal age limit that differentiates, conceptually, between adults and children might seem to offer a theoretical solution to the problem of age—of when a child is not a child—the CRC definition is extraordinarily difficult to put into practice in any meaningful way. Ostensibly included within this singular concept of the child are, for instance, dependent infants and young people who may well have children of their own! Any commonality of interest between these infants and young people would be hard to find. Moreover, in the United States pregnant teenagers constitute a social problem that requires social interventions of some kind (Klerman 1991), while in parts of India marriage at thirteen or fourteen years of age for girls, followed quickly by pregnancy, is not considered unusual. Even within one age grade, as this example underlines, different social experiences and contexts may create such diversity in children's childhoods that age-based comparisons become meaningless.

Writing as a developmental psychologist, Woodhead offers one way to address the problem of age and its definitional role in relation to children. He has argued strongly that we must try to separate out which aspects of children's experiences are clearly determined by their age and developmental stage and which are shaped by social experience. Not to do so, Woodhead believes, would make the universalizing claims of traditional developmental theory sanction a "spurious veneer of coherence on diverse childhood realities" (1996, 8). Such research is particularly important in relation to assessments of psychological development that are modeled on normative assumptions about children's physical growth. Charts of physical growth may easily underestimate the importance of social and cultural experiences for children's intellectual and emotional development. As he goes on, "*Development* implies a uniform progressive growth process towards an implicit, normative image of maturity; *early childhood* suggests that this is (or should be?) a common thread in the experience of young children (girls and boys, deprived and indulged, revered and abused, and so on) whatever their life circumstances" (8–9).

Though in no way wishing to argue against there being some universal biological and psychological needs that all children share, Woodhead rightly suggests that what are often taken as "fundamental needs are actually about socially constructed, contextual needs" (1996, 91). For Woodhead, there is no simple correlation between age and developmental stage. To assume such a correlation risks missing the importance that environmental contexts can have on the ways children mature (see Chapter 4). It also risks obscuring what, in different cultural contexts, is to be regarded as "social" maturity in the child. Thus, "while scientific research offers some universal principles that can inform developmentally appropriate practices, much that is taken to be 'developmentally appropriate' is based on the particular cultural niche in which dominant, expert early child development knowledge has been generated" (Woodhead 1996, 91).

As Woodhead notes, exactly what is social and particular and what is biological and universal may in practice be rather hard to disentangle. This difficulty should not prevent us, however, from asking about the relative weight to be given to each of these spheres for the ways childhood is envisaged in different contexts and about the policies for children that, as a consequence, follow. Nor should it dissuade us from asking how children themselves encounter and experience age-related definitions of themselves and what effect this encounter has on their everyday lives and experiences. As I shall explore later, for example, the rights of sick children to participate in decisions taken about their treatment—rights that in the United Kingdom are enshrined in the Children Act 1989—are rights often tempered by age-related constructions of the self-as-child.

The potential of such an approach has been particularly well illustrated by Archard (1993) in his discussion of children's rights. As he notes, the use of age eighteen as a marker to separate off the world of children from that of adults by denying rights is "based on an alleged correlation between age and some relevant competence" (58). Indeed this lack of rights has become definitional of childhood, setting children apart from the adult world and subjecting them to the hegemonic control of adults. He suggests further that "the young are denied rights because, being young, they are presumed to lack some capacities necessary for the possession of rights" (58). According to Archard, however, age-linked competence is arbitrary on at least two points. First, if rights are associated with achieving the age of eighteen, "then this means seventeen-year-olds on the eve of their eighteenth birthday lack the right but acquire it the next day," even though only a few hours have passed (58). Second, some fifteen- and sixteen-year-olds may well have competencies that a twenty-year-old lacks. The correlation of age with competence is not, therefore, a reliable indicator of whether rights can—or should—be granted in accordance with age. Maturity and social context are key variables here. Though it cannot be disputed that children everywhere develop along roughly the same trajectory en route to adulthood, some children may mature earlier or later than is normal or expected. Furthermore, the purpose or social context within which such maturity or competence might come to matter varies extensively both among and within cultures. For example, in the United Kingdom huge disparities exist between the ages at which the welfare system and the criminal-justice system deem children responsible for their actions. The welfare courts set the marker at sixteen; the criminal system lowers it to ten.

Key Concepts in Childhood Studies

Childhood studies understands the importance of a focus on age not simply because of the empirical questions it raises in relation to social policy. Nor is it of interest only because children's everyday experiences are structured by age through the denying or granting of access to certain aspects of the social world. Over and above these issues, a theoretical focus on age allows us to explore, analytically, how childhood comes to be constituted for children in the social world and, therefore, how we might properly grasp a child's perspective on the social world that takes this cultural shaping of children's experiences into account.

Listening to children's voices is a key feature of the paradigm that lies at the heart of childhood studies, and it is fast becoming a mantra in the policy field. However, as we listen to children we need to be careful that we know how to hear what they are saying, through acknowledging that their words and ideas may be filtered, obscured, or muted by the constructs of childhood that shape our conceptualization of the life course. (See also Roberts 2000.) Age is one of the key filters, if not the most important of such filters.

The concept of the child is an age-related concept. Wherever the boundary is drawn between adults and children the very fact that a boundary can be drawn—and given a numerical definition—is, in itself, significant. Beings of a lesser age are, it would seem, what children are! However, if we were to rest content with this age-based definition of the child and to regard it as simply an unproblematic fact, we would not be acknowledging the import that this peculiar form of ageism can have for children in their everyday lives. A central task for childhood studies is therefore to think about the age-based concept of *child* and the ways it is used and enacted in our constructions of childhood.

Clear distinctions have to be made, for example, between the three concepts—childhood, children, and child. Often these terms are used uncritically, so that *the child* as a singular term comes to represent an entire category of people—children. Such a conflation would never happen in relation to adults except, ironically, with the elderly. Indeed, the idea that *the adult* could be used as a concept to represent adults in general contradicts the very notion of the individual as a fundamental constituent of adulthood in the United States and other developed societies. For young people, however, such generalizations have, traditionally, been seen as unproblematic. Children, it would seem, can be united under a singular umbrella phrase, *the child*. This formulation not only dismisses the individuality of children but also, by collectivizing children, reduces their significance as social actors. This generalization has seemed unproblematic precisely because of our strange obsession with developmental age. It is as if children's growing-upness was the only interesting aspect of children's lives!

Formulations and nomenclature are important. So our social model of disability gives rise to a criticism of the term *the disabled* when used to describe disabled people because it assumes that their disabled bodies define their personhood. Perhaps now is the time for childhood studies to argue against the uncritical use of an age-based term, *the child*, to confer identities on children. In order to make this change, childhood studies has first to address the theoretical and practical outcomes of the interrelationship between the terms *childhood*, *children*, and *the child*. Irrespective of disciplinary perspectives, the consequences of not addressing these theoretical and practical issues would be, as suggested below, to remain firmly locked into the developmental paradigm that has, for so long, held a deterministic grip on our thinking about children.

The term *childhood* is the only one of the three that embraces the temporality of the developmental aspects of children's lives. At its most general level, the concept of childhood works as an analytical term to mark out a particular space in the life course, the temporal space that follows infancy and precedes adulthood. The term *children*, then, is the classificatory label given to the category of people who inhabit that temporal space or time of life called childhood. The term thus becomes an analytic one, used to refer to a collection of individuals who can be structurally grouped together by virtue of their sharing a set of assumed characteristics. Some of these characteristics may be biological (being small, being sexually immature) or developmental (having limited linguistic competence, for example), but other characteristics may be much more social in origin or orientation. Indeed, this social and cultural perspective is part of the process of constructing childhood, framing our conceptions of schoolchildren or street children as opposed to other kinds of children, and enabling us to identify particular kinds of cultural artifacts as belonging specifically to children rather than to adults. Thus, children's television and children's literature, for example, are culturally identified as different by virtue of the content deemed suitable for consumption by children in particular cultural contexts. The fact that this is a social rather than a developmentally-based, age-based distinction can be illustrated by comparing the access to sex-education materials permitted to children in the United Sates and the United Kingdom with the access given to children in Scandinavia and Holland (Hockey and James 2002).

The term *child* should be used to refer to the individual social actor, to the young person whom one meets on the street or the schoolyard. Although as a descriptive label the term *child* does indicate a young person's position in the life course and his or her potential membership in the category *children*, this term is primarily descriptive rather than analytic (unlike childhood or children). It can be argued that our day-to-day encounters with the individual child are necessarily informed by our understanding of the analytical concepts of childhood and children, but they are not—or should not be—dependent on them. If we fail to acknowledge this important point, then, as I argue below, we shall fail to grasp a child's perspective on the social world, whether that of any particular child or of a group of particular children.

Only this dialectical relationship between child and children allows us to make judgments about the competence of this eight-year-old child—the one who stands in front of us—by comparing her competence with our general knowledge of the competence of other eight-year-old children. And our judgement may be that she is advanced or backward *for her age*. But—and this is the crux of the matter—if we were to bracket off age from this understanding, then our judgment and understanding of this child would have to be made according to other kinds of parameters—skill, efficiency, eloquence, or communication of ideas, for example. Thus Solberg (1994) argues that children involved in the fishing industry in Norway, who baited long fishing lines alongside adults, took on the role of worker. Their age-based child status was temporarily suspended and their skill was judged in accordance with the task at hand. In India, children's labor provides subsistence needs and is "essential to ward off the effect of starvation wages on individuals as well as on the families of which they are a part" (Nieuwenhuys 1994, 120).

This is not, however, to suggest that age should always be ignored. Such an undertaking would be absurd and indeed potentially detrimental to children's well-being. However, the possibility of holding age in abeyance as an overarching and determining aspect of who children are and what any particular child might do or say may go a long way to aid us in not just listening to children's voices but also hearing clearly what they have to say, even though prejudices based on class or culture or both may still have a part to play.

Alderson's (1993) research into children's consent to surgery illustrates this point well. It depicts the complex and varied social context within which children of different ages are facilitated or hindered in giving their consent to surgical procedures. In this research, some parents and medical staff were willing to listen to what children had to say about their feelings with respect to their prospective surgery and to respect these feelings in the process of decision making. In other cases children's views were given little credence, the assumption being that the children were not old enough to make informed and competent choices. Alderson depicts the pitfalls of an age-based model of children's competence that ignores their social experience (154):

> One surgeon thought, "The variation is absolutely enormous. I know lots of adults who can't make decisions." . . . [He had] "come across a couple of children who are able to make decisions remarkably well" at eight years, and thought some thirteen-year-olds were "much more sensible than their parents." He repeated the terms "manage" and "deal with," referring to the child's emotional maturity to cope with hard concepts: "If they ask an appropriate question leading on from the information, I think you can assume that you are able to communicate something they've taken in, and understood and can deal with."

As Alderson concludes, "Competence is more influenced by the social context and the child's experience than by innate ability." To respect children means we must not "think in sharp dichotomies of wise adult/immature child, infallible doctor/ignorant patient, but to see wisdom and uncertainty shared among people of varying ages and experience" (1993, 158).

Conclusion: The Future of Childhood Studies

As argued so far, the concepts of childhood and children bear the legacy of deterministic age-based models of the child. They often work to frame our everyday

social relationships with children and thus work as interpretative devices or filters through which children's views and perspectives must pass. Demonstrating
how this process occurs and raising questions about it from a range of disciplinary perspectives has been central to the development of childhood studies. However, another task remains for the future: exploring and understanding how *this*
child—the one who stands in front of us—helps to shape our ideas of childhood
and our expectations of what children can or cannot do. The investigation of
this reciprocal relationship is important for childhood studies and for the attention it can draw to children's perspectives. As one instance of the generalized
category, this child can tell us something about all children and may, through
his or her actions, lead us to shift our thinking about who children are and what
childhood is like. We need to give attention to the dialectical interplay between
these different concepts, for that interplay is at the heart of the construction of
childhood that childhood studies seeks to uncover.

To see children as social actors is core to childhood studies. From that perspective, one sees children both as individuals who participate in the social world
and as members of a social category defined by particular social, historical, and
ideological processes. To take a child's perspective is therefore more than simply listening to the voices of children. It is also acknowledging the temporality
and the processes of change that define the being and becoming of a child. Children contribute to this definition from their own experiences and perceptions.
We need to know much more about their unique contributions.

References

Alderson, P. 1993. *Children's Consent to Surgery*. Milton Keynes, U.K.: Open University
    Press.
Archard, D. 1993. *Children: Rights and Childhood*. London: Routledge.
Aries, P. 1962. *Centuries of Childhood*. London: Cape.
Briggs, J. 1982. "Living Dangerously: The Contradictory Foundations of Value in Cana-
    dian Inuit Society." In *Politics and History in Band Societies*, edited by E. Leacock and
    R. Lee. Cambridge: Cambridge University Press.
Burman, E. 1994. *Deconstructing Developmental Psychology*. London: Routledge.
Christensen, P., and A. James. 2001. "What Are Schools For? The Temporal Experience
    of Children's Learning in Northern England." In *Conceptualizing Child-Adult Rela-
    tions*, edited by L. Alanen and B. Mayall. London: Falmer Press.
de Mause, L., ed. 1976. *The History of Childhood*. London: Souvenir.
Ennew, J. 1986. *The Sexual Exploitation of Children*. Cambridge: Polity Press.
Gorky, M. [1913] 1974. *My Apprenticeship*. London: Penguin.
Hendrick, H. 1990. "Constructions and Reconstructions of British Childhood: An In-
    terpretive Survey, 1800 to the Present." In *Constructing and Reconstructing Childhood:
    Contemporary Issues in the Sociological Study of Childhood*, edited by A. James and A.
    Prout. Basingstoke, U.K.: Falmer Press.
Hockey, J., and A. James. 2002. *Social Identities across the Life Course*. London: Palgrave.
James, A. L., and A. James. 2001. "Tightening the Net: Children, Community and Con-
    trol." *British Journal of Sociology* 52(2): 211–228.

James, A., and A. L. James. Forthcoming. *Teaching Children to Be Children: How Law and Education Policies Instruct the Child*.

Kessen, W. 1979. "The American Child and Other Cultural Inventions." *American Psychologist* 34:815–820.

Klerman, L. V. 1991. "The Association between Adolescent Parenting and Childhood Poverty." In *Children in Poverty*, edited by A. C. Huston. Cambridge: Cambridge University Press.

Ladurie, R. 1980. *Montaillou*. London: Penguin.

Nieuwenhuys, O. 1994. *Children's Lifeworlds: Gender, Welfare, and Labor in the Developing World*. New York: Routledge.

Pollack, L. A. 1983. *Forgotten Children: Parent-Child Relations from 1500–1900*. Cambridge: Cambridge University Press.

Prout, A., and A. James. 1990. "A New Paradigm for the Sociology of Childhood? Provenance, Promise and Problems." In *Constructing and Reconstructing Childhood: Contemporary Issues in the Sociological Study of Childhood*, edited by A. James and A. Prout. Basingstoke, U.K.: Falmer Press.

Qvortrup, J. 1990. "A Voice for Children in Statistical and Social Accounting: A Plea for Children's Right to Be Heard." In *Constructing and Reconstructing Childhood: Contemporary Issues in the Sociological Study of Childhood*, edited by A. James and A. Prout. Basingstoke, U.K.: Falmer Press.

Rafky, D. M. 1973. "Phenomenology and Socialisation: Some Comments on the Assumptions Underlying Socialisation." In *Childhood and Socialisation*, edited by H. P. Dreitzel. London: Collier-Macmillan.

Richards, M., and P. Light, eds. 1986. *Children of Social Worlds*. Cambridge: Polity Press.

Roberts, H. 2000. "Listening to Children: And Hearing Them." In *Research with Children*, edited by P. Christensen and A. James. London: Falmer Press.

Solberg, A. 1994. *Negotiating Childhood: Empirical Investigations and Textual Representations of Children's Work and Everyday Lives*. Stockholm: Nordic Institute for Studies in Urban and Regional Planning.

Woodhead, M. 1990. "Psychology and the Cultural Construction of Children's Needs." In *Constructing and Reconstructing Childhood: Contemporary Issues in the Sociological Study of Childhood*, edited by A. James and A. Prout. Basingstoke, U.K.: Falmer Press.

Woodhead, M. 1996. *In Search of the Rainbow: Pathways to Quality in Large-Scale Programmes for Young Children*. The Hague: Bernard van Leer Foundation.

Children as Philosophers

Chapter 2

GARETH B. MATTHEWS

Sᴛᴇᴠᴇ, ᴛʜʀᴇᴇ ʏᴇᴀʀs ᴏʟᴅ, watched his father eating a banana.

"You don't like bananas, do you, Steve?" commented the father.

"No," agreed Steve; "if you wuz me, you wouldn't like bananas either."

Steve reflected a moment. He began to look puzzled. "Then who would be the daddy?" he asked, simply.

Steve's puzzle is profound. It is a puzzle about what philosophers call "counterfactual identicals." If I were you, who would you be? If George Bush were Al Gore, who would be president now? If Bach were Beethoven, would great romantic symphonies have appeared already in the early eighteenth century, or would the B Minor Mass be a nineteenth-century composition?

In the last several decades philosophers have made significant progress in understanding counterfactual conditionals by appealing to the idea of possible worlds. Consider the counterfactual conditional 'If Steve had been fed bananas as an infant, he would like bananas now.' According to one suggested line of analysis, that conditional is true if, and only if, Steve likes bananas in the possible world otherwise most like our actual world, except that in that world Steve is fed bananas as an infant. Can we understand Steve's own counterfactual conditional ('If you were me, you wouldn't like bananas either') this way? It seems not. The reason is that there is apparently no possible world in which Steve's father *is* Steve. Try supposing there were, and then ask Steve's question: "Then who would be the daddy?"

I should perhaps add that there are a few discussions of counterfactual identicals in the technical philosophical literature that might seem to offer a good basis for responding to Steve's question. But I find none of them satisfactory. I myself have tried several times to write a discussion of the question that I am happy with. I have not succeeded, but I have not given up trying.

38

Steve's question is a wonderful example of philosophical perplexity. Consider now another example, this one from my first book on philosophy and children, *Philosophy and the Young Child*. Ian, six years old, was watching TV when friends of his parents arrived for a visit. His parents' friends had brought along their three children, who immediately took over the TV from Ian and changed the channel from his favorite program to theirs. Annoyed and upset, Ian went out to the kitchen to complain to his mother. "Mother," Ian asked in frustration, "why is it better for three people to be selfish than for one?" (Matthews 1980, 28). Ian's mother told me this story when she learned that I was interested in philosophical thinking in children. She had remembered the occasion quite vividly because, as she told me, she had felt that her response to Ian had been inadequate. She had first reacted to the child's expressions of annoyance and frustration by making some comment to the effect that the three visiting children would, no doubt, not have enjoyed watching Ian's favorite program. This way, at least, three people were enjoying themselves instead of just one—namely, Ian.

Ian's reply to his mother, born of his own frustration and annoyance, presents a serious challenge to classical utilitarianism. According to classical utilitarianism we should always choose the option that would maximize utility, which is usually thought of as total pleasure or happiness. Many of us have the strong intuition that we should produce as much happiness as we can—and as little pain and suffering. It is the strength of this intuition that makes utilitarianism, as an ethical theory, so plausible.

Utilitarianism has not had clear sailing in philosophy. In fact, I think it is correct to say that no interesting philosophical theory has ever had completely clear sailing. I won't stop here to list the difficulties that plague utilitarianism. But I will say that I myself consider Ian's annoyed question an interesting basis for an important criticism of utilitarianism, and in this I am not alone. The renowned English philosopher Elizabeth Anscombe, who was herself a lifelong critic of utilitarianism, once used Ian's question in a lecture at Oxford on what's wrong with utilitarianism. For Anscombe an ethical theory is defective to the degree that it claims we have the obligation to produce as much overall happiness as we can, even if we thereby encourage selfishness. Ian's question suggests that very point. And thus the question of a six-year-old has taken its place in the long debate over the sufficiency of utilitarianism as an adequate account of morality.

I don't know whether Ian was himself in the grip of philosophical perplexity when he asked the question. Perhaps he raised it simply to win a debater's point with his mother. We have no way of finding out now, so many years later. But at least we can say that anyone who finds classical utilitarianism plausible and seeks to defend it against objections had better try to think of a good response to Ian's question.[1]

What should we do when the children around us become perplexed? Or get us perplexed? If the perplexity rests on simple ignorance of some relevant fact, we should doubtless enlighten the child or seek help ourselves in a reliable reference work—say, an encyclopedia. But suppose the perplexity is philosophical. Suppose your own child, or a child in your classroom, is perplexed about counterfactual conditionals such as 'If I were you, who would you be?' or about the adequacy of utilitarianism for dealing with moral problems. In that case the best response is to have a discussion with the child. Discussion honors the child by taking the child's question or challenge seriously. Adult and child together may be able to work out a reasonably satisfactory solution. And, even if they don't, they can have some good philosophical fun together trying.

OUR STANDARD WAY of thinking about childhood owes much to Aristotle. Aristotle, as you may know, tells us that there are four different sorts of causality.[2] One of the four is Final Causality, and another is Formal Causality. Aristotle thinks of the Final Cause of a living organism as the function that organism normally performs when it reaches maturity. He thinks of the Formal Cause of the organism as the form or structure it normally has in maturity, where that form or structure is what enables the organism to perform its normal functions well. According to this picture, a human child is to be understood as an immature specimen of the organism type *human*, which, by nature, has the potential to develop into a mature specimen with the structure, form, and function of a normal or standard adult.

Although most adults in our society have never read any Aristotle, they tend to think of children in this Aristotelian way. A child is for them primarily a potential adult. Thus we often say, "I wonder what kind of person she will be," or "I wonder how he is going to turn out." Having this conception of childhood in mind, adults consider that their fundamental responsibility toward their children is to provide the kind of supportive environment those children need to develop into normal adults. Normal, mature adults are supposed to have the biological and psychological structures in place that enable them to perform the functions we assume that normal, standard adults can perform.

One trouble with this Aristotelian picture is that it makes no room for philosophy. And one reason it does not is that normal, standard adults in our society are not philosophical. If they have had a college education, they might have taken a philosophy course or two. But, in the typical case, that philosophy course has little effect on what they think about in the course of the day or on how they orient themselves to their experience, to the world they live in, or to the society they think they ought to have.

Because most adults do not concern themselves with philosophical questions, it is hardly surprising that, typically, they fail to pick up on the philosophical questions the children around them raise or the philosophical comments they make or the philosophical reasoning they develop. Nor is it surprising that adults usually make no effort to raise philosophical questions with their children or set aside time to reflect with children on philosophical issues.

In fact, what I am calling the "Aristotelian conception" of childhood insulates adults from appreciating the philosophical comments, questions, and reasoning that the children around them come up with. Being themselves, presumably, mature specimens of the species *human being*, adults naturally assume that they must have the cognitive means immediately available to them to deal with any significant issues their children can formulate. Because these adults won't, typically, have worked out any very good responses to philosophical issues, they often simply do not hear what is philosophically interesting or challenging about what their children have to say. Moreover, it doesn't occur to them that it might be appropriate to venture into unfamiliar territory and explore issues with their children that normal, standard adults do not, as a general thing, spend any time thinking about. But by ignoring the possibility of philosophical reflection and dialogue with their children, adults impoverish their relationship to those children, underestimate the cognitive capacities of children, and make their days of childcare and teaching much more dreary and boring than they need to be.

There are other, nonphilosophical, respects in which the Aristotelian conception of childhood impoverishes our relationship with our children and deprives those children of the respect they deserve. It is quite clear, for example, that, as children of four or five or six years of age, each of us was much more likely to produce a painting or drawing of genuinely aesthetic value than we are now at forty or fifty or sixty. But, for most adults, the recognition of this fact goes no further than assuming that it is appropriate to put a child's drawing up on the refrigerator door or display it in the schoolroom for parents' day. In general, adults are much more likely to denigrate the art of Paul Klee or Joan Miró or Jean Dubuffet for being childlike ("My child could paint that!") than they are to assign real aesthetic value to a child's work for being Klee-like or Miró-like or Dubuffet-like (Fineberg 1997).

But my theme here is children as philosophers, not children as artists or, for that matter, children as poets or linguists, though they are also, on average, much better at writing poetry and learning languages than the average adult. So let me buttress my case by giving examples of what happens when one deliberately encourages children to reflect on philosophical questions.

THE WORLD, AS SOCRATES tried to tell us, and as many children independently recognize, is a perplexing place. The world is a place in which things like this are true: "If I concentrate on making as many people happy as I can, I might just end up making more people selfish." Or "If you were me, you wouldn't like bananas, either, even though, it seems, there is, in fact, no possible world in which you are me."

In addition to respecting perplexities our children naturally give expression to and sometimes discussing those perplexities with them, even when we aren't at all sure how to resolve them, should we ever try to introduce an interesting perplexity to our children? Of course we should, especially when the perplexity is a profound one that, in our best judgment, children ought to think about. In my book *Dialogues with Children* (Matthews 1984), I report on a philosophy class in St. Mary's Music School, in Edinburgh, Scotland, in 1982–1983 in which I did just that. I made up stories for that class that presented recognized philosophical issues as questions that a child might raise and get perplexed about.

More recently I have made up stories that give expression to perplexities more clearly tied to specific texts from the history of philosophy. Plato is a good source for such stories. Consider this passage from Plato's dialogue *Gorgias* (494cd):

SOCRATES: Tell me now, [Callicles,] whether a man who has an itch and scratches it and can scratch to his heart's content, scratching his whole life long, can also live happily.
CALLICLES: What nonsense, Socrates. You're a regular crowd pleaser.
SOCRATES: That's just how I shocked Polus and Gorgias and made them ashamed. You certainly won't be shocked, however, or ashamed, for you're a brave man. Just answer me, please.
CALLICLES: I say that even the man who scratches would have a pleasant life.
SOCRATES: And if a pleasant one, a happy one, too?
CALLICLES: Yes, indeed.

Now here is a story I made up based on the Platonic passage:

Total Happiness

"What happened in school today, Tony?" asked Tony's mother as she served him his helping of spaghetti and meatballs. The Allen family was seated around the dinner table for their evening meal.

"Actually, there was something kind of cool," replied Tony. "This new kid in the class, I think his name is Roy, he cracked everybody up by something he said."

"What did he say?" asked Tony's sister, Heather.

"Well, you see," explained Tony, "our teacher, Ms. Hernandez, was talking about this story in which some kid said that she wanted to be totally happy. Ms. Hernandez asked us if we could think of a time when we were totally happy."

"That's an interesting question," put in Tony's father.

"Yeah, well, what this kid, Roy, said was that if he had an insect bite on his seat, you know, on his rear end, and it itched like crazy and he could scratch it as hard as he wanted to, he would be totally happy."

"That's pretty gross," said Heather, making an ugly face.

"Yeah, it was pretty gross all right," Tony agreed, "but it cracked everybody up. Kids laughed so loud you couldn't hear Ms. Hernandez trying to get us to shut up."

"That was a disgusting thing to say," said Tony's mother disapprovingly.

"Yeah," agreed Heather, "it was a yucky thing to say, but, you know, it's right! If scratching a very itchy insect bite gives you so much pleasure that, at that moment, you don't want anything else, then you're totally happy."

"I wouldn't call that total happiness," protested Tony.

"Why not?" insisted Heather; "total happiness is just enjoying something, it doesn't matter what it is—scratching an insect bite, stuffing yourself with chocolate cake, whatever—enjoying it so much that you don't at that time want anything else. Do you have some other explanation of what total happiness is?"

Tony decided to change the subject. He wished he hadn't told his family about what Roy had said in school. He didn't think Heather was right about what total happiness is, but he didn't know how to prove she was wrong. She was always winning arguments. He hated that.

Still, Tony was puzzled about what happiness is and especially about what total happiness would be. Would it be just enjoying something so much that the thought of everything else is blanked out? Somehow that didn't seem right to him. But what could he say about total happiness that he could use as a defense against Heather?

I discussed this story with a group of fifth-graders in an elementary school in Northampton, Massachusetts. Here is a summary of that discussion.

Simon began the discussion by stating Heather's thesis: Total happiness is enjoying something so much that you don't want anything else. Juliane then made a comment that made clear how limited the idea is. "Total happiness," she said, "is enjoying what you are doing right now and not thinking of all the other things that you want." Andrew brought home this limitation with a simple example. "You could be playing with something at your desk and not paying attention to anything else," he pointed out, "and that would then count as total happiness."

Matt didn't want to accept the idea that one could be totally happy at the moment by just being totally satisfied at that time. For total happiness, he required some major accomplishment, such as playing football and being the best wide receiver ever. If you did that, he said, you could be happy for life. Nathan seemed to agree. "Even after you retire," he said, "you could have the satisfaction of knowing that you were the best."

Marissa was skeptical. "You can get bored doing what you do best," she said. Maya had reservations of another sort. "You can't be happy forever," she said, simply; "sad things will happen." Kristhle put the point more poetically, "Happiness," she said, "fades like a smile."

Mary suggested that if you concentrate on yourself, you might succeed in making yourself totally happy. "But if you are rich and famous," Juliane warned, "some people won't like you." Mary emphasized the vulnerability of us all to bad fortune. "Something bad can always happen," she warned, "something not in your control."

In the end, the children in this class decided that the idea of total happiness was an illusion. "You can be overall happy," they agreed, "but not totally happy."

ANOTHER STORY I WROTE for that same group of children took its inspiration from Book IV of Plato's *Republic*, where Socrates offers an argument for saying that the soul, or self, must have different parts. Here is the story I wrote:

Parts of Yourself

ANNA: "Dad, do you think that you've got parts?"

FATHER: "Well, of course, Anna. I have two legs, two arms, a body, and a
    head. Those are all parts of me." Anna's father was just settling into his
    recliner in front of the TV to watch a football game.

ANNA: "No, that's not what I mean. Like when we were just eating
    Thanksgiving dinner earlier today, I had already eaten so much that I
    was about to pop. But Mom had made brownies to go with the ice
    cream for dessert and she said that since it was Thanksgiving and all, I
    could eat as many as brownies I wanted. So I ate two of them. Then,
    you could say, part of me wanted another brownie, but part of me said I
    had better stop so I wouldn't get sick. Do you think I really have differ-
    ent parts like that, one that wants to eat more and more brownies and
    one that is sensible and says that I had better stop?"

FATHER: "Well, why not say that? Why not say you have a greedy part of
    you that always wants to eat more brownies and a reasonable part that
    tells you when to stop?"

ANNA: "That's what my friend Tony says. He says you have different parts,
    and one part wants to do one thing and the other part wants to do
    something else instead. We were having an argument about that at
    lunch yesterday in the school cafeteria. I said that saying things like
    that was, you know, just a way of talking. We don't really have any

parts like that, I said. It's just that we have different wants, you know, different desires. And sometimes we realize that we can't satisfy all our desires. We can't, for example, satisfy the desire to eat more and more brownies and also satisfy the desire not to get sick. So the desire to have another brownie fights with the desire not to get sick."

FATHER: "That sounds pretty sensible to me."

ANNA: "But get this! What Tony said was that desires don't just float around in your mind like leaves on a pond. You don't have a desire unless it's you that wants something. But it can't be both you that wants another brownie and also you that wants to stop eating them to avoid getting sick."

FATHER: "Why not?"

ANNA: "Well, Tony said that that would be like saying that you are sitting still and you are also moving. Part of you could be moving, like your hand, and part sitting still. But you, as a whole, can't be doing both. Do you want to know what I said to that?"

FATHER: "Sure, tell me, Anna."

ANNA: "I said, and I'm really proud of myself for thinking of this, I said you can be sitting in the school bus and all of you could be sitting still in your seat, but yet all of you could be moving because the school bus is moving."

FATHER: "That's pretty clever, I have to admit."

ANNA: "Yeah, but Tony had an answer to that too. He's so smart. He said that you can't, all of you, be both moving and sitting still with respect to the same thing. So you can't, all of you, be both moving and also sitting still with respect to the ground. Similarly, with respect to the last brownie sitting on the plate in front of you, you can't, all of you, both want it and not want it. But part of you can want it and another part not want it. Do you think he's right about that?"

FATHER: "I don't know, Anna. But I want to watch the football game now."

ANNA: "Oh Dad, I wish you'd help me. . . . I guess I'll just have to figure this out for myself. Do I really have different parts like that or not? That's what I want to know."

I discussed this story with fifth graders in two different classes. Both classes began their discussion by focusing on the analogy in the story between bodily movement and desire. Tony, in the story, had said that you can't be both sitting still and moving at the same time. But, he had added, part of you—say, your hand—could be moving and the rest of you sitting still. Anna had pointed out that you could be sitting in a school bus that was moving. Then all of you might be both sitting still and also, at the same time, all of you moving. But the sitting still and the moving would be with respect to different things. Thus all of you could be sitting still with respect to the seat, she said, yet moving with respect to the ground. One child immediately wanted to know what "with respect to" means. I tried to dramatize the idea of sitting still with respect to the seat and moving with respect to the ground by pretending I was in a bus. I probably looked rather foolish. The kids seemed amused. But I think they got the idea.

What seemed to interest these children was the idea of one's body being somehow both moving and being still at the same time. They began to think about whether your body is ever completely at rest. "You could be sitting still and yet your heart would be beating," said Jason. "A human body can never do nothing," announced Esther. "Even if you're breathing, you're doing something," put in Carl.

Plato, in the passage from the *Republic* that inspired my story, had chosen a cleaner analogy than my example of sitting still in a bus that's moving. Plato used the idea of a perfectly spinning top. I must admit that all the tops I can remember spinning for my children either wobbled inelegantly or, even if they remained perfectly upright for a few seconds, still floated around the floor on their point while spinning. But I can imagine a top doing what Plato described—namely, spinning so perfectly in place that you might think it was magically standing still on its point. In such a case one could say, with Plato, that the top was both moving and at rest; it would be moving with respect to its outer surface, but it would be at rest with respect to its axis because it was spinning perfectly in place.

In making up my story I had thought I would choose a simpler analogy than the spinning top. But the kids smoked me out. Even with respect to the seat of the school bus and sitting perfectly still, one might have moving parts—for example, the heart, or even, as one child suggested, a blinking eye. As long as we are alive, we are never perfectly still. A rider would have a pumping heart and perhaps even a blinking eye. I had to agree that as long as we are alive, we are never perfectly still.

What about the main idea of the story—that every self has different parts? Several students seemed to find that idea immediately plausible, even natural. Unprompted, Alex even identified the parts in true Platonic fashion as reason and appetite. Yet he seemed not to be simply passing on something he had been told because he made up his own terminology for reason and appetite. "There is a *wiser* one," he said, choosing his words carefully, "and a *wanting* one; the wanting one wants something and the wiser one says no." The contrast Alex drew between reason and appetite runs through the whole history of Western philosophy. Yet it seemed that Alex was inventing it afresh. Several children mentioned the idea of conscience. But they were not entirely sure how to think of conscience. Is it an inner agent? Is it a kind of censor? Or just a "voice within"?

In the second class I discussed this story with, Laura suggested that each of us has an "angel" whispering in one ear and a "devil" whispering in the other. Lilly and Eddy pooled ideas they had about neurophysiology to suggest that when we have conflicting desires, different and conflicting messages are coming to the brain. One message, they thought, might come from the tongue that tastes the sweetness of the brownie that Anna talks about in the story and invites the brain to see to it that she eat another brownie. Another message might come from the stomach, which, let's suppose, was getting stuffed and was beginning to warn of the possibility of throwing up. The children seemed to think that this neuro-physiological story was more scientific than the story about the angel and the devil.

Cory fastened onto the idea of there being different thoughts that go to the brain, rather than different parts of the self. "It's not so much different parts as it is different thoughts," he said, "and the brain has to decide which thought to go with." At this point in the discussion a few others suggested that there could be more than just two competing desires. That suggestion, ordinary as it may seem, harbors a profound critique of the traditional account of conflict in de-sires as a battle between reason and appetite. Sometimes we realize that there are two or more good things we want to do, though we can do only one. Or we realize that there are two or more equally bad things we want to do, even though we can, at most, do only one of them. We cannot then understand what is go-ing on as a contest between reason and appetite or between an angel and a devil. There may be two angels in conflict with each other or two devils—or three or seven or any number. The profound conclusion is that a conflict in desires *need* not be a conflict between a good desire and a bad one.

The model of desire-conflict that these youngsters found themselves at-tracted to is thus much more flexible than the traditional Platonic story. If, think-ing of the mind as the brain, we understand the situation as one in which different messages come to the brain and the brain realizes that it can't make the body act on them all, then we can allow for much more variety in motiva-tional conflict. Perhaps the messages often do come in pairs: "This is sweet, so eat this!" and "This will make you sick, so stop eating this!" But in principle messages may come in triples or quadruples. And even if they come in pairs, it may not be the case that one speaks for the wiser self and the other for the greedy self.

I left those two classroom sessions thinking that, interesting and provoca-tive as those two discussions were, they hadn't dealt with the question I had meant to pose in the story I had brought with me. I had hoped that we might get on to the issue of whether talk about parts of the self is a cop-out. Saying that a part of me wants another brownie and another part wants to stop eating brownies seems to leave *me* out of the picture. St. Paul, in the biblical book of Romans, says, "It is not I that do it, but sin that dwells in me." Now if I overeat or perhaps take more than my share of brownies, I might try to escape censure by saying, in the fashion of St. Paul, "It wasn't I that did it, but that greedy appetite acting in me."

On the way home I realized that the students in those two classes had, after all, dealt with the problem of responsibility. They decided that it's not so much that we have parts, one wanting to do something and another wanting not to do it. It is, rather, that different messages come to the brain—that is, to the mind. "You don't do anything unless the mind agrees to it," one of them had remarked. If the mind is in charge, then I certainly can't get myself off the hook by saying that it was that greedy part of me that made me do it. The greedy part sends a tempting message to the brain, but nothing happens unless the brain agrees to act on the greedy suggestion. That idea is certainly worth thinking about.

Incidentally, another way to discuss some of these same issues with children (or adults!) is to read together Arnold Lobel's simple yet profound story "Cookies," from his collection *Frog and Toad Together* (Lobel 1979, 30–41). That delightfully whimsical story focuses our attention on perplexities in the notion of willpower. The story is simple enough to be understood by a four- or five-year-old. But the perplexity it invites is sufficiently deep to occupy a graduate seminar in what philosophers call weakness of will, or *akrasía*.

SOME MONTHS BEFORE the story about total happiness I had written a story based on the discussion of time in Augustine's *Confessions*, Book XI. Augustine's discussion echoes skeptical concerns that go back to Book IV of Aristotle's *Physics* and perhaps even earlier. Because I planned to use the story with children in Oslo, I tried to give the characters in the story Norwegian-sounding names.

Time

MOTHER: Hi, Tor, how was school today?

TOR (throwing down his school pack and beginning to take off his jacket): Oh, all right, I guess. But we have this girl in my science class who thinks she knows everything. She was in Switzerland last year. I think her father is a big scientist or something. He was working in a lab there. Her name is Ingrid. Do you know what she said today?

MOTHER: I don't have a very good way to guess from what you've told me so far.

TOR: Well, the teacher, Mr. Knudsen, was saying something about space and time and this Ingrid, she raised her hand and said in this sickly-sweet know-it-all voice of hers, "You know, Mr. Knudsen, there really is no such thing as time."

MOTHER: What did Mr. Knudsen say to that?

TOR: Well, you know how he always likes to humor students, especially the smart ones, so he just smiled and said, "What makes you say that, Ingrid?"

MOTHER: Did Ingrid have a good reply?

TOR: Well, she started off by saying, "You know, Mr. Knudsen, if there really were such things as times, some of them would be long and others would be short."

MOTHER: Did Mr. Knudsen agree to that?

TOR: Of course. But then this Ingrid said in her sassy way—I really can't stand her—"But you know, Mr. Knudsen, the past doesn't exist anymore. So there is nothing of the past to be either long or short. And the future doesn't exist yet. So the future isn't there to be long or short either."

MOTHER: That sounds pretty interesting. Did Mr. Knudsen have a good reply?

TOR: Well, he said, "What about the present, Ingrid? That exists, doesn't it?" And you know what Ingrid said to that?

MOTHER: No, son, tell me.

TOR: Well, she said, "You might think a whole day or a whole hour or at least a whole minute could be present. But really," she went on, "even though it's now Thursday, some of Thursday is already past and some is future. So some of it doesn't exist any more and the rest doesn't exist yet."

MOTHER: What did Ingrid say about the present minute? Surely none of the present minute is already past or still future.

TOR: Oh yeah, she had an answer for that, too. She said, "So and so many seconds are already past and the rest are future. All that is really present is something like a knife edge of time. That's not either long or short. It's just a knife edge. So," she concluded, "since, if there were such a thing as time, there would have to be long times and short times, and no such things ever exist, there is no such thing as time."

MOTHER: I can tell Ingrid is very smart. Did Mr. Knudsen have a good answer for her?

TOR: Well, he said we were all to go home and think about what Ingrid had said. Tomorrow we are each supposed to come up with the best response we can. I wish I could think of something that would blow her out of the water. She thinks she's so smart.

MOTHER: Well, you could go over and talk to Olaf's big sister. I think she has done a little philosophy at the university.

TOR: No, I want to figure this out for myself. I want to show that Ingrid isn't really the smartest kid in the class. She just thinks she is.

The discussion in the Northampton fifth-grade class began in a rather uncertain way. Simon commented that "Ingrid was using philosophy." That was a
rather promising starting point so I wrote it on the poster board for later discussion. Three of the next four comments, however, focused on the psychological
dynamics of the story. Thus Juliane pointed out, what is surely correct, that "Tor
wants to have a response to show that Ingrid wasn't right." Maya added that
"Tor is jealous of Ingrid," which is highly plausible. And Andrew expressed the
reasonable thought that "the continuation of the story should show that Ingrid
isn't as smart as she thinks she is."

In the midst of these comments, Kristhle raised her hand and, with a frown
on her face, blurted out, "I don't get it." I responded by writing on the board "I
don't get it," with her name afterward. Several children giggled, and Kristhle
blushed a bit, but I tried to reassure her that that was a good thing to say and
that we would try to deal with it once we had all the initial comments on the
board.

So far there had been two good goads to further discussion: Simon's comment, "Ingrid was using philosophy," and Kristhle's comment, "I don't get it."
The other comments had more to do with what is called "reading comprehen-
sion." Still, I wasn't completely disappointed because I had built the element of
jealousy into the story to help motivate the search for a good reply to what is,
after all, an abstract bit of philosophical reasoning. It was good to be assured
that the students had understood the psychological dynamics of the story.

There is a more general issue here. I write story beginnings like this one
and ask the children how the story should go on to try to present philosophical
perplexities as problems they themselves can have. In this case the question is
what Tor should say in response to Ingrid. It is important to the enterprise I
want to foster that the students do not say at the end, "Now tell us what the
answer is." And, in fact, they never do that. They soon take these problems on
as their own. They may or may not be able to handle them to their own satisfaction. But the aim is, if possible, for them to take ownership of the problems.
The aim is most definitely not to get them to learn some famous solution to the
problem under discussion. It is not even to get them to recapitulate the history
of philosophy, though that is often what they do. It is rather to help them become self-reliant thinkers who have the ability to address difficult and fascinating philosophical issues and work out articulate and well-argued responses.

But I am jumping ahead of my story. The first five comments did not tackle
the philosophical issue the story raises. At this point I wondered whether I had
made a mistake in bringing such a difficult bit of reasoning to these fifth graders. After all, the solution Augustine eventually offers is not one that many
people find satisfactory. In addition, many commentators think that Aristotle
offers no solution to the problem at all, either in the *Physics* or elsewhere in his

writings. So why should I expect a group of fifth graders with no previous training in philosophy to be able to figure out an interesting response to a problem Aristotle apparently was not able to solve and Augustine responded to only in a fashion many people find disappointing?

Naïve or not, my faith was rewarded. In the back of the classroom Owen screwed up his face, twisted his body a bit, and raised his hand. "If the past doesn't exist," he said carefully, weighing each word, "I couldn't have started this sentence since I wouldn't have existed then." I was excited by his arresting insight and by my own anticipation about where this observation might lead us. While the others were talking, Owen had clearly been working away in his own mind at a response to Ingrid's argument. And his response was an excellent one. Jason immediately jumped on it and expanded it: "If the past didn't exist, nothing would exist now." In its full generality, Owen's idea is that if the past doesn't exist, then there is nothing that could have brought anything that now exists into being—this sentence I am writing, the people who are now talking about this philosophical question, the world around us, anything at all that now exists! It was a stunning move.

In the discussion that followed, a few others tried to think about the specific kind of reality that the past has. Jason was particularly persistent in this effort. "The past sort of exists," he said at one point, "because we experience it." He didn't exactly have Augustine's idea that the past exists in our memory. His idea seemed to be that the past exists in a way that makes it possible for us to know things about it.

Later on, Jason wanted to say more about the "sort of" existence that the past has. His idea at this point seemed to be that the past is settled, determinate, always one way or the other. It couldn't have the definite character it has, he seemed to be saying, if it didn't exist at all. His notion echoes the traditional notion, to be found in Aristotle, that the past has a kind of necessity; it is the necessity of the unchangeable. Talk about whether the past could be changed introduced the issue of time travel. Several students had ideas about time travel and whether, if you went back in time, you could change something that had happened, rather than simply being an ineffectual observer.

Talk about the kind of existence the past has also introduced a question about the kind of existence the future has. Some of her classmates seemed prepared to accept Ingrid's claim in the story, that the future simply has no existence at all. But some seemed to want to assign it some existence as well. A summary way of putting their point would be this: the future sort of exists, too, because the same thing that is now present was future.

Kristhle, who first blurted out, "I don't get it," came to take an animated part in the discussion. It seems to have been important to the discussion as it developed that she had been fearless enough to say at the beginning that she didn't get it. But eventually she certainly did get it and she made an important contribution.

Early on we returned to Simon's comment that Ingrid was using philosophy. I asked the students how they knew that Ingrid was using philosophy. Someone who had paid close attention to the story pointed out that Tor's mother had suggested that Tor talk with someone who had studied philosophy at the university to get his problem solved. That observation was certainly a textually astute comment. I think it was Simon, however, who picked up on his own comment and explained rather impressively that what Ingrid was doing was philosophy because it was giving reasons for something, not just making a blanket statement. He then made two or three rather eloquent comments about how it wasn't enough just to have an opinion about something; one needs to be able to give reasons.

One of the last comments was simple yet, in its own way, also profound. A boy who hadn't participated much in the discussion, Matt, eyed the clock and commented, "There's a time when school gets out; so time exists." Matt was making a point very much like one the English philosopher G. E. Moore was famous for early in the twentieth century. J.M.E. McTaggart, like Ingrid, had argued that time is unreal. Moore replied that he knew he had had breakfast that morning, so time must exist. Moore went on to say that he had much more certain knowledge that he had had breakfast that morning than he could possibly have that McTaggart's rather complicated argument for the unreality of time was sound.

WHAT CONCLUSIONS SHOULD one draw from these examples of children doing philosophy? One conclusion I have suggested already is that our common conception of what it is to be a child, the Aristotelian conception, is inadequate. Children certainly are proto-adults, but they are not just proto-adults. Their essential nature is not given by saying simply what they will normally become. They may now be much more free, open, inquisitive, and, yes, philosophical thinkers than they will ever be when they grow up. Respecting them as thinkers and encouraging their thought, even their philosophical thought, promises at least three rewards. First, it may make them better thinkers throughout their lives, including their adult lives. Second, it may give the adults around them, especially their parents and teachers, a fresh perspective on the world. Being able to see the world freshly through children's ideas by engaging in noncondescending discussions with them is one of the finest gifts teachers and parents can receive from their children. And, third, having a genuinely two-way conversation with a child about something the child realizes is perplexing in some deep and important way is one of the best ways to enhance intergenerational relationships.

When I give workshops for parents and teachers about doing philosophy

with children, I sometimes get the complaint that it is hard for an adult un-
trained in philosophy to recognize that a comment, question, or bit of reasoning from a child is philosophically interesting. The complaint is well founded.
My own books on philosophy and children are attempts to help adults recognize, by example, what a philosophically interesting remark or question from a
child might be like. Some of the examples in this chapter might help too. But I
suspect that the biggest stumbling block to appreciating the philosophical interest our conversations with our children might have is our very conception of
childhood. We don't think of our children as being capable of having philosophical thoughts or as being interested in pursuing them.

So, as I have maintained in this chapter, we need to get a better model of
childhood by going beyond the Aristotelian model. At the same time, we also
need a better model of adulthood, one that will allow for the real possibility
that the freshness, inventiveness, openness, inquisitiveness, and imagination of
childhood will be preserved, even enhanced, in adult life, rather than simply
displaced by routinized competencies, no matter how vital those competencies
are. If we had such a model of adulthood, perhaps it would be easier to develop
a concept of childhood that makes a proper place for children as philosophers.

Notes

1. For other examples of children's philosophical comments, questions, and reasoning,
   see Matthews 1980 and 1994.
2. Or perhaps it is Aristotle's claim that the Greek word *aition*, which, in English, we
   translate as "cause," has four different senses.

References

Fineberg, J. 1997. *The Innocent Eye: Children's Art and the Modern Artist*. Princeton, N.J.:
   Princeton University Press.
Lobel, A. 1979. *Frog and Toad Together*. New York: HarperCollins.
Matthews, G. B. 1980. *Philosophy and the Young Child*. Cambridge: Harvard University
   Press.
Matthews, G. B. 1984. *Dialogues with Children*. Cambridge: Harvard University Press.
Matthews, G. B. 1994. *The Philosophy of Childhood*. Cambridge: Harvard Univer-
   sity Press.

| | Children as |
| Chapter 3 | Theologians |

EILEEN W. LINDNER

Mark had just turned nine years old during the summer of 1973, but his was not the summer of other third graders. Bald and ashen, he lay in bed in Chicago's celebrated Children's Memorial Hospital diagnosed with leukemia. He had just returned to the hospital after a furlough day at home where he had celebrated his birthday, the one that would be his last, with his family and a few friends. His excitement almost counteracted his exhaustion and returned some color to his cheeks as he told of the festivities. The high point had been his birthday gift, the dog he had hoped for and had dreamed about. The Polaroid pictures showed a typical birthday table festooned with trimmings. Centered in the picture was a bald boy in a baseball cap and at his side a dazed looking mongrel, complete with birthday hat. I was a young student hospital chaplain paying a pastoral call on Mark; and I had to struggle for enough composure to admire the dog, concealing the emotion that welled up within me in contemplation of the weeks ahead.

During the waning weeks of that summer more than thirty years ago, Mark and his dog had infrequent personal visits but many opportunities to view each other through the floor-length windows in the hospital's ground-floor lobby. Their friendship and affection seemed to blossom even without the physical contact so characteristic of boy-dog relationships.

Mark's parents knew he was dying but would not disclose his condition to him, being certain that the horror of such a reality would add to his suffering. Rather, they reasoned, he should be permitted the opportunity to make plans for a future he would never see and to enjoy whatever elements of a normal boyhood his failing health would allow. His parents did not object to my stopping by to visit him. They were not practitioners of any faith nor were any of their children, but they held no grudge against religion either and sometimes took my brief daily visits as an opportunity to grab a quick cup of coffee or lunch.

Mark's conversation began to take on some new characteristics in the warm days of early August. Hours of bedridden boredom had led Mark to contemplate the ceiling tile in his hospital room. Characteristic of hospitals of that era the tiles were a white synthetic material with hundreds of tiny holes punched out in neat rows. Having just recently mastered the rudiments of multiplication, Mark often tried to count the holes in one tile and then to calculate the total number of holes in the ceiling of his room. Sometimes losing count because of being interrupted or falling asleep or simply blinking and failing to find his place again, Mark was persistent in his self-designed vocation. On one of these visits, Mark asked me whether there was a name for a number higher than any number anyone had ever counted. I was clearly on unfamiliar mathematical ground but suggested that the number might be what was known as infinity. To be certain, he asked whether infinity could be used to describe the biggest number known plus one. When I assured him that it could be, he breathed a sigh and then engaged me in what can only be called a theological exploration of death and afterlife.

It soon became apparent that Mark knew he was dying. Just as his parents thought Mark was ignorant of his condition, he insisted that his parents did not know he was dying and that they should not be told in order to protect *them* from the pain of anticipating the death of their son. In the absence of conversations with his parents about death, Mark discerned a meaning of death and beyond from studying the tiny holes in the ceiling tiles. He assured himself that the existence of these holes was real and their number determinable, but in addition there was more to this reality, there was a reality that could be given the name *infinity*. In the days that followed, our conversation made it clear that he extended that insight to life as he was living it. He spoke about his belief that beyond what could be counted (and seen) was another reality in which the holes in ceiling tiles participated and, by implication, there was a reality for boys and dogs that extended beyond his own experience.

As he prepared himself for his death, Mark conjured up a rather compelling systematic theology, or at least a spirituality, in which ceiling tiles, boys, and dogs go on forever even when they are out of view. He never mentioned God or heaven or any of the culturally rich constructs about the afterlife. Mark believed that because boys and dogs are made to specifications as exact as ceiling tiles, they must be of some cosmic consequence and would find eternal manifestation beyond their present condition.

Late in August, Mark died. I attended a secular service for him at his elementary school. I never saw his parents after the week of his death and know nothing of what became of his family and his dog. I do know that Mark has lingered these three decades in my memory specifically because of his personal theologizing and his doing so in a *Sitz im Leben* (situational context) that would be daunting to any pastor or theologian. Mark's example is all the more impressive when it is recognized that he had not been "formed" by any religious training or in any religious tradition. Mark was my first introduction to a child theologian, but he was not the last.

In this chapter I examine the religious thought of children, limited though it is, especially in relation to their respective communities of faith. In keeping with the book's overall theme, this chapter examines children's lives with special attention to their spiritual needs and their often unrecognized but substantial capacity to address those needs. The theological capacity of children—their ability to articulate ontological concepts and order their perspectives of God and of spirituality appears to offer fresh and authentic insight to the question of children's agency. Moreover, children's capacity to design and promulgate both rituals and rites to express solemnity and piety can be seen as further evidence of their theological capacity.

The growing religious pluralism of the United States offers a unique and dynamic environment in which to study the relation of children to a variety of religious traditions, communities, and affiliations. My own tradition is one of classic Protestant Christian belief. Although this is a dominant form of religious affiliation within the United States, it has its own particular views and engagement with children. And even though mainline Protestantism has enjoyed cultural hegemony in the United States, some cautions are warranted. First, not all the experiences of mainline Protestantism in relation to children can be generalized to other religious traditions and other religious communities. Second, the great rise in religious pluralism has been relatively recent, and only slowly do religious communities arrive in this country in sufficient numbers to provide living laboratories for the consideration of children and religious faith.

For these reasons the observations in this chapter should be assumed to reflect Christian thought and practice unless otherwise noted. Inferences drawn will likely be of the greatest usefulness in applications to monotheistic faiths and particularly the three Abrahamic traditions of Judaism, Christianity, and Islam. The thoughts below are offered not so much to illuminate the practices of other faiths and traditions as they are to prompt questions that others will need to address in relation to both historic faiths and emerging new-age belief systems.

Children in the Community of Faith

It has long been axiomatic that any religion lives one generation from extinction. Most religious traditions place special importance on the continued survival of the community of faith. As a result, a preponderance of religious traditions hold sacred their own rites and rituals of initiation, which graft the young onto the religious tradition of their culture. In many religions this initiation takes place in infancy or early childhood and is sometimes associated with naming ceremonies. Socialization in this view is provided to the child and in it the child is understood to have neither voice nor agency. Sometimes these rituals are closely related to the coming-of-age traditions that are a hallmark of adolescence. The specific content of such rites need not concern us here. Whether it is a bris or an infant baptism or christening or, later, a bat or bar mitzvah or confirmation or first communion, the initiation of the young is a communal cause for rejoicing. Throughout history religions have looked to children for the survival of both the community of faith and the faith itself. In this regard children and their childhood must increasingly be perceived as fully human, not simply potentially human.

Religious communities have so much at stake in the acculturation of the young that theological disciplines and religious education have been slow to recognize the socially constructed character of childhood. The emergence of childhood studies offers the theological disciplines both new insight and new tools to share with other disciplines in an exploration of children's own role in shaping childhood. At least two foci of this approach—children's rights and the acknowledgement of their own voices (as described by Allison James in Chapter 1)—will be of interest within the religious community.

Despite sacred language that suggests otherwise, communities of faith often fall prey to the objectification of children as much as do other institutions within the culture. Along with schools, health institutions, the media, and others, religious bodies often make two assumptions that aid in the objectification of children.

First, children are frequently perceived as potential subjects or agents but are not accorded the dignity of being regarded as fully formed persons or as being agentive in the present moment. Because of the importance attributed to chronological age and developmental theories, children are often viewed as those who will attain full personhood at some future time but not as those who enjoy such status at this moment (a point developed in the Introduction). Indeed, in the name of protection of the child this assumption is often codified into law (as described by Alice Hearst in Chapter 14 and by Barbara Woodhouse in Chapter 13), where children are ordinarily viewed as unemancipated minors. A second assumption is closely related to the first and likewise is often codified in law: absent any finding of abuse or neglect, children are often viewed (both culturally and legally) as the chattel of their parents and guardians. Taken together, these assumptions work to erode the perception of children as agents within the society. In religious communities in which this notion of "not yet" is linked with an ethic of love and concern for the child, this belief is so strong that early religious training of children is referred to as "formation." These communities believe that only through such a process of formation can the raw material of humanity, a child, be transformed into the culmination of human striving, a mature believer.

More than enough has been written elsewhere about the necessity, methods, timing, and content of religious formation. But children and their own agency have not been central to the conduct of such formation studies. There is an often unnoticed irony here. Although children's own contribution and agency have not been encouraged or integrated in programs and practices of formation until recent years, many remarkable child-serving agencies have been founded within religious communities in furtherance of programs that have the express purpose of allowing children to live the lives for which they were created and to live them, presumably, in the present. The range of these agencies is considerable. They include foundling hospitals, orphanages, group homes, colleges, training academies, and a host of programs and institutions addressing the needs of children who live with disabling conditions and in difficult circumstances. Rhetorically, at least, religious agencies have long held a theological commitment to the child's dignity and worth even when their working assumptions have not taken the child's voice and agency fully into account.

Judaism and Christianity have had remarkable successes in serving the educational needs of children, and both have given rise to research closely associated with educational and therapeutic programs designed to foster the development of children. The benevolent intent of these environments has not meant, however, that the children's religious voice was tolerated, much less heard. On the contrary, it has all too often meant that children's beliefs were subordinated to the broader religious and theological conceptualizations of the adults around them.

Although religious education, Hebrew schools, Sunday schools, mosque schools, church-related colleges, and the like have been an essential expression of faith communities, they have not been instituted at the expense of other ministries. Faith groups of all sorts run social activities for children and teens and often operate leisure activities such as summer camps. Extensive research in church-housed childcare (Lindner 1983) demonstrated that most out-of-home early-childhood group care takes place in church-owned facilities. Service activities for older children and youth are also important features of the practice of faith for a wide variety of religious traditions.

In recent decades contemporary ideas about worship have led many Christian churches to reform their worship practice for children. Sometimes such change is attempted through the provision of "children's worship kits," which constitute a kind of ecclesiastical Happy Meal. Packaged locally and distributed to families with young children as they arrive at worship, these kits often contain crayons, Bible pictures to color, a small snack, and sometimes a picture book.

Another option for accommodating young children in worship is the institution of a "children's moment," in which children gather near the altar for a brief, often interactive, sermon centered around an ethical or even theological question. Typically children are asked a question about the nature of God or about an ethical decision. Their spontaneous responses are audible to the whole congregation—and are often a source of amusement more than an opportunity for reflection. The children then often leave the sanctuary and retire to a church school, choir rehearsal, or recreation period as the adults continue with worship.

A more sweeping approach to accommodating families and children in worship is the institution of an "alternative" worship service in many mainline churches. Characteristically such services take place earlier in the day than the regular service and are attended by families in casual clothing. Gone from such services are robed choirs, pipe organs, clerical garb, and other formalities. A more free-flowing and lay-led order of worship is often followed. Singing lots of songs with repetitive lyrics and simple tunes to the accompaniment of a "praise band" comprised of electronic keyboard and electric guitar makes hymnals unnecessary. Once the sole province of Pentecostal fellowships or charismatic Catholics, such informal services are now conducted in large numbers of mainline congregations. Although more attuned to children's tastes than regular worship, these services remain adult driven in their religious content.

All these strategies are intended to make church attendance more attractive than it now is to families with children and youth. The hour, musical selection, and liturgical content at such services are all based on assumptions about the spiritual and intellectual needs of the families in attendance. The success of these services suggests that some of the assumptions utilized in planning have been on target. There is little doubt that such services are more accessible to children and youth and therefore more pleasurable for the family as a whole. Yet some caution is warranted especially as regards young children. Do these services meet the spiritual needs of children or merely the logistical and social needs of their families? It may be that such services will ultimately prove to be no more appropriate to the pastoral needs of children than were the classical services and practices they replaced.

In 1997, the National Council of Churches conducted a small study to assess the perceptions of children and pastors about the need for children's pastoral care—that is, counseling and prayer offered by priests or ministers ("When Did We See Thee Hungry" 1998). Asked to identify the key occasions at which young children require the ministry of the church, the pastors offered the following in descending rank order:

Day of baptism
First day of school
Day of first communion or confirmation
Day of departure for college or armed forces
Wedding
Death of parents or grandparents

Children aged six through sixteen were asked as well to list the occasions on which they felt the need for a minister's presence or counsel. These girls and boys listed a different set of occasions from the ministers. In descending rank order, they were:

The day your best friend moves away
When you get left back in school or aren't selected for a team
When parents divorce
When your dog/cat/pet dies
When a kid you know dies
When parents or grandparents die

The striking differences in the responses of pastors and children offer strong evidence that the religious ideation of children varies substantially from that of the pastors who are called to minister to their spiritual needs. The small size of the sample and some additional methodological considerations dictate caution in generalizing these findings. Yet the fact that these two groups appear to speak with different voices compels us to do more research on the views of the laity and of the clergy about spiritual needs and occasions for ministry. Despite rapidly expanding sociological research on religion and interfaith matters and the substantial body of research on the development of moral reasoning, scant attention has been given to children's own views of religion and their spiritual life.

The absence of such research must be attributed, in part at least, to the failure of the religious communities to recognize that children have spiritual needs that may differ from the ones imagined by adults. Churches often do child-related research only to determine the kind of educational processes that will facilitate religious formation. Frequently, research on pastoral care is not sorted by demographics. Methodological progress in assessing children's thoughts independent of test response is not well known among those who conduct religious research. Perhaps the greatest disincentive to the conduct of such research is the widespread assumption that children are largely unaware of, or at least incapable of, articulating their own spiritual and religious longings. Indeed, many would question whether children have the requisite cognitive capacity to formulate conceptual understandings of existential realities, their own or those of others.

A review of standard rabbinical and seminary courses of study for those planning to enter the ministry suggests that pastoral care is seldom a matter of serious inquiry by candidates for the most primary congregational leadership roles. Such classes often offer training in the "how tos" of wedding and funeral preparation, family counseling, and the like.

Courses that focus on children's religious life, and to some degree on youth programming, are designed to meet the needs of those preparing for careers in religious education. Whatever the content of such courses in relation to the pastoral-care needs, mission aspirations, or worship preferences of children, their content is unlikely to be shared with those who have the most authority in and responsibility for these areas of ministry. Many who begin their careers in youth ministry later abandon this child focus so that they can move upward in church leadership, exchanging their youth ministry for the higher status role typically accorded to the senior pastor and preacher. This career drift is a vivid index of the relatively low status of children's ministry within religious communities generally. Moreover, institutionalizing this low status contributes to the problems that cause us to deny the integrity of children's religious thought.

Although historically child and youth ministry has been seen as a low-status assignment, some religious bodies are beginning to rethink their relationship to the spiritual lives of children. The growing incidence of children, some of them quite young, taking part in violent crimes has been the source of somber reflection. School shootings, culminating in the Columbine High School disaster, have done much to call the attention of clergy to the real existential turmoil of their more youthful members. Even with this renewed interest, adequate research and scholarly leadership lag far behind the needs of most religious communities. As we enter a new century, most religious communities continue to struggle with either offering religious education and formation programs to the exclusion of all other ministries with and for children or investing in the kinds of study and research that are likely to produce new insights in the field. How each community makes these choices is likely to turn on the community's assumptions about the intellectual capacity of children and therefore about their aptitude for serious spiritual, moral, and religious thinking. The whole field of developmental theory is poorly attended to in the literature of religious thought and probably offers a less than adequate framework for nurturing children as agents in their own spiritual and theological development. Like those in secular fields, religious thinkers have had a peculiar and oft-changing view of child development.

The Capacity for Theological Inquiry in Childhood

Jean Piaget's pioneering work in formulating a theory of cognitive development has been foundational to present assessments of children's capacity to engage in theological thought, and Piaget's methodological contributions continue to influence much of religious education to the exclusion of other perspectives. In brief, Piaget posited that children's capacity to explore the moral and spiritual dimension of their lives grows in direct proportion to their capacity to understand the laws of nature and of physics and chemistry. In essence, one cannot inquire about the miraculous until one knows what is normative. A limitation in this approach when applied to the work of theology is that it establishes the misimpression that religious thought is primarily about the miraculous and dismisses broader ontological concerns from consideration. Although Piaget's work focused primarily on moral precepts and religious reasoning, subsequent theorists have applied his findings more generally to the religious and theological thought of children.

Working from Piaget's methodological orientation and his theories of cognitive developmental and children's cognition of death, Kohlberg (1968) developed a typology of moral thought among children. Kohlberg asserted that moral development is the result of an increasing ability to perceive and organize social experience. In the same decade Goldman ([1965] 1970) applied Piaget's theories and concluded that young children are essentially in a prereligious state. He concluded that children have little capacity for moral thought because they are underdeveloped cognitively: "We need to have lived long enough to have experienced the real problems of the human condition before we see the point of what religion offers" (49–50). Goldman believed that only at the onset of the teenage years does religious thinking begin to develop in children.

The work of Piaget, Kohlberg, Goldman, and others therefore provides a somewhat narrow basis for the exploration of children's moral reasoning. This literature does much to identify the capacity of children to acquire and integrate the religious thought and moral precepts to which they are exposed. But ethical discernment and doctrinal acquisition do not exhaust the field of theological thought. Nor does such a focus begin to address the areas of spirituality. Hence, a relatively narrow focus and basis for the exploration of children's religious lives was established early and has left largely uncharted a broader range of religious agency on the part of children. Particularly limiting have been those theories that link developmental theory to religious sentiment and then pronounce some children to be "prereligious." Although such children may, like Mark, be predoctrinal, they may be deeply spiritual, albeit uniquely and originally so. Indeed broader acceptance of the philosophical capacity of children (as discussed in Chapter 2) would enrich a discussion of theological voice and agency.

This narrowness of focus has had consequences not only in theoretical and conceptual matters but in the practical fields of ministry as well. Absent attention to children's own theological contributions, ministry to children has continued to be conceived of and practiced in ways that objectify them. Those engaged in these ministries have tended to show little concern for eliciting children's own thoughts and questions. For the most part, they have perpetuated the notion that their task is "forming" children within their inherited religious tradition.

The highly significant and influential work of Fowler (1981) and his colleagues on proposed stages of moral development marked a substantial departure from earlier work. It led to a significant downward revision of the ages at which children are thought to begin to take a proactive stance in framing questions about the meaning of the world around them. Fowler reasoned that shortly after their second birthdays children begin to construct personal stories in order to give coherence and a framework of meaning to the persons and events in their lives. The integrative form of these stories emerges with considerably more power in the early teen years. In early adulthood, narrative stories begin to yield to a deeper capacity for abstract thinking. In these mature years the demand for a logical explanation of all existential matters begins to yield to a willingness to relinquish control over the events of life. Ironically the magical thinking of childhood, which is unchecked by a sense of the enduring laws of nature, is mirrored at this higher level of development by the choice to acknowledge the profound and enduring existence of mystery as an alternative to logical necessity. Although still developmental in its essence, Fowler's construction refashions the perception both of the extent and variety of religious thought throughout development and of young children's capacity to be generative within these realms.

Fowler's work was published during the 1980s amid a growing body of work emphasizing both the dignity and capacity of children. Theorists of religious education like Berryman (1991) applied Fowler's insights to the study of children and worship. The attention given to a new appreciation for children's cognition fostered increased interest in the subject. Coles's two landmark works, *The Moral Life of Children* (1986) and *The Spiritual Life of Children* (1990), brought new depth and fresh research to questions about the moral thinking and spiritual content of children's lives. Although often criticized within the academy, Coles's approach is equally often well received among practitioners and within theological circles, perhaps, in part, because of his own theological training; during his psychiatric residency he audited a class taught by the great Protestant theologian Paul Tillich. Bringing together the insights of psychoanalytic thought and contemporary theological sensitivities, Coles trained his listening ear to the rhythms of the lives of children, finally offering an abundance of fresh insight concerning the capacity of and activity of children in moral thinking (1986).

Coles's work *The Spiritual Life of Children* (1990) is a model of an interdisciplinary approach to childhood. His own cross-disciplinary training in psycho-analysis and theology (at Union Theological Seminary) led him to break meth-odologically and theoretically with orthodox psychoanalytic thought in his work with children. Referring to Sigmund Freud's dismissive generalizations regard-ing religious ideation, Coles notes, "This is the kind of naïve and gratuitous reductionism we have seen relentlessly pursued these days in the name of psycho-analysis" (1990, 2). He goes on in a confessional tone to lament, "Even today I recall with sadness and remorse some of the thoughts I had, the words I used, as I worked with children who had their own moral concerns, their philosophical interests, their religious convictions. I tended to focus on their 'psychodynam-ics' unrelievedly to the point that they and I became caricatures"(10). Coles made his confession with such passion that it inspired similar acts of repentance from others and gained him a following among scholars in theological disciplines. His preservation and careful interpretation of children's drawings and his clinical methodology demonstrate children's profound capacity for voice and agency in moral, theological, and spiritual thinking.

Since the early 1980s, the work of Coles and of those inspired by him has established the theoretical and methodological basis for a broad and carefully nuanced inquiry into the moral, theological, and spiritual lives of children. Such inquiries might well inspire others to both greater depth and breadth than those displayed by previous work, including that of Coles. Indeed, Coles has been criti-cized for evaluating religious ideation according to the standard of preexisting theological constructs rather than with a keen eye for originality in theological and spiritual thinking. Religious pluralism itself offers new opportunities to ex-pand the breadth of such studies.

Not all spirituality is religiously based and so special care must be taken in any such studies. Children themselves must be afforded the opportunities to de-sign research and even assist in the analysis. In 1978, Bluebond-Langner's *The Private Worlds of Dying Children* demonstrated both a methodological approach for listening to what children are saying. and a valued insight into their lives. Although an important contribution to the field, this work was not significantly instrumental in altering adult attitudes, in part because it dealt with children in exigent circumstances. Garbarino and his colleagues took a much broader ap-proach in *What Children Can Tell Us* (Barbarino, Stott, and the Faculty of the Erikson Institute 1989). This work and others like it advance substantially our capacity to seek out and heed the voice of children and to interpret that voice in a context and by methods that maintain their sense of meaning. More study is needed to provide a more valid conceptual and theoretical framework for child-hood studies.

In thirty years of pastoral ministry I have frequently presided over last rites and funeral services for numerous of God's critters. Some of the deceased have been the household pets of my children. Others were unfortunate birds, squirrels, frogs that just happened to breathe their last in the environs of our home. With two clergy parents, our sons have often felt obliged to offer our pastoral and mortuary services to other children in their hours of bereavement for their pets. For this reason I have served as celebrant in various interfaith services when the children (and presumably their pets) were of a faith tradition other than our own family Presbyterianism. In such settings children often readily disclose the symbolic meanings of various rites, rituals, and ceremonies. On more than one occasion I have been struck by the historically and theologically accurate information shared with me. Religious educators would no doubt take pride in the extent to which children both internalize and at the same time find new meaning in their faith's traditions. I have been impressed as well when children appear to have invented their own rituals and ceremonies to mark special transitions in life and in death.

The prayers of children deserve a special note both for their content and for the confidential and confident way in which they are offered. Although adults often struggle to obtain and maintain meaningful spiritual lives, children generally find the idea of conversing with God neither more nor less mystical and mysterious than speaking to a distant grandmother by telephone. They approach the encounter with God giving little thought to whether the technology is in place to permit direct and immediate communication. Their assumption appears to be that God has neither a pressing schedule nor any interests more treasured than the immediate conversation. Such readiness to pray and to intimately express hopes and fears is an exercise in deep self-expression and spirituality.

Existential Angst and Children's Spiritual Lives

As some of the other chapters in this book attest, all is not well with children. Society seems ill-prepared to deal with the childhood it has constructed. More of our children are poor than are members of any other age cohort. In the United States, more than twelve million live in poverty. Many lack health care, nutrition, opportunity, and hope. Children of color are routinely offered small futures in comparison with white children. The public education system is under assault. Nor is affluence a shield against damaging experiences in childhood. Crime and violence, suicide and mental illness now touch children in ways that were uncharacteristic only a generation ago. The exploitation of children for commercial gain silently robs them of their dignity and fosters a poor self-image and lack of confidence (as Enola Aird suggests in Chapter 8). Many children in our culture have loving homes, moral guidance, and physical protection, but all too many do not. Children are the canaries within the mineshaft of modern societies. Across social class, region, and age children are adversely influenced by society's larger inequities and excesses.

A number of cultural influences have coalesced to place on all our children new pressures and stresses that disrupt their own natural rhythms and subject them to demands for behaviors that lie beyond their years. Developmental theories and theorists who inform the therapeutic interventions to which nonconforming children will be subjected continually define "developmental norms" and "age-appropriate" behaviors too narrowly and, worse, may not describe the trajectories of many children's experiences. These pressures occur across the culture and are manifested in a variety of ways by children in different social locations. Popular literature, such as David Elkind's *The Hurried Child* (2001), now in its third edition, argues that our children are being pressured to exhibit adult behaviors and attitudes too fast and too soon. In their fragile struggle for self-esteem children mimic adult practices even while longing for their childhood and yearning for innocence. It is hard to argue with such a sentiment, yet it may not capture the fullness of children's angst. It may not be innocence that children long for but rather their enfranchisement as humans with an integrity, dignity, perspective, and generational culture of their own.

All institutions share culpability for permitting our culture to feed on its own young. For its part, the religious community must face some hard choices to maintain its integrity. Child molestation by priests amply illustrates the problem. Whether sexually, economically, or psychologically, children are too frequently used to satisfy adult longings. Childhood is surely socially constructed, yet across these constructions childhood must be perceived as an epoch of special significance for humanity with unique requirements for the unfolding, as opposed to the formation, of what it means to be human.

Religious communities exercise substantial moral authority in the United States, and they have the capacity to advocate for children in the broader society. Moreover, they are often instructed to do so by their own deepest religious convictions. Jewish, Christian, and Muslim sacred texts, for example, all give prominence of place and special attention to the poor, the unpropertied, and the vulnerable, to "the widow, the fatherless and the sojourner in the land" (Deut. 24:19). Those who are mature in the faith are expected to bind up the wounds and provide for children who are in need. In the United States, which prides itself on individualism, material achievement, and rapid advance through the developmental hurdles of life, coming to the defense of childhood and children is suspect, both politically and socially. Yet the dignity of that protected journey to adulthood may be endangered, and religious communities must recognize this reality.

The consequence of childhood's demise is unthinkable. In a gesture of defiance and hope, faith communities and others of goodwill must declare themselves and their institutions to be sanctuaries for both the children in their midst and children within the broader society. They must establish countercultural institutions that nurture, protect, and mentor others on the steps of life's way and in the ways of life. Such mentoring should be undertaken with a profound and operational respect for the voice (self-expression) and agency (self-actualizing activity) of children. A sanctuary movement for children would, in essence, declare a time, place, and space in which children could live in closer congress with the biological, spiritual, and psychological rhythms of their nature.

Conclusion

In the awful and immediate aftermath of the events of September 11th our community and congregation, like hundreds of others in the New York metropolitan area, discovered that horror had come home and that friends and family members were missing. One boy waited to hear word of his father, whose office had been high in Tower 2 of the World Trade Center. The days were growing long for a five-year-old, and all the attitudes and activities around him told him the adults were frightened and troubled. His mother, feeling profoundly unable to address the now certain fact that his father was dead, asked the pastor to be her surrogate. In the conversation, the boy said, "My mom says that something bad happened at my dad's work and that he is lost, but I think he died and went to God." Somewhat astonished the pastor replied, "I think you are right. But what makes you think he died?" "Oh," he responded, "you don't know my dad; he never gets lost!"

In his own terms this boy had done the theological work that a nation full of people, many his chronological senior, were grappling to do. His own thinking led him to resolve the tension of the moment in eschatological terms typical of his family's religious tradition: he posited the theory that his father was now in God's safekeeping. In doing so he rejected what was, to him apparently, the far worse possibility that his father was lost in some never-ending ambiguity. In this boy's telling, the resolution came about not by God's grace (the traditional belief of Christianity) but by some strength in his father's character. A theological acuity that holds such capacity to at once make sense of events, connote meaning, and bring comfort constitutes a voice worth heeding.

Religious communities, then, have a twofold challenge as they rethink childhood and children. First, through both participation in and consumption of interdisciplinary childhood studies, their understanding of and approach to children should honor children's voice and agency. Second, through exercise of moral authority and social advocacy, religious institutions should be in the forefront of urging reform in society's perception and practice regarding children.

Through many interdisciplinary attempts, we must regain our own ethical and moral moorings. Childhood and children are best treasured as respected elements of our community whose voice is sought and whose agency is honored.

Public and private policies urgently need to be measured for their capacity to make our culture more receptive to both.

References

Berryman, J. W. 1991. *Godly Play: An Imaginative Approach to Religious Education.* San Francisco: Harper.

Bluebond-Langner, M. 1978. *The Private Worlds of Dying Children.* Princeton, N.J.: Princeton University Press.

Coles, R. 1986. *The Moral Life of Children.* Boston: Houghton Mifflin.

Coles, R. 1990. *The Spiritual Life of Children.* Boston: Houghton Mifflin.

Elkind, D. 2001. *The Hurried Child: Growing Up Too Fast Too Soon.* 3d ed. Cambridge, Mass.: Perseus.

Fowler, J. W. 1981. *Stages of Faith: The Psychology of Human Development and the Quest for Meaning.* San Francisco: Harper & Row.

Garbarino, J., F. M. Stott, and the Faculty of the Erikson Institute. 1989. *What Children Can Tell Us: Eliciting, Interpreting, and Evaluating Information from Children.* San Francisco: Jossey-Bass.

Goldman, R. [1965] 1970. *Readiness for Religion: A Basis for Developmental Religious Education.* Reprint, New York: Seabury Press.

Kohlberg, L. 1968. The Child as Moral Philosopher. *Psychology Today* 2 (September): 24–30.

Lindner, E. W. 1983. *When Churches Mind the Children.* Ypsilanti, Mich.: High/Scope.

"When Did We See Thee Hungry: Implications for the Pastoral Care of Children." 1998. In *Sermons from Haley.* Privately published at the Haley Farm Conference Center of the Children's Defense Fund.

Chapter 4

Action, Voice, and Identity in Children's Lives

JACK A. MEACHAM

Many readers will find the concepts of action (or agency) and voice to be unremarkable. Parents and teachers commonly describe two-year-olds as assertive, four-year-olds as stubborn or unpredictable, middle-school children as passionate for sports or music or literature, and adolescents as having a direction or mission in life. Thus the purpose of this chapter is not to make the case for action and voice, which are widely accepted, but rather to show that there are different kinds of action and voice. When we describe children's lives, we implicitly draw on four primary metaphors: the metaphors of essence, organism, machine, and historical context. Each has the power to frame and guide how we describe children's lives and how we define the concepts of action and voice. If we don't distinguish among these metaphors, then we will not be speaking, writing, and communicating clearly. The challenge is to know which metaphor has been adopted and so which meaning of action and voice is intended.

Heredity, Environment, and Children's Actions

Most discussions of children's development turn, sooner or later, to a consideration of causes, determinants, factors, or influences in development. Typically, only two categories of causes are considered: heredity, nature, biology, maturation, or internal influences, on the one hand; and environment, nurture, culture (including socialization and education), or external influences, on the other. This notion leads to the question, Which is more important in children's development, heredity or environment? Unfortunately, this question is badly phrased and, by neglecting the role of action in development, can never lead to a correct answer.

Parents, teachers, and child-development professionals frequently note the importance of children's actions in furthering their own development. They refer to children's actions and developmental processes with terms such as self-reflection, being aware, and seeking insight; self-organization, coordination, and self-regulation; behaving, having goals and plans, and self-control; and interpreting, constructing identities, and making commitments. Early in life, these processes become functionally autonomous from and at least as powerful as heredity or environment in children's development. If these processes—which can be included together (along with agency) under the general term *action*—are of such significance as developmental causes, why are children's actions often neglected when we consider the lives of children? One answer, explored in the following paragraphs, is historical, social, and cultural: neglecting the role of action in children's lives and emphasizing merely heredity and environment serve to maintain social inequalities associated with differences in race, gender, and social class (Meacham 1981).

People often ask whether children's characteristics have their basis in heredity or environment. The answers typically given, both incomplete and incorrect, reflect either biological determinism or cultural determinism and neglect three important principles for children's development. First, neither heredity nor environment can be a sole determinant of development, for both are always essential (principle 1) (Carmichael 1925; Meacham 1981). Second, because genes and environments always interact, children's genetic backgrounds cannot be evaluated as "good" or "bad" in isolation, without specification of the environments within which these genes are functioning. Similarly, environments cannot be evaluated as "good" or "bad" without specification of the genetic factors through which the environmental influences are mediated (principle 2).

Third, the possibilities for change—for modifying the course of development and improving children's lives—are independent of whether heredity or environment is the major influence in the interactive process of development (principle 3). The two notions, that modifying the course of development must be difficult if heredity is a major influence in development and that modifying the course of development must be relatively easy if the environment is a major influence, are both based in the erroneous belief that either heredity or environment alone can influence the course of development (violating principle 1).

Unfortunately, the implication that heredity alone could be a cause of children's problems has been taken to imply that some children's heredity must be "bad" (violating principle 2) and thus modification and improvement of children's prospects for development are not possible (violating principle 3). This false reasoning lets society incorrectly assume that it is relieved of responsibility for developing policies and committing resources for preventing and remediating children's problems. Legal and ethical reasons are cited in the case of prevention of "hereditary" problems, and the incorrectly assumed difficulty of modification is cited in the case of remediation. The mere suggestion that heredity plays a role in development—as it does in all development—has been a convenient rationale for racism, sexism, and other political views that encourage the maintenance of social inequalities. In counteracting these views, one must make clear that although behavior and development are always under genetic control, their being so does not mean that modifying and improving the prospects for children's lives are difficult. The fact that heredity plays a role does not limit what can be accomplished through improving physical and social environments for children and through encouraging the influence of children's actions on their own development.

Overemphasizing the role of the environment (socialization and education) in determining children's lives, to the exclusion of heredity and action, can also be a serious mistake. Environmental determinism can, unfortunately, support arguments for maintaining social inequalities that make the naturalistic fallacy— that is, the argument that what happens to be the case also ought to be the case. Similarly, environmental determinism can support arguments that power or might (for example, having control over the allocation of social and cultural resources) makes right. In the search for equality and justice, arguments grounded in both inherent and essential human qualities and in the liberating power of human action have been effective against environmental determinism. That was the case with Jean Jacques Rousseau's opposition to tyranny and Immanuel Kant's defense of freedom. Human individualism and freedom are grounded philosophically and in practice both in our heredity and in our capacity for creative, constructive, and emancipating action.

Emphasizing the developmental role of action and neglecting heredity and environment can also create distortions in our understanding of children's lives. That kind of imbalance neither guarantees progress toward overcoming problems in children's lives nor provides a vision of equality of opportunities for children. To be sure, an emphasis on children's actions may promote an optimism that children can and should, through their own efforts, pull themselves up by their bootstraps, overcome adversity, and improve their conditions and prospects. But ignoring environmental shortcomings (e.g., poorly funded schools) and only emphasizing children's actions can readily lead to criticism and neglect of children who are experiencing difficulties in their development. One might naïvely claim, for example, that such children are lacking in some force or drive for action. Neglecting heredity and environment and focusing exclusively on action can conveniently shift the blame for problems in children's development to the child or, as Ryan (1976) has described the process, can lead to "blaming the victim." Once again, the powerful segment of society is freed of its responsibility for children's lives and for considering changes that would ameliorate existing inequalities.

Why can it sometimes be difficult to recognize that children's actions can be developmental causes along with heredity and environment? The answer is that our implicit folk notions about heredity and environment have come largely from agricultural research. The discovery of genes resulted in part from Gregor Mendel's observation of successive generations of garden peas, not of children. In the first half of the twentieth century, new knowledge about genetics was applied largely to the improvement of vegetables and grains. Agricultural experimentation involves control of heredity through selection of seeds from plants with desirable characteristics and control of environments through variation of soil types, amount of water, and fertilizers. Understanding the interaction of heredity and environment within agricultural science does not require consideration of action because seeds and plants cannot act on the environment to change the conditions for their development. A kernel of corn planted in poor soil cannot direct the application of fertilizer or move itself to a nearby field with better soil. Children, however, continually act on and introduce multiple changes into both their physical and their social worlds, changes that can powerfully influence the course of their own development.

Accepting the proposition that action, along with heredity and environment, is a third primary cause of children's development raises intriguing and significant questions regarding the nature of children's actions, how and when capacities for action emerge, and how children's actions interact with heredity and environment to influence and change the course of their development. However, there can be great variation in the answers to these questions depending on the relative importance attributed to heredity, environment, or action and how these three causes are understood to interact with each other.

Logically, six developmental models can be constructed to represent the interaction of these three primary causes, depending on their relative influence: (1) heredity is most important in development, followed next by environment, followed by action as least important; (2) heredity is most important, followed by action and then environment; (3) environment, then heredity, then action; (4) environment, action, heredity; (5) action, heredity, environment; and (6) action, environment, heredity. How children's actions are conceptualized and what role actions are thought to play in interaction with heredity and environment in children's development can be quite different depending on whether action is thought to be of minimal importance (models 1 and 3) or of major importance (models 5 and 6).

Four Metaphors for Action and Voice

Which of these six developmental models parents, teachers, and child-development professionals find most appealing depends on which of four primary metaphors they choose; each metaphor implies different roles for heredity, environment, and action. The metaphors of essence, organism, machine, and historical context are loosely derived from Pepper (1942) and from two papers I have published (Meacham 1991, 1994). The meanings hidden within these metaphors can influence significantly how and what we think about children's lives, how we interact with children and make decisions that affect their lives, and how we design and implement policies and interventions that we hope will address problems in children's lives and improve their prospects. When the metaphorical meanings are transferred into discussions of children's lives, they lead to describing and understanding children primarily (and respectively) according to their intrinsic qualities, according to the general properties of living systems, according to children's behavioral repertoires, or according to children's interpretations of the events in their lives. Furthermore, each of the four metaphors by implicit comparison or analogy leads us to describe and understand children's action (or agency) and voice in particular ways and to give less emphasis to other possible understandings. From the perspective of each of these four metaphors, action can be understood variously as self-reflection, self-organization, behaving, or interpreting. Similarly, voice can be understood variously as self-awareness, conversation, speaking, or cooperating. Table 4.1 provides a summary and comparison of the metaphors on the basis of the understanding each provides.

THE ESSENTIALIST METAPHOR

Why does an orange taste like an orange and not like a lemon, apple, or peach? Well, it just does. It's in the intrinsic, unchanging, indispensable nature of an orange to taste like an orange. This is an orange's distinguishing property, attribute, trait, or feature—in short, its essence. Within the essentialist metaphor, the method for describing and understanding children's lives is to identify and compare and contrast the intrinsic essences—the attributes, traits, and features—of individual children and groups of children.

From this essentialist perspective, action is self-reflection on, awareness of, and seeking insight into one's attributes, traits, and features. A child who is feeling that he or she is, for example, smart, shy, athletic, lonely, or creative is engaging in essentialist action. An adult who uses the essentialist metaphor in thinking and talking about children similarly labels individual children or groups of children as, for example, intelligent, introverted, masculine, difficult, or of a particular race, ethnicity, or religion. Both the child and the adult are referring to presumably essential, relatively unchanging traits of a child or a group of children.

From an essentialist perspective, "to have voice" (Gilligan 1982) means to be aware of one's experiences and feelings and to discover the attributes and qualities that represent who one is. Those who advocate an increased voice for children would like children to understand that they can and do have a point

Table 4.1.
Four Metaphors for Understanding Children's Lives

	Metaphors			
Understandings	ESSENCE	ORGANISM	MACHINE	HISTORICAL CONTEXT
Children understood primarily by . . .	Their intrinsic qualities	General properties of living systems	Their repertoires of behaviors	Interpreting their life events
Children's action understood as . . .	Self-reflection	Self-organization	Behaving	Interpreting
Children's voice understood as . . .	Self-awareness	Conversation	Speaking	Cooperating
Children's identity development understood as . . .	Discovering who one is	Growing into one's potential	Being made by others	Making oneself

of view. They urge us both to recognize that children have an inner life of experiences and feelings and to encourage children to become aware of who they feel themselves to be and why.

The essentialist metaphor assumes the importance of heredity in bringing about and maintaining the relatively stable traits identified by adults and assumes that the environment and children's actions have little or no role. The essentialist metaphor aligns well with the first of the six developmental models, in which heredity is most important, followed next by the environment and then by the child's action. Within this essentialist metaphor, what the child experiences or whether the child feels smart or lonely is unlikely to alter the assumption that heredity determines the child's abilities and personality.

The use of essentialist metaphors and models for describing children's lives is increasingly rare among child-development professionals. Only a few of them advocate understanding children merely in terms of a list of inherent and stable traits. And only a few maintain that personality traits, moods, or styles of behavior persist from childhood into adulthood without being substantially modified by the influence of parents, teachers, peers, and the media. By contrast, the essentialist metaphor can frequently be detected in discussions among parents and teachers and in media presentations on child and adolescent development.

THE ORGANISMIC METAPHOR

We are immersed in a biological world of living organisms, both plants and animals, including ourselves. Living organisms are organized, self-regulating, and actively functioning systems. Just as a seed planted in favorable conditions is expected to unfold and mature into a tree, so a child provided with a supportive environment is expected to mature into a productive and responsible adult. Within this organismic (living-organism) perspective we can understand children's lives by asking how they maintain an adaptive balance between acting on the environment and being acted on and supported by the environment.

From this organismic perspective, action is self-organization, coordination, and self-regulation. A child striving to coordinate and balance his or her own needs and desires with the expectations of parents, teachers, peers, society, and culture is engaged in organismic action. The child's coordinating and balancing actions are important in resolving the competition and conflict among multiple desires and needs and between what the child would like and what the adult world expects. An adult who thinks and talks about children from an organismic perspective focuses on the difficulties, conflicts, and turmoil of childhood and adolescence and on how these might be alleviated and resolved.

From an organismic perspective, to have voice means to be able to participate in conversation, exchanging thoughts and feelings with others, when some voices are loud and others soft, some are dissonant and others harmonious. For children to have voice is to acquire conversational skills for taking turns, listening, persuading, debating, negotiating, and resolving conflict. With skills such as these, children become able to accommodate others' points of view in conversation without losing sight of their own.

The organismic metaphor of living, biological systems is consistent with the second developmental model, in which heredity is most important, followed closely by the child's actions, with the child's environment as relatively less important. However, the relative influence of these three is more nearly equal than it is within the essentialist perspective. From the organismic perspective, heredity and the environment can present competing and conflicting demands that can be resolved only through the child's own coordinating, mediating, and balancing actions.

The use of the organismic metaphor is evident in many common notions of child and adolescent development. For example, a typical organismic notion is that child development reflects the unfolding of a biological plan marked by critical periods during which specific learning experiences are important. A second example is the notion that child development is determined primarily by physical maturation, to which the social environment responds with increased expectations for the child's actions. A third example is the notion that proper development is a matter of coordination or self-regulation by the child in order to maintain an adaptive balance between heredity and the physical and social environments.

THE MECHANISTIC METAPHOR

Not surprisingly, given the technology of the nineteenth and twentieth centuries—steam engines, telephone switchboards, internal combustion engines, electric motors, and computers—the machine has frequently been adopted as a metaphor for thinking about children's development. Machines are typically described according to the parts from which they are assembled—for example, gears, transistors, chips. Independent of their constituent parts, machines remain at rest until energy is supplied. Within the machine, or mechanistic, metaphor, we seek to understand children's lives by identifying the component parts and processes of childhood and by observing how children's development is a response to stimulation from the physical and social environments.

Within the mechanistic metaphor, action is behaving, forming goals and plans, and engaging in self-control. A child who is laughing, running, speaking, studying, or crying is, in each of these, engaging in a mechanistic action. An adult who adopts a mechanistic perspective focuses on children's behaviors—actions—that are directly observable and on what motivates children to behave. When parents and teachers think and talk about children's thoughts, they consider these thoughts to be similar to behaviors. Thoughts are not directly observable and so they must be inferred from behavior; but otherwise there is little difference between overt behaviors and thoughts. From the mechanistic perspective, children's action, behaving, and thinking reflect primarily the causal influence of the physical and social environments. Those with a mechanistic perspective commonly assume that if the environment is of foremost importance in bringing about and maintaining the individual child's repertoire of behaviors, then that repertoire ought to be readily malleable (violating principle 3).

From the mechanistic perspective, to have voice means to be able to speak one's thoughts and to be able to communicate so that others can understand. Those who advocate increased voice for children from this mechanistic perspective would like children to feel comfortable expressing their points of view; and they would like adults to listen with sensitivity and respect to what children have to say. However, the mechanistic perspective on voice is less conversational and dialogic than the organismic and contextualist perspectives are. The emphasis is more on the children's ability to speak and less on the listener's role.

The mechanistic metaphor aligns well with the third developmental model (in which environment is most important, heredity is next, action is least) and the fourth model (in which environment is most important, but action is next, and heredity least). The child's own actions—how the child behaves and what the child believes about the social world and his or her own abilities—have relatively little influence in determining the child's abilities and personality, compared with the strong role played by the social environment. The notions that the mind of the infant is a tabula rasa, or blank slate, that is written on by the environment and that the child's behavior is a product of selective reinforcement by parents, teachers, and peers or by other environmental contingencies are consistent with this mechanistic metaphor.

THE CONTEXTUALIST METAPHOR

Historical events—for example, an election, revolution, or war—have no significance when considered in isolation. The significance of any particular event depends on its context—that is, its relationship with other events that precede and follow it in time and the interpretations that people construct for and ascribe to this sequence of events. Historians select among many events, contexts, and interpretations and weave these into coherent and significant stories (Meacham 1984). Within this historical-context, or contextualist, metaphor, we can increase our understanding of children by considering how they interpret various events in their lives, as well as the way they weave these events and interpretations into personal identities and life stories that are meaningful and significant. From the contextualist perspective, action is a matter of interpreting events, constructing identities, and making commitments. Commitments require three components: first, expectations of attainment of goals; second, a free choice among alternative means for attaining those goals; and, third, potential consciousness of these goals and means. They create cultural as well as personal integrity (as Wade Boykin and Brenda Allen describe in Chapter 6). The child anticipates not only intended consequences of the actions in which he or she is engaged but also some potential unintended consequences. For this reason the child is prepared to accept responsibility for these consequences and for his or her actions (Eckensberger and Meacham 1984).

Children are engaged in action from a contextualist perspective when they are constructing and choosing among alternative identities for themselves—that is, constructing life stories that provide coherent and acceptable explanations of where they have come from and who they used to be, who they feel and believe themselves to be now, and the trajectory of their aspirations and prospects for the future. Adults who adopt a contextualist perspective when thinking and talking about children focus on being good listeners. When children reveal their emerging identities and life stories, these adults try to alert children to potential internal contradictions. Through conversation they try to help children and adolescents understand the importance—indeed, the necessity—of accepting personal responsibility for the choices they are making in the personal narratives they are constructing.

From the contextualist perspective, to have voice means being able to cooperate with others in setting an agenda for action. For children, having voice also means having the ability to construct and contribute interpretations, critiques, and insights that can enrich family, group, and community life. Adults can facilitate the development of children's voice by including them within a caring community where they can share their visions and goals for the future and work together with others to make those goals become reality. Children who are acquiring increased voice understand the potential they have, through working together with others, to construct communities and to gain knowledge more encompassing and more powerful than they might have accomplished working alone.

The contextualist metaphor is consistent with both the fifth developmental model (in which action is most important, heredity is intermediate, environment is least important) and the sixth model (first action, then environment, then heredity). To a greater extent than the other three metaphors, the contextualist metaphor incorporates children's actions as a cause of their own development. Neither heredity nor environment ensures opportunities for or constitutes unassailable barriers to children's development. Children's personally constructed narratives and the significance they ascribe to perceived opportunities, barriers, and prospects in their lives matter the most. Discussions of children's development based on the contextualist metaphor focus on children's interpretations of their experiences, their creation and invention of new knowledge, and their construction of a sense of identity in adolescence and young adulthood.

Metaphors and Identity

The four metaphors—essentialism, organicism, mechanism, and contextualism—frame and guide how we describe and understand action and voice in children's lives and are the perspectives through which children seek a deeper and more complete understanding of their own experiences. The examples that follow illustrate both how adults use the four metaphors in describing children's lives and how children and adolescents can use these same metaphors in striving to understand themselves. The four metaphors lead directly to four perspectives on the nature and significance of identity in children's lives. A child's sense of identity reflects both the child's understanding of being a unique individual, with relatively stable and enduring characteristics, and the child's feeling of belonging to a group or community with others who share some or many of these characteristics (see the fourth row in Table 4.1).

ESSENTIALIST IDENTITY AS BEING

From the essentialist perspective, one's identity is simply who and what one is as determined primarily by heredity. Identity development is a process of discovering this inherent identity. The child's actions play little or no role in establishing identity, although the action of self-reflection can be important in discovering one's essential qualities. The essentialist metaphor for identity development corresponds well with commonplace, popular notions of identity, according to which identity development is a solitary process by which isolated individuals discover who they truly are, deep inside, at the core.

This essentialist perspective on identity is illustrated in Lydia Minatoya's (1993) account of growing up in Albany, New York, as the only Japanese-American she knew outside her own family. Minatoya describes the awkward efforts of her peers to discover the essential attributes behind her facial features: "I was nervous the first day of school. I wanted to belong. . . . 'What religion are you?' asked a fair-haired, freckled boy. . . . The other children stiffened. I knew this was the test" (29–30). Later, as a young adult, Minatoya visits Japan and meets the patriarch of her family: "The old man looked at me. He turned and studied my face. For a long and breathless time, his keen eyes seized and held me. 'This is who you are,' he said. 'Remember and be proud'" (101). Minatoya's self-reflections do contribute to her identity, but the essentialist reactions of others to her physical attributes are also important.

The essentialist perspective on identity is illustrated in Henry Louis Gates's (1994) account of growing up in a small town in West Virginia. Gates explicitly rejects this perspective when he expresses his dislike of being perceived primarily in racial stereotypes: "One reason is a resentment at being lumped together with 30 million African Americans whom you don't know and most of whom you will never know. Completely by the accident of racism, we have been bound together with people with whom we may or may not have something in common, just because we are 'black'" (xii). . . . "I rebel at the notion that I can't be part of other groups, that I can't construct identities through elective affinities, that race must be the most important thing about me" (xv).

ORGANISMIC IDENTITY AS GROWING

From the organismic perspective, a sense of identity emerges gradually as a process of growing and becoming. Heredity and environment combine to provide opportunities for identity development or, said differently, potential identities or destinies toward which the child grows and matures. The child's action in identity development involves the growing into, or unfolding of, a mature identity that is an adaptive balance among the conflicting demands and expectations of heredity and environment, of biology and culture.

In recounting her experiences as a young girl in Puerto Rico and later in New York City, Esmeralda Santiago (1993) describes a culture with strong expectations for the gender roles that boys and girls will move into as they grow and mature physically. "Men, I was learning, . . . had no shame and indulged in behavior that never failed to surprise women but caused them much suffering. . . . All the females were wives or young girls who would one day be wives" (29). When Santiago was a young teen, her mother told her, "You're almost senorita. You should know how to [care for children and do housework] without being told" (124). As Santiago developed biologically and matured from a girl into a young woman, the expectation within her social environment was that her identity and her destiny were principally to be a sexual object for men and to fulfill childcare and household responsibilities. Santiago's actions in support of the development of her identity were secondary, limited to her efforts at organizing, coordinating, and balancing the competing and conflicting expectations of biology and culture.

MECHANISTIC IDENTITY AS BEING MADE

From the mechanistic perspective, one's identity is what one is made to be as a result primarily of environmental influences. A child's identity develops as a reflection of what significant others—parents, teachers, peers—think about the child and as a consequence of their actions toward the child. The child's own actions play little or no role in establishing identity, for identity is primarily imposed on the child by the social and cultural environment. The child needs merely to be shaped and guided by others and to learn what others believe his or her identity to be.

Yezierska's (1925) largely autobiographical account of Sara Smolinsky, the youngest of four daughters in a Jewish immigrant family in New York City, illustrates the mechanistic perspective in highlighting the strong influence of others, rather than the child's own actions, on identity development. While still a young girl, Sara laments, "Maybe if I could only live like others and look like others, they wouldn't pick on me so much" (181). Russell Baker's (1982) story of growing up during the Depression and experiencing the awkwardness of adolescence includes several examples of how his mother and teachers guided him toward an identity as a writer and a career in journalism. "I began working in journalism when I was eight years old. It was my mother's idea. She wanted me to 'make something' of myself and, after a level-headed appraisal of my strengths, decided I had better start young if I was to have any chance of keeping up with the competition" (17). Significant events in the development of Baker's identity as a writer included various teachers expressing delight at his papers, reading his stories aloud to classmates who laughed appreciatively, and being encouraged to pursue a career in journalism. Baker's actions in support of his own identity development are limited to a particular behavior—that is, writing. It falls to others in the social environment—his mother, his teachers, his peers—to shape, guide, and create Baker's particular identity as a journalist.

CONTEXTUALIST IDENTITY AS MAKING ONESELF

From the contextualist perspective, identity is made by oneself through choices and commitments and through constructing a life narrative about oneself. The child's actions—constructing and choosing among alternative identities, making and maintaining commitments, filling roles in relationship to others, and constructing a coherent and meaningful life story—are fundamental and necessary in this creative process of identity development. From an essentialist perspective, identity development is a process of discovering one's personal attributes, while from a contextualist perspective, identity development is a process of creating and constructing one's attributes. Whereas from an essentialist perspective identity development is a solitary activity, a looking inward, from a contextualist perspective identity development is a social process. It includes considering alternative roles for being in relationships with others in society, choosing among those roles, accepting responsibility for one's choices, and making a commitment to enduring and positive relationships with other people.

This contextualist perspective on identity development as making or constructing oneself is illustrated by Sara Smolinsky (Yezierska 1925), who as a mature and confident young woman declares that her identity will be the result primarily of her own actions as she constructs a role for herself in relationship to others in society: "I want to learn something. I want to do something. I want some day to make myself for a person [sic] and come among people" (66). The contextualist perspective on identity implies the development of will, which involves the construction of a set of personal values and the strength to act consistently with those values. Sara illustrates the development of will and the ability to make and maintain commitments when she confronts and leaves her father, who continues to cling to his traditional values: "You made the lives of the other children. I'm going to make my own life. . . . My will is as strong as yours. Nobody can stop me. I'm not from the old country. I'm American." Primarily as a result of her own actions, she succeeds: "Nothing had ever come to me without going after it. I had to fight for my living, fight for every bit of education" (218). "I, Sara Smolinsky, had done what I had set out to do. I was now a teacher in the public schools. And this was but the first step in the ladder of my new life" (241). Her understanding of her identity as a teacher reflects not primarily heredity or environment but instead her own actions, including constructing a realistic interpretation of her family and social context, creating a potential identity for herself as a teacher, and making and maintaining commitments to being industrious and to working together with others to achieve her life goal.

The primary importance of children's actions, rather than heredity and environment, in the development of identity is evident in Charlayne Hunter-Gault's (1992) account of becoming a broadcast journalist. When a mob of loud and violent students protests her presence as a black student on a previously segregated college campus, she finds that "the newfound sense of mission that now motivated us evolved for me out of a natural desire to fulfill a dream I had nurtured from an early age. With a passion bordering on obsession, I wanted to be a journalist, a dream that would have been, if not unthinkable, at least undoable in the South of my early years. But no one had ever told me not to dream, and when the time came to act on that dream, I would not let anything stand in the way of fulfilling it" (4). Through her own actions, she was able to overcome the apparent obstacles of heredity (skin color) and environment (racism). The similarities in the process of identity development for both Smolinsky and Hunter-Gault are consistent with the contextualist perspective. Each constructs a personal set of values and a potential identity or dream, making a commitment to these values so that they become inseparable from her self, and each pursues her dream with will power and determination.

One can compare the strong role of children's actions in contextualist identity development—interpreting, constructing, choosing, making commitments, pursuing—with the relatively minor role of children's actions from the other three perspectives. At the mid-point of Minatoya's (1993) story, her essentialist self-reflection (action) and self-awareness (voice) of who and what she has become are at a low level: "I never asked myself, 'Do I want this?'" (68). It falls to one of her students to advocate that she adopt a more contextualist approach: "The point simply is to make an initial act toward what you want to become. Stop ruminating and consider your life in terms of actions you can take" (69). Yet Minatoya's action in response to the student, at this point in her story, does not rise to the level of passion and determination so evident in Smolinsky's and Hunter-Gault's accounts: "And so I set out on my journey, trying to change discomfort with my choices into comfort with unknowing" (69). Nor is the role of Baker's (1982) action in his mechanistic account of the formation of his identity as a writer—"It was my mother's idea" (17)—as powerful as in Sara Smolinsky's and Hunter-Gault's contextualist accounts.

The conclusion of Santiago's (1993) autobiography leaves the reader with the impression that she has rejected the organismic perspective and is adopting a more proactive, contextualist perspective on identity and life. "I decided that I had to get out of Brooklyn. Mami had chosen this as our home, and just like every other time we'd moved, I'd had to go along with her because I was a child who had no choice. But I wasn't willing to go along with her on this one" (260). When she yells at her mother, "I hate my life," her mother yells back, "Then do something about it" (261). Santiago writes, "I felt the force of her ambition without knowing exactly what she meant" (263), but subsequently she obtains library books to expand her English vocabulary and applies to and gains acceptance into a high school performing-arts program that leads eventually to college and success in her adult role in society. Thus Santiago's organismic destiny in relation to gender roles, strongly determined by biology and culture, is replaced with a contextualist dream that she makes into a reality through her own actions of constructing new interpretations of the social environment and entering into more positive relationships with others.

Similarly, Gates's rejection of the essentialist perspective on identity—"I rebel at the notion that I can't construct identities through elective affinity" (1994, xv)—enables him to adopt a contextualist perspective in which his own interpretations and commitments become primary determinants of his identity. The evidence is apparent at many points in his autobiography: "I was more aggressive around white people than Daddy" (85); "I personally integrated many places at Rehoboth Beach that summer" (195); and on his college application, "Allow me to prove myself" (201). (Additional examples of using autobiographical accounts to illustrate processes in child development are provided in Meacham 1999a, 1999b.)

Conclusion

Increasing our understanding of children's lives and doing our best to overcome problems and to improve the prospects for children require maintaining our vigilance against incomplete and incorrect claims that call attention to only one or two of the three determinants of children's development: heredity, environment, and children's actions. In particular, the role of children's actions has been too often neglected and must be more fully acknowledged. How we believe these three determinants come together within one of the four metaphors of essence, organism, machine, and historical context can lead to markedly different understandings of children's lives and of the role and significance of the processes of action and voice. It may be fashionable, but it is no longer sufficient, to merely describe and praise children's use of action and voice as though we all understand these terms and agree about their meaning. Further progress in understanding the lives of children requires that we be far more precise. By children's action, do we mean self-reflection, self-organization, behaving, or interpreting? By children's voice, do we mean self-awareness, conversation, speaking, or cooperating? The way we answer those questions will have significant impact on how we understand children and on the prospects for children's lives both now and in the future.

References

Baker, R. 1982. *Growing Up*. New York: Signet.
Carmichael, L. 1925. "Heredity and Environment: Are They Antithetical?" *Journal of Abnormal and Social Psychology* 20:245–260.

Eckensberger, L. H., and J. A. Meacham. 1984. "The Essentials of Action Theory: A Framework for Discussion." *Human Development* 27:166–172.

Gates Jr., H. L. 1994. *Colored People*. New York: Knopf.

Gilligan, C. 1982. *In a Different Voice*. Cambridge: Harvard University Press.

Hunter-Gault, C. 1992. *In My Place*. New York: Farrar, Straus & Giroux.

Meacham, J. A. 1981. "Political Values, Conceptual Models, and Research." In *Individuals as Producers of Their Development: A Life-Span Perspective*, edited by R. M. Lerner and N. A. Busch-Rossnagel. New York: Academic Press.

Meacham, J. A. 1984. "The Individual as Consumer and Producer of Historical Change." In *Life-Span Developmental Psychology: Historical and Generational Effects*, edited by K. A. McCluskey and H. W. Reese. New York: Academic Press.

Meacham, J. A. 1991. "The Concept of Nature: Implications for Assessment of Competence." In *Criteria for Competence: Controversies in the Conceptualization and Assessment of Children's Abilities*, edited by M. J. Chandler and M. W. Chapman. Hillsdale, N.J.: Erlbaum.

Meacham, J. A. 1994. "Identity, Community, and Prejudice." *Journal of Adult Development* 1 (3): 169–180.

Meacham, J. A. 1999a. "Autobiography, Voice, and Developmental Theory." In *Change and Development: Issues of Theory, Method, and Application*, edited by E. Amsel and K. A. Renninger. Hillsdale, N.J.: Erlbaum.

Meacham, J. A. 1999b. "Transforming a Developmental Psychology Course to Reflect Students' Diversity." *Transformations* 10:26–38.

Minatoya, L. 1993. *Talking to High Monks in the Snow*. New York: Harper Perennial.

Pepper, S. C. 1942. *World Hypotheses*. Berkeley: University of California Press.

Ryan, W. 1976. *Blaming the Victim*. New York: Vintage Books.

Santiago, E. 1993. *When I Was Puerto Rican*. New York: Vintage Books.

Yezierska, A. 1925. *Bread Givers*. New York: Persea Books.

Part II

Voice and Agency in Education

"Do You Know You Have Worms on Your Pearls?"

Chapter 5

SUSAN ETHEREDGE

Listening to Children's Voices in the Classroom

Pᴜʙʟɪᴄ ᴇᴅᴜᴄᴀᴛɪᴏɴ ɪɴ ᴛʜᴇ United States is immersed in a standards movement. Curriculum and instructional standards and assessment measures are current and recurring themes in the national and local discourse and debate. School systems throughout the country are reforming their curricular and instructional practices to align them more directly with national and state standards in the language arts, mathematics, science, social studies, and other disciplines.

A close reading of the national standards in each of the academic disciplines reveals that all these standards have a similar, overarching goal: to prepare students to be critical and creative thinkers and problem solvers and knowledgeable, active, cooperative, and reflective members of their learning communities. For example, the *National Science Education Standards*, published in 1995, in articulating one of its teaching standards, charges teachers to do the following (45–46):

> Teachers of science develop communities of science learners that reflect
> the intellectual rigor of scientific inquiry and the attitudes and social
> values conducive to science learning. In doing this, teachers
> - Display and demand respect for the diverse ideas, skills, and experiences of all students.
> - Enable students to have a significant voice in decisions about the

content and context of their work and require students to take
responsibility for the learning of all members of the community.
- Nurture collaboration among students.
- Structure and facilitate ongoing formal and informal discussion
  based on a shared understanding of rules of scientific discourse.
- Model and emphasize the skills, attitudes, and values of scientific
  inquiry.

The focus of this standard is the social and intellectual environment that must be in place in the classroom if all students are to succeed
in learning science and have the opportunity to develop the skills and
dispositions for life-long learning. Elements of other standards are
brought together by this standard to highlight the importance of the
community of learners and what effective teachers do to foster its development. A community approach enhances learning: It helps to advance
understanding, expand students' capabilities for investigation, enrich
the questions that guide inquiry, and aid students in giving meaning to
experiences.

Classrooms as Communities of Learners

This science teaching and learning standard, as well as the national standards
in the other academic disciplines, reflects the universal call in the research literature on best practices in teaching and learning: to create classrooms that function as communities of learners. These are classrooms where inquiry, discourse,
sense making, reflection, and shared understandings and respect are central. In
such a learning community, investigation is encouraged. Children and teachers
act as researchers together, immersed in authentic, real-world contexts and problems. In a true community of learners, children pose questions and create, debate, and negotiate their theories. Teachers extend, build, and elaborate on
children's questions and theories. In a classroom learning community active exchange is expected, modeled, practiced, and sustained by the teacher and the
children. This active and rich exchange leads to the building of relationships
within the classroom. Understanding, respecting, and valuing others' perspectives, experiences, and expertise, as well as one's own, grow out of the interdependence created in such a reciprocal environment. Individual differences among
learners and their ways of knowing and experiencing the world are reflected,
respected, and embraced.

Implicit in this call for classrooms as communities of learners is the belief
that learning is socially constructed activity. This paradigm places a great emphasis on the social context for cognitive, social, and emotional development
in the school setting. Vygotsky's (1978) work highlighting the social roots of
learning and the important presence of the expert hand to scaffold another's
learning has strongly influenced pedagogical practices in the early-childhood

education and elementary school. The social-cognition, or sociocultural, perspective (Vygotsky 1978; Wertsch 1985; Lave 1988; Rogoff 1994) sees the child as an active, social constructor of knowledge. The teacher's role in this model is to mediate actively the child's developing understandings, to provide the scaffold for the child's growing knowledge structures, and to facilitate peer collaboration in the classroom. To perform this role well, teachers must know how to listen to children and how to provide place and space in the classroom for the child's voice to be heard.[1]

In such classrooms, teachers must rethink the traditional and practiced role of teachers as "transmitters of knowledge" and move to pedagogical models that recognize the power and potential of the social context for promoting cognitive development, a reflection of the view of the child as an active, social constructor of knowledge. This is not an easy shift for most teachers to make. The "teacher question—student answer—teacher response" cycle is the communication pattern most students experience in the typical public school in the United States. Teacher-education programs have traditionally highlighted the objectives and lesson-plan approach, a prescriptive, procedural approach to teaching. Building a community of inquiry and discourse in a classroom replaces a procedural approach and requires a complex set of understandings and skills on the part of the teacher. It calls for a different conception of teacher, student, and classroom than the one we have traditionally held, and it calls for a different conception of curriculum and instruction as well.

Models of Practice

We therefore need models of practice, pedagogical and philosophical examples of how teachers create such classroom environments. Novice, veteran, and future teachers have few models, if any, in their own learning histories to understand what a community of inquiry in a classroom truly is. The research on teaching illustrates that teachers are most inclined to teach in the ways they were taught. Models continue to be the most powerful teachers for the preservice teacher; and the "teacher question—student answer—teacher response" pattern of communication is usually the one teachers know best.

The difference in these pedagogical models is illustrated in the following two vignettes of the early-morning activity in two different elementary school classrooms:

Vignette I. It is 8:30 A.M. on a November morning. The children enter the classroom to begin their day at school. They shed their coats and jackets, hang them in their cubby spaces, and head toward their desks. Some visit and exchange greetings as they make their way to their desks. A few engage in a bit of harmless mischief with each other along the way. Others go directly to their seats and talk to classmates seated around them. The teacher is busy at her desk at the front of the room, organizing papers, checking her plan book, taking attendance, and writing the day's assignments on the board. At 8:45, the teacher asks the children to stand to recite the Pledge of Allegiance. When they finish the pledge, she tells them to open their math books to page 88 and asks a child to begin reading at the top of the page. The child reads a paragraph that reviews the procedures for solving arithmetic word problems. The teacher asks the children to solve the first problem on the page and reminds them to work quietly at their desks. She waits while they work independently. When most of the children have completed the problem, the teacher asks for the answer. Many hands go up. She calls on one student to give the answer, asks whether others got the same answer, confirms that the answer is correct, and then assigns the next six word problems. The children work at their desks while the teacher works at hers. The school day has begun.

Vignette II. It is 8:30 A.M. on a November morning. The children enter the classroom to begin their day at school. The teacher stands by the classroom door and greets the children and family members who have accompanied children to school. The children shed their coats and jackets, hang them in their cubby spaces, and busily exchange personal anecdotes and assorted belongings with classmates. The teacher freely engages in conversations with the children. She asks them about the things they have brought to school or follows up on unfinished conversations from the day before. Children mill about the room, some going directly to do the class jobs they are responsible for that week (taking attendance, taking chairs off the desktops, watering the plants). By 8:45, most of the children have made their way to the rug in one corner of the room where they begin the school day with a morning meeting. The teacher asks them all to take their places in a circle on the rug. She takes her place in the circle, says good morning, welcomes the children to school, and asks them to begin the morning rituals (lunch and milk count, calendar, review of the day's schedule that is posted on the board, sharing of class news or a poem). When the children and teacher complete the morning rituals, the teacher asks the children to partner with their math buddies. She tells them that they will continue the previous day's work on arithmetic word problems. Together they review what they did the day before, and then the teacher assigns them three problems to work on, first independently and then with their buddies. She encourages them to use the math manipulatives or to draw pictures if they need to while they work to solve the problems, and to discuss their strategies and solutions with their math partners. The teacher also tells them that they will have to describe their solution strategies to the rest of the class later in the morning. She says that she is looking forward to hearing about all the different mathematical ways they approach the problems. The children get to work while the teacher observes them and circulates around the room, checking in with individual children as needed. The school day has begun.

These two vignettes illustrate different classroom environments that we can find in any public elementary school in the United States. The classroom in the first vignette is the one we more typically come across. The "teacher question—student answer—teacher response" communication cycle there reflects a routine, procedural, and scripted approach to teaching and learning. Wells, Chang, and Mahar (1990) describe such an approach as unidirectional. The teacher and the texts are the transmitters of information to students in such classrooms, and the students are the receptors of the information. Little or no emphasis is placed on student discussion and exchange, investigation, or problem solving.

And yet a substantial and convincing body of educational research indicates that children score higher on measures of academic achievement and social skills in classrooms where they are engaged in collaborative learning, critical and creative thinking and problem solving, and explicit instruction and practice in social skills (Brown and Campione 1996).[2] Common to these kinds of classrooms is an emphasis on dialogical exchange and reflexivity, communal activity and shared learning goals, support and respect for individual inquiry processes, and active reflection on learning processes and outcomes—objectives that are espoused in the current national standards in all academic disciplines. We find such a classroom environment in the second vignette, where children's voices and activity have place and presence.

In these classroom environments, teachers understand and respect children's agency. They embrace the notion that children are negotiating complex social worlds and constructing multiple identities as they engage in these worlds. They believe that school is a place for children to explore important personal, social, cognitive, and cultural connections and, most of all, that the classroom is a place of social and intellectual relationship.

Studying a Model Learning Community

This chapter is about what I saw, heard, and experienced in such a classroom, a specific classroom in a specific school. It is a story of Jane's classroom in the Easton Road School, a classroom where the child's voice is central to the mission and vision of her philosophy and practice as a teacher.

The Easton Road School is a public elementary school in a city with a population of about thirty thousand in the northeastern United States. One of four elementary schools in the city, it currently serves 337 children in preschool through grade five. Students of color make up 35 percent of the population; 40 percent of the student body qualify for free and reduced cost lunch. The principal is committed to small class size and has worked tirelessly to maintain classrooms of twenty or fewer children. In Jane's classroom of seventeen six- and seven-year-olds, seven first languages are represented: Albanian, English, French, Italian, Portuguese, Spanish, and Vietnamese.

I began this observational study with the general question "What is going on in this classroom?" For a number of years I had been hearing stories of this teacher; community members (parents, principals, teachers, student teachers, and colleagues) described her as someone who "really listens to children"; "presents curriculum that is meaningful and relevant to children's lives and the 'real world'"; "connects with children, parents, and community"; "gets children to think"; "is multicultural in her approach"; "challenges the status quo in classrooms." I was intrigued. I was curious. I wanted to know what she did and how she did it. Jane had been teaching for four years; this was not the case of a veteran teacher who had had many years of practiced observation, experience, and study.

My research methodology combined observation, participant observation, and informal interview. I spent time observing in Jane's classroom during the first four months of the school year, most weeks spending a morning or an afternoon and, occasionally, a full day.[3] I accompanied Jane on some home visits before the first day of school. I was in her classroom on the first day of school. I went to the family night in the fall, an evening for family members to be in the classroom and meet the teachers. I went to a family potluck lunch in December and observed as the children read some of their work aloud to their families. I had many conversations with parents of children in Jane's class (past and present), with community members and school administrators who know her professional practice well, and with student teachers (also past and present) who have learned under her tutelage. I assumed the supervision of the student teacher in Jane's classroom at the end of the semester, so I found myself experiencing the same classroom also through the eyes and the reflections of the student teacher. I met with Jane often throughout the semester, at her home and at school, to discuss the curriculum, her practice, and the children. We also had many telephone conversations over the course of the semester.

The Principles of Good Practice

At the finish of my research, my intent was to construct a portrait of this classroom and its inner workings. As I began to review and reflect on my field notes after a number of days of observation, I saw that the child's voice is present and central to all that was happening there. It is heard loudly and clearly and is expected, invited, and embraced not only by the teacher but by the children as well. My initial question—"What is going on in this classroom?"—then evolved into a more specific question: "How is the child's voice invited, heard, and responded to in this classroom?" When I organized and coded my observational and interview data, a set of seven principles, or beliefs, emerged that defined and guided Jane's daily praxis in consistent and regular ways:

The fundamental need for relationship and reciprocity
The central role of autobiography
The power and potential of ordinary classroom moments
The construction of common purpose
The structure and design of the physical environment
The curricular emphasis on inquiry
The goal of self-efficacy

In this chapter, I frame the discussion of each guiding principle with the question "How is the child's voice invited, heard, and responded to in Jane's classroom?" I use verbatim quotes and classroom vignettes, as recorded in my field notes, to describe and provide examples of each principle. I intentionally use many examples from the first weeks of the school year because I wish to provide a picture of how the teacher consciously sets the context and expectations for children's voices to be heard and listened to, starting during the first days of school.

THE FUNDAMENTAL NEED FOR RELATIONSHIP AND RECIPROCITY

"Do you know you have worms on your pearls?" a child asks me one morning as I sit in the corner trying to be invisible, observing and scribbling away in my notebook. I am taken by surprise. I look up from my notebook, and there's Anna standing in front of me, pointing to my handcrafted necklace of Slinky-like cording, interspersed every so often with white pearls. The school year has been in session for about a month. Jane had introduced me to the class the first day of school as a college professor who wanted to know more about how teachers teach children in first and second grade. I had become the visitor, the outsider, the person who came once a week, who sat and watched, who wrote in a notebook, and who never talked (except to the teachers). Anna was going to change that. She did. I responded, and we started a conversation. From that day forward, I became a participant observer when I visited this classroom. It was too difficult, impossible actually, not to become a member of this classroom community.

Seeking and building relationships and connections within the classroom and with the community outside of the classroom are fundamental aspects of Jane's philosophy and practice. She begins to know her children and families before the school year starts. She visits them in their homes. This is not a schoolwide practice. Jane visits families because she believes it is important. It demonstrates her desire to know the families of her students and the value she places on building relationships with them.

"Who knows the child better than the parent?" Jane asks me as we drive to a student's home. "I learn an enormous amount about each child when I meet them with their families in their homes." She asks the parents or guardians to be sure that the children are there when she visits. And she talks directly to the child when she arrives at the house. She begins listening to the child on that day.

We arrive at Oscar's house. Jane introduces herself to Oscar and his parents. Oscar announces that he doesn't want to go to school because he doesn't like school. (He is beginning second grade.) Jane asks him what he doesn't like about school. He tells her that his teacher yelled at him a lot in first grade. She says that she is sorry to hear that and engages him in a conversation about what kind of place he wishes school would be for him. "I really like to read," Oscar tells Jane. "I like to read really good books, not the baby books my teacher made me read last year. And I like to draw a lot."

Jane asks Oscar to tell her about some of his favorite books. He does. The conversation continues, with Oscar doing most of the talking. He digs out some of his drawings from under a pile of papers on the dining-room table. He tells Jane about the drawings. A neighborhood friend comes to the door to invite Oscar to play outside. Jane tells him how much she looks forward to seeing him in school in a few days. They shake hands, and Oscar bounces out of the room with a smile on his face to join his friend in play.

Oscar's parents then openly share their concerns about the difficult year Oscar had in first grade. Jane listens intently. She invites Oscar's parents to check in with her often, especially during the first few weeks of school, and she promises to do the same. She invites them to spend time in the classroom.

We return to the car. Jane begins to discuss her impressions of Oscar and his shaky relationship with school. I realize that Jane has recorded Oscar's favorite book titles and a few of his other likes and dislikes. She intends, she tells me, to put some of Oscar's favorite books on the classroom library shelf the first day of school.

The emphasis Jane places on forging and nurturing relationships with her students and their families builds a base for an ethos of care and concern in her classroom. She models an open and inviting style that affirms the presence of every child and family in the class. By doing so, she also increases the likelihood that her students will succeed academically. The research on family involvement in education shows that children have a greater chance of academic success if their parents or primary caregivers are integrally connected to their schools and classrooms (Henderson and Berla 1994). Jane's classroom is a place of such connection.

THE CENTRAL ROLE OF AUTOBIOGRAPHY

It is the first day of school. Jane has written a message on large chart paper on the easel:

Dear Students,

Welcome and good morning. Today is Wednesday. It is the first day of school. We are very excited to see new and old friends!

Our leaders today are Maria and Efraim. We have a special this morning. At 10:00 we will go to music.

We will have snack after music and then go to recess at 11:00. Lunch is at 12:50 every day.

We are glad to have you here!

Love,

Your teachers

Jane calls the children together on the rug. They sit in a large circle. She welcomes each child by name. She introduces the other adults in the room. Then she directs the children's attention to the morning message and reads it aloud, asking them to read along with her.

"You know, girls and boys, that in this classroom we are very lucky. We have children who speak lots of different languages: Albanian, English, French, Italian, Portuguese, Spanish, and Vietnamese." Jane writes each language on the board as she says it aloud. "Let's count how many languages are spoken by the children in this classroom. 1, 2, 3, 4, 5, 6, 7! This year, we are going to learn how to say some words in each one of these languages, and some other languages too. Every morning I will write you a message like this [points to the day's message on the easel]. One day it will be in English, and the next day it will be in Spanish."

"I'm kinda scared," Nina blurts out.

"Who had a hard time sleeping last night?" Jane asks. "Put your hand up if you had a hard time sleeping last night."

Almost all the hands shoot up. Jane tells them to look around the circle.

"Why? Were you scared, nervous, excited?"

At this point, children begin to share their stories of first-day-of-school jitters.

"I was so scared I threw up a little."

"I couldn't eat breakfast."

"I got up at 5 o'clock this morning. I was so excited!"

Jane shares her story of how she has butterflies in her stomach. The expectation that this classroom is a place for telling your stories is thus born on the first day of school, during the first minutes of the school day.

Jane introduces the class "story bag." She pulls Corduroy, a stuffed and well-loved bear out of the bag. "Corduroy has been in my class ever since I started teaching," she says. She then takes out two copies of the picture book *Corduroy*, one in English and one in Spanish. With great animation, Jane explains that Corduroy's story bag will accompany a different child home each night. In the bag is a journal. The child who takes home Corduroy and the journal writes or dictates a story about or draws a picture about Corduroy's adventures at his or her home. The child or family member who writes about Corduroy's adventures can do so in any language. The child shares his or her entry with the class the next day.

Jane continues, "Write in the book about what happens when Corduroy visits your house. Corduroy can do whatever you and your family are doing, at suppertime, at playtime, at bedtime. He has pretty good manners, you know. Oh, one other thing—there is a letter in the story bag written in both English and Spanish that tells your family all about the story bag."

Nina is one of the first students to take Corduroy home with her. Here is Nina's entry about Corduroy's visit to her house:

> It was a hot day. Corduroy was happy to get out of the bag and take a look around Nina's new house. We had fun going up and down the stairs. Then we watched *The Ketchup Vampire*. In the beginning I held Corduroy cause it was a scary video. When it was over I asked Corduroy what he wanted to be for Halloween? He said a bat! Then we had Mommy pull us to the park in the green wagon. We went to the forest and he thought it was his home. There was no honey but there were flowers and bees. BZZZ. We went to the playground at the YMCA. Corduroy liked the slide and swing. We went home for water and pasta. Then off again to stroll around the block to my babysitter's house. Now Corduroy and I are ready to snuggle in bed. Sweet dreams.

The use of story or narrative to make meaning, to order and organize concepts, and to discover central themes is well established in the literature related to teaching and learning. Sillick (1997) writes, "Story is the primary structure through which humans think, relate, and communicate"(64). Bruner (1986) reminds us that the narrative mode, the telling of stories, is the way human beings express their understandings about the world. Story transcends culture; it is a universal construct. In Jane's classroom, the story bag journal becomes a means for a dynamic exchange of family stories, of autobiographies. It provides a window through which to see the daily lives of Jane's students beyond the classroom walls.

THE POWER AND POTENTIAL OF ORDINARY CLASSROOM MOMENTS

It is the second day of the new school year. Jane's classroom is a busy place. Many adults come in and out throughout the day to work with individual children or to assist the teacher. There is also a student teacher. Jane hears Aisha ask Adam, "Now who are the teachers in here anyway?" She senses confusion and frustration in Aisha's question. The next day, Jane takes time during morning meeting to talk about the various adults who spend time in the classroom each day. She also sends a letter home to parents (in English and Spanish), describing the daily schedule and introducing them to the adults who participate in the daily life of the classroom. This is an example of how the words of children are considered seriously and heard in Jane's classroom. Ordinary moments of classroom conversation between and among children hold the power and potential for curricular response on Jane's part. She listens carefully and pays attention.

Another illustration of how Jane takes advantage of ordinary classroom moments is the story of the dead bee. Having found a dead bee on the way to school, Jane shows it to the class during morning meeting. She had thought it would be interesting to look at and then develop conjectures about how it had died. Instead, the children are inspired to move the conversation in another direction:

"It's alive!" exclaims one child, who is sure he saw it move.

"It came back to life!" says another.

"It's a miracle!" concludes a chorus of voices, almost in unison.

This round of observations leads to further discussion about miracles, perceptions, and spiritual and scientific explanations. What Jane had initially thought would be a quick look at an interesting insect becomes a philosophical discussion about death and the nature of miracles.[4]

Jane understands the importance of taking time during the day to pursue "the unplanned" with her children. She is willing to put aside her scripted lesson plan to follow up on a child's hunch, observation, or question. During these moments, she tells me, she comes to understand how her children think, what they are thinking about, and how they put ideas together. She gets to know her children better and, in turn, can be more responsive to their needs and learning styles. These unplanned conversations also serve as fodder for future curricular pursuits.

THE CONSTRUCTION OF COMMON PURPOSE

It is the second week of school. Jane introduces the word *goal*. "Does anyone know what a goal is?" Jane inquires. Together the class generates examples. Jane moves the discussion to the importance of having goals for the school year, individual goals and group goals. She asks children to reflect on their individual goals. They discuss them together in the circle, and then go to their desks to record their goals in words and pictures:

"I want to have fun playing with my friends."

"I want to learn new math and make new friends."

"I want to learn more stuff about the world."

"I want to play with money and pretend I'm rich."

"I want to learn more science."

Jane displays each child's articulated and illustrated goal on the classroom walls. The goal is always in the child's words; Jane does not rewrite them.

The following day, during morning meeting, the children carry on the tradition that has been set since the first day of school: Each child says good morning to the child next to him or her, calls the child by name, smiles, and makes eye contact. This ritual is repeated, child by child, all around the circle. Then they read the morning message together. Jane tells them that she wants to hear everyone reading the message aloud. "It's a shared reading," she says. "Every voice is important."

Then children share personal artifacts they have brought from home. Jane has set one rule: no toys allowed. She stays in the background during the sharing. Children ask each other questions about their artifacts. They manage their own conversation. Jane intervenes only when they need reminding about how to listen well to one another and take turns.

Jane explicitly teaches her children skills for living and working together in respectful and caring ways. There is a sense of a shared, common purpose among these children and this teacher. They come to know each other's aspirations and goals, and they learn about and reflect on their own in the process. Research indicates that positive interdependence is developed in classrooms through the setting and articulation of mutual goals, and it results in increased student learning (Bereiter et al. 1997; Brown and Campione 1996; Good and Brophy 1999).

THE STRUCTURE AND DESIGN OF THE PHYSICAL ENVIRONMENT
Five posters are on the classroom walls:

Activism: An activist is someone who wants something to change, but they don't just sit there and wish it. They try and change it, like Martin Luther King. An activist makes it happen.

Exploit: Telling someone else to do all the work, so you get rich.

Organize: Getting a plan ready in order to protest and make change.

Protest: Argue, speak, or take action against something unfair. Could be violent or non-violent.

Cooperate: Work together with friends and others.

Underneath each poster are illustrations and descriptions of these concepts, which Waddell presents in his book *Farmer Duck* (1996). These posters, illustrations, and descriptions are the words of the children in Jane's classroom. They worked in groups to define the concepts of activism, exploit, organize, protest, and cooperate. They then dictated their definitions to Jane, and she recorded their words.

On another wall is a world map and the following quotation: "Learn, Reflect, Question, and Work to make the world a better place"—the words of researcher Sonia Nieto (1999). Next to that display is a poster of Albert Einstein with his words: "In the middle of difficulty lies opportunity." On yet another wall are photographs of twelve leaders of civil rights movements. And clipped to a clothesline that is strung from one classroom wall to another are the handprints of each child, in an array of skin colors and tones, with an accompanying explanation: "We used paints [primary colors] and color theory to understand melanin and how skin color is part of identity."

In this classroom, the children's words and images are displayed alongside the works and words of great thinkers, leaders, and artists. There are no cute, Hallmark-type decorations on these walls. The physical environment reflects and respects the child's voice, hand, and mind. There is an implicit message in this space that says to children, "What you have to say is important." The curriculum is evident through the child's translation and representation. The physical environment functions as a teacher of sorts. Jane consciously and actively uses the physical environment as a teaching and learning tool.

THE CURRICULAR EMPHASIS ON INQUIRY

"Kids need food, drink, warm and safe places."

"We couldn't survive if no one cared about us or loved us."

"If no one gave you food, you would just die."

These are children's responses to a question Jane posed as she was ready to launch a unit on nutrition: "What do kids need?" She likes to start new curricular units with questions. But most of all she wants to find ways to engage children immediately through questions that they can answer based on their prior knowledge and experience.

She finds another way to capture a spirit of inquiry by having the students keep "moon journals." The children observe the moon at night, from their own windows or yards at home, and, noting the time and date, they describe the moon with words and pictures.

> JACK: "8:30 P.M. It looks like the moon is a robber stealing the earth, carrying it in its arms."
>
> JOSE: "The old moon is in the arms of the new?"
>
> JANE: "Jack, did you hear the connection that Jose made to what you said?"

Jack nods. Jose looks pleased.

ELIZA: "Jack, I looked for the moon at 8:30 P.M., and I didn't see no moon
out there."

JANE: "Hmm, that is an interesting observation, especially if we're
looking at this from multiple perspectives. What do I mean by
'multiple perspectives'?"

By building the curriculum on what children already know and can do, Jane
provides meaningful entry points for all the children. Each child can find a way
to engage that makes sense to him or her; every perspective is valuable; and every question is valued. Communal literacy and inquiry are at work here. Wells
(1999) defines inquiry as "an approach to the chosen themes and topics in which
the posing of real questions is positively encouraged, whenever they occur and
by whomever they are asked. Equally important as the hallmark of an inquiry
approach is that all tentative answers are taken seriously and are investigated as
rigorously as the circumstances permit" (11). Jane continually searches for the
child's question and nurtures and sustains it throughout the curricular frame-
works, the prescribed framework as well as the emergent one.

THE GOAL OF SELF-EFFICACY

Ricardo loves the natural world. He is always bringing insects, leaves, and other
plant parts to school to share with his classmates. He relentlessly seeks out classmates to (in his own words) "do science research" with him on his found objects. His dream is to become a scientist. Although he struggles with reading,
he organizes "research teams" of classmates so that those who can read become
his readers. Jane is always searching for easy-to-read science books for him. She
also works hard to integrate stories about scientists of color into the curriculum. One day, immediately after a class viewing of a videotape of Puerto Rican
scientists doing research in the Yunque Rainforest, Ricardo anxiously asks Jane,
"Can I still be a scientist if I'm only *half* Puerto Rican?"

Jane is committed to helping children discover their power, potential, capacity, and competence. She seizes opportunities to engage children in reflection about who they are and how they can affect their immediate world in
important ways. Jane wants them to use their skills and understandings effectively and thoughtfully.

At the end of a recycling unit, the children suggest to Jane that they invite
the head of the school system's food services to their class to ask him about some
cafeteria practices they have concluded are not environmentally sound. The children prepare questions for the department head and arguments as well. On the
day of his visit, a child quickly reminded her classmates before he enters the
room, "Remember, we don't want to scare him!"

The children debrief one another after the department head's visit. They decide that they should have had more facts and figures at their fingertips to argue their positions more knowledgeably and forcefully. They will be better prepared for a similar visit in the future, they agree. A child concludes, "We have to ask more 'what if' questions next time."

Jane wants her students to develop an active social consciousness. She wants them to understand that they can make a difference in the world, individually as well as collectively. Jane's curriculum engages students in socially responsible thinking and doing.

Conclusion

The children in Jane's classroom are not passive recipients but active constructors of their classroom community. Their life narratives shape the curriculum. Each voice is needed and honored. All together, these voices create a community of inquiry and discourse that nourishes individual identity and spirit while also building and sustaining a collective group identity.[5] Teachers do not create communities of inquiry in their classrooms; the children and the teacher together construct community over time. In this classroom, the ever-present, tacit understanding is: "You matter. Your stories matter. Your life inside and outside of school matters. What you have to offer matters."

A teacher-made poster has a place of honor in Jane's classroom: "Studying is, above all, thinking about experience, and thinking about experience is the best way to think accurately. One who studies should never stop being curious about other people and reality. There are those who ask, those who try to find answers, and those who keep on searching. To study is not to consume ideas, but to create and re-create them" (attributed by the teacher to Paulo Freire). In this intellectually vibrant classroom community, teacher and children do just that: create and re-create ideas. They actively produce knowledge, inquiring and imagining together. They seek, consider, and negotiate multiple perspectives and interpretations. They are a community in search of "worms on pearls."

The philosopher of education John Dewey (1938) believed that education is not only a matter of garnering knowledge and skill but of learning how to use that knowledge and skill effectively in daily life, "to know, to care, and to act" (Banks 2002, 32). The children in Jane's classroom are indeed thinking, learning, and working together in ways that will prepare them for a lifetime of critical thinking, cooperative teamwork, engaged citizenship, and respectful exchange in their workplaces and communities. The model of the learning community put in place here has demonstrated its effectiveness.

Notes

1. The world-renowned early-childhood schools of Reggio Emilia, Italy, provide a state-of-the-art model for what researcher Carla Rinaldi calls "a pedagogy of listening" (unpublished lecture, Lesley College Reggio Institute, Cambridge, Mass., May 1997). The teacher's role in these schools is to be a facilitator and to provide a scaffold. In the Reggio Emilia model, young children collaboratively pursue long-term projects that engage their different learning styles in complex and sophisticated ways. They construct knowledge through exploring and representing concepts and ideas in multiple modalities and sign systems (drawing, painting, sculpture, music, drama, music, movement, oral language). See Edwards, Gandini, and Forman 1998 for an extensive collection of readings about the philosophy and practices of the Reggio Approach.
2. In addition to Brown and Campione, see Banks 2001, Bereiter et al. 1997, Chapter 6 in this book, Good and Brophy 1999, Johnson and Johnson 1992, Nieto 1999, Slavin 1996.
3. I wish to acknowledge and thank the Jean Picker Fellowship Program at Smith College for its generous support of this research project.
4. Jane applies a philosophy curriculum in her teaching practice. She is inspired by the writings and research of philosophers Gareth Matthews and Thomas Wartenberg.
5. Jane is an example of a teacher who adopts and applies the contextualist metaphor (as described by Jack Meacham in Chapter 4). She holds an image of the child as an interpreter, a maker of meaning, and a knowledge constructor. She provides opportunities in her classroom for children to invent, create, and affirm their identities. She listens to children and supports their goal setting and choices.

References

Banks, J. C. 2001. *Cultural Diversity and Education: Foundations, Curriculum, and Teaching*. Boston: Allyn & Bacon.

Banks, J. C. 2002. *An Introduction to Multicultural Education*. Boston: Allyn & Bacon.

Bereiter, C., M. Scardamalia, C. Cassells, and J. Hewitt. 1997. "Postmodernism, Knowledge Building, and Elementary Science." *Elementary School Journal* 97:329–340.

Brown, A. L., and J. C. Campione. 1996. "Psychological Theory and the Design of Innovative Learning Environments: On Procedures, Principles, and Systems." In *Teaching for Transfer: Fostering Generalization in Learning*, edited by A. McKeough, J. Lupart, and A. Marini. Mahwah, N.J.: Erlbaum.

Bruner, J. S. 1986. *Actual Minds, Possible Worlds*. Cambridge: Harvard University Press.

Dewey, J. 1938. *Experience and Education*. New York: Macmillan.

Edwards, C., L. Gandini, and G. Forman 1998. *The Hundred Languages of Children*. 2d ed. Norwood, N.J.: Ablex.

Good, T., and J. Brophy. 1999. *Looking in Classrooms*. Boston: Allyn & Bacon.

Henderson, A. T., and N. Berla. 1994. *A New Generation of Evidence: The Family Is Critical to Student Achievement*. Washington, D.C.: National Committee for Citizens in Education.

Johnson, D. W., and R. Johnson. 1992. "Implementing Cooperative Learning." *Contemporary Education* 63 (3): 173–180.

Lave, J. 1988. *Cognition in Practice: Mind, Mathematics and Culture in Everyday Life*. London: Cambridge University Press.

National Science Education Standards. 1996. Washington, D.C.: National Academy Press.

Nieto, S. 1999. *The Light in Their Eyes: Creating Multicultural Learning Communities*. New York: Teachers College Press.

Rogoff, B. 1994. "Developing Understanding of the Idea of Communities of Learners." *Mind, Culture, and Activity* 1 (4): 209–229.

Sillick, A. 1997. "The Telling of the Story." *NAMTA Journal* 22 (1): 64–80.

Slavin, R. E. 1996. "Cooperative Learning in Middle and Secondary Schools." *Clearinghouse* 69 (4): 200–204.

Vygotsky, L. 1978. *Mind in Society: The Development of Higher Psychological Processes*, edited by M. Cole, V. John-Steiner, S. Scribner, and E. Souberman. Cambridge: Harvard University Press.

Waddell, M. 1996. *Farmer Duck*. Cambridge, Mass.: Candlewick Press.

Wells, G. 1999. "Dialogic Inquiry in Education: Building on the Legacy of Vygotsky." In *Vygotskian Perspectives on Literacy Research: Constructing Meaning through Collaborative Inquiry*, edited by C. Lee and P. Smagorinsky. London: Cambridge University Press.

Wells, G., G. Chang, and A. Maher. 1990. "Creating Classroom Communities of Literate Thinkers." In *Cooperative Learning: Theory and Research*, edited by S. Sharan. Westport, Conn.: Praeger.

Wertsch, J. V. 1985. *Vygotsky and the Social Formation of Mind*. Cambridge: Harvard University Press.

Cultural Integrity and Schooling Outcomes of African American Children from Low-Income Backgrounds

Chapter 6

A. WADE BOYKIN
BRENDA A. ALLEN

How can schools better serve children from diverse backgrounds to enhance educational outcomes so that diversity becomes an asset rather than a liability?[1] In this chapter, we seek answers to this question by focusing on how to create resilient schools. Such schools function well, yield more educational success stories than not, and thrive because they produce academic talent; and they do so even though the children served may be from low-income backgrounds, dwell in inner-city communities, or come from ethnic/minority/cultural groups who historically have not fared well in public schools. The quest for resilient schools is not new. Indeed, calls for "culturally responsive pedagogy" (Ladson-Billings 1994), "equity pedagogy" (Banks and Banks 1995), "culturally congruent instruction" (Au and Kawakami 1994), "culture centered schooling" (King 1994), and "liberatory pedagogy" (Gordon 1997) indicate that our efforts to help students at risk for educational failure need to shift focus from fixing the child to fixing the educational process.

Until recently, researchers have viewed children from poor backgrounds or from marginalized groups in terms of what they do not know, cannot do, and do not get at home (Ausubel 1966; Battle and Rotter 1963; Bereiter and Engelmann 1966; Davidson and Greenberg 1967; Deutsch 1965; Marans and Lourie 1967; Hunt 1968; Katz 1973; Silverstein and Krate 1975). But a growing chorus of educational scholars and practitioners maintain that our preoccupation with potential deficits fails to acknowledge the possible benefits of knowing what these children know and can do. Moreover, the deficit model does not acknowledge that protective factors that these children get at home or from their neighborhoods could foster educational achievement (Boykin 2000; Boykin and Allen 2002; Hale 2001; Michaels 1986; Perry and Delpit 1998). Using this knowledge to inform us about the schooling process is the first step in creating resilient schools.

Cultural Integrity

Some have characterized the potential capital that children from poor backgrounds or marginalized backgrounds (or both) bring to educational situations as cultural or social differences; and they view these differences not merely as signs of uniqueness but as an indication of strength (Baratz and Baratz 1970; Gay and Abrahams 1972; Hale 2001; Michaels 1986; Stewart 1970; Williams 1974). We intend to balance the claim that there are strengths in children's cultural experiences by claiming that there is psychosocial integrity within their cultural heritage (Boykin 1996; Boykin and Allen 2002). We argue that just as it is too simplistic and uninformative to characterize children's experiences and modes of functioning solely as pathologies, inadequacies, or weaknesses, so too is it superficial to characterize them as differences, uniqueness, or strengths. The concept of psychosocial integrity balances strengths as well as weaknesses, positives as well as negatives, uniformity and inconsistency, as well as similarities and dissimilarities with other groups. Psychosocial integrity implies that children's experiences and modes of functioning are complex, coherent, and meaningful. From this perspective, the goal is to understand the members of a targeted population on their own terms, as they strive to make sense of their lives and as they attempt to interpret, coordinate, and negotiate successfully their perceived and experienced realities. We share with many who press for resilient schools the belief that this integrity is based in the experiences, habits, values, and beliefs that these children bring with them to the classroom.

We have pursued effective ways of building on the cultural integrity of various domestic cultural groups in order to enhance educational outcomes. This integrity-based approach, we believe, offers two fundamental insights into children's educational experience. First, evidence suggests that dishonoring the cultural integrity children bring with them to school can lead these children to acts of resistance in the classroom. The classic work of Piestrup (1973) furnishes an illustration. Efforts to suppress Black English during literacy lessons by correcting and punishing its use lead on the one hand to its increased use by first-grade low-income black children and on the other to comparatively low reading levels. Elsewhere Towns (1998) has documented resistance behaviors in low-income urban black children in response to what she has termed "structural hypocrisy." For Towns, this form of hypocrisy is evident in the contradiction between the rhetoric of inclusion and the reality of cultural exclusion. Black children often react to this hypocrisy by actively and passively resisting the majority culture's efforts to teach them skills and beliefs that are at odds with black culture. Because the majority skills are defined as critical to school success, black children tend to suffer the unfortunate consequence of unsuccessful school performance. Black and Latino youngsters often resort to protective and defensive practices when they feel that their ethnicity or culture is being disrespected, misunderstood, minimized, devalued, or ignored in their classrooms (Sheets and Gay 1996). Their ensuing behavioral disruptions suspend the conduct of the academic lesson. When teachers act as though there is no justification for such displays, their energies are focused on the disruptive behavior and not on the underlying cause. In the end, the integrity of the children's culture goes unrecognized, and they fail to thrive educationally.

Second, the theoretical validity of pursuing an integrity-based perspective can be derived from scholarship examining the interface of cognition and context (Greeno and the Middle School Mathematics Through Application Group 1997; Rogoff and Chavajay 1996; Sternberg 1986; Serpell and Boykin 1994). These same researchers have persuasively argued that the processes of human performance, cognition, and thinking are not taught in isolation. They are situated within contexts of application. Contexts are constituents of culture. Contexts owe their organization and meaning to the cultural themes within which they exist. Some culturally structured contexts have more potency for a given person than others. Batting averages or points per game may help American male children understand how to calculate and use arithmetic average, but they may be of little use to most male and female children in Thailand, where baseball does not figure so squarely within the popular culture. If a child from Thailand is slow to understand the concept of arithmetic average when baseball analogies are used as the context for teaching, it would be a mistake to conclude that Thai children have difficulty with math. A more reasonable conclusion would be that the cultural context provided for learning did little to build on the cultural themes familiar to the Thai child.

There are several reasons for this pedagogical linkage. First, culturally familiar contexts, in contrast to unfamiliar contexts, are more likely to trigger access to problem-solving strategies, relevant skills, competencies, and solution techniques. They lead to the increased likelihood of an effective outcome because of the child's familiarity with and prior experience in similar contexts. Second, the information a context affords can vary from highly relevant and functional to highly irrelevant and inconsequential. Greater familiarity and prior experience can lead to the increased likelihood that one will tune into functionally consequential information and appropriate task demands and definitions. Third, the context likely conveys perspectives, postures, and values that will seem important and appropriate to the person. Contexts that are personally significant and are as well associated with positive, enjoyable, and efficacy-based experiences may well enhance motivation and sustain the effort to learn because their cultural integrity has been engaged.

In spite of its potential heuristic value, this integrity-based perspective must overcome one particularly daunting challenge. When the notion of culture is presented for explanatory purposes, it is generally used to account for the expressions and experiences of small-scale or relatively homogeneous societies, where cultural manifestations are relatively uniform across the indigenous population. Examples can be found in traditional societies like the !Kung of the Kalahari desert (Bruner 1966) as well as within the complex societies of a dominant majority population in a Western country (Berry 1984; Super and Harkness 1986; Rogoff 1990). Cultural integrity is less often invoked as an explanation for performance in multicultural, multiethnic, and multiracial settings or societies. Particularly ignored in these diverse societies are the cultures of those domestic subpopulations that function in a subordinated fashion and whose status is dictated by the cultural imperatives of the dominant group. African Americans, especially those of low-income status, constitute such a population in the United States. Making sense of their cultural integrity within a multiplex and hierarchical society requires thinking about culture in innovative ways. In this chapter we attempt to describe cultural integrity within such a society by first depicting important aspects of the cultural process and its application to African American experiences. We then present examples from our research that illustrate how task contexts that capitalize on the cultural integrity of African American experiences can enhance the performance of black schoolchildren.

The Process of Culture

E. B. Tylor (1871) defined culture as the knowledge, beliefs, arts, morals, laws, customs, and other capabilities and habits acquired by people as members of society. Since Tylor, many have attempted to provide a crisper definition of culture, but a satisfactory conceptualization continues to be elusive. We prefer to offer an entry-level, admittedly simplified, definition that is obviously circular yet illuminating for our purposes: culture is that which is cultivated. Because in any group many things can be cultivated and for many reasons (Boykin and Allen 2002), we consider culture to be multidimensional.

Boykin and Allen (2002) present a more elaborate depiction of the multidimensional nature of culture than the one we use here. But we would like to examine the value of adopting this circular definition. At its most general level culture is the result of how reality gets codified and perceived as a world-view or as a coordinated set of beliefs or as a belief system (or as some combination of these). Belief systems and world-views refer to vantage points or perspectives from which individuals come to understand, interpret, and experience reality. A given world-view embodies a corresponding set of core cultural values. Values are interests, priorities, preferences, and goals that are foundationally and intrinsically esteemed, emphasized, and looked on favorably by a group of people. To bring us full circle, these core cultural values in turn inform particular behavioral expressions, inclinations, or regularities. Core values lead us to seek out and be receptive to those experiences and human contexts that are consistent with our own world-view and value system.

Cultural transmission is the mechanism by which culture comes to influence one's outlook, preferences, and styles. We find the notion of theme appropriation particularly useful in describing this process. Themes can be understood as blueprints for living, as designs for engaging life. Themes help to give meaning to one's existence. Cultural themes structure the social worlds within which individuals participate. Children appropriate these cultural themes and incorporate them into their emerging meaning systems as they participate in social worlds structured by given themes (Ortner 1984; Pachter and Harwood 1996; Peters and Boggs 1986; Super and Harkness 1986). For instance, a cultural theme like communalism, where emphasis is placed on the social connectedness of people, may be manifest in children's lives through their everyday practice of fictive kinship (Fordham and Ogbu 1986) and through child-rearing practices that are more focused on the relationships among members of society than on objects (Hill 1997). A cultural theme will be salient, have positive affective associations, and come to occupy a relatively central place in a child's meaning system if it is associated positively with significant others and with a sense of personal efficacy.

Theme appropriation may be culture-neutral if not culture-blind during early development. Children can incorporate themes from a variety of sources into their meaning repertoires. However, the most central, positively coded, and salient themes are likely those children acquire early in life as they function within the proximal realities of home and neighborhood. As developing children participate in such proximal experiences, the salient themes come to inform their values, perceptions, attitudes, and behaviors. These themes then culturally structure events within which children learn and through which they develop, events that rehearse competencies and cognitive skills. The proximal experiences of early childhood are later broadened when children enter school, where they may well encounter new beliefs and values.

Psychosocial Integrity and the African American Experience

Culture as used here can help us understand the psychosocial integrity of African American experiences. We conceive of African American culture as encompassing three distinct realms of experience: the mainstream, the minority, and the Afrocultural (Boykin 1983, 1986; Boykin and Allen 2000). The mainstream experience entails participation in institutions of the wider society. These include the economic, legal, and educational systems of the United States. In the mainstream, children may encounter and access cultural themes like competition, individualism (in many forms, such as self-contained individualism, acquisitive individualism, rugged individualism); materialism, and the preeminence of thinking over feeling (Ani 1994; Greenfield 1994; Katz 1985; Spence 1985). The minority experience is linked to themes of marginalization and victimization caused by racism, the denial of opportunities, and low social status. It entails the development of adaptive strategies or defense mechanisms designed to shield the self from oppressive forces (Harrell 1980; Jones 1997; Steele 1999). The Afrocultural realm is the link between contemporary African Americans and traditional African cultural legacies. Some Afrocultural themes are communalism, spirituality, the interdependence and co-importance of cognition and affect, and a premium placed on music, poly-rhythms, and percussion along with movement expressiveness (Boykin 1994; Dixon 1976; Gay 1978; Lee 1994; Nobles 1991; Richards 1989).

The three realms of experience constitute three distinct and largely nonoverlapping social domains for African Americans. African Americans are appropriating values within three distinct cultural realms, each of them with themes that are at times incompatible if not contradictory. A significant aspect of psychosocial integrity among African Americans is the attempt to integrate the mainstream, minority, and Afrocultural realms into one coherent meaning system.

Boykin (1983, 1986) refers to this phenomenon as the "triple quandary" and argues that there is coherence and meaning in African Americans' effort to negotiate among these three realms. However, integrity is also present in their efforts to appropriate the demands of each realm independently. Appropriation is thus one mechanism at work, but Boykin also speaks of a second form of "impositional" integrity in African Americans' efforts to negotiate a mainstream culture whose themes are at odds with other aspects of their cultural lives. This is the adaptive integrity associated with African Americans' ability to adjust to an imposed circumstance and to make sense of the often senseless nature of an oppressive environment. Finally, a third form, proactive integrity, is derived from living within the Afrocultural realm. Indeed, aspects of this proactive integrity are examined in much of the work on the strengths and distinctiveness of black culture (Baratz and Baratz 1970; Gay and Abrahams 1972; Hale 2001; Michaels

1986; Stewart 1970; Williams 1974). Although each type of cultural integrity may provide some insight into the schooling experiences of African American children, the third type, proactive integrity, promises the most insight into the creation of resilient schools. We will focus the remainder of our discussion on this aspect of cultural integrity.

The main elements of the Afrocultural legacy are manifest in cultural themes linked to traditional Africa. African Americans can appropriate these enduring themes, but their appropriation, while probable, is not certain. Moreover, these themes are now part of the American social context; thus they are in principle available for all Americans to appropriate, but in practice they are not equally available. Even among African Americans, Afrocultural themes are only more or less accessible, pervasive, effective, and attractive. Afrocultural themes are generally most likely to be attended to by the African Americans most disenfranchised or cut off from participation in the mainstream of American life. But there is no guarantee that any of the themes will be picked up by any given person. Race is not equivalent to culture. Still, given the African origins of Afrocultural themes and the racial stratification of American society, the probability that people of African descent will appropriate these themes is high.

How could Afrocultural themes have survived the temporal and physical separation of contemporary African Americans from traditional African legacies? Their survival seems especially unlikely in the face of two major facts: the social forces that value the majority culture and black peoples' continuing need to cope with marginalization and oppression. The answer to the question may be found both in the way cultural themes are acquired and in the enduring nature of meaning systems. Cultural themes can be transmitted through participation in a cultural system. Themes are persistent; they remain available in culturally structured contexts via the informal interactions and interpersonal routines of everyday life that take place in family settings, in neighborhoods, and among peer groups. They are persistent and available within formal institutions in the form of artistic/creative and social/recreational endeavors. Moreover, they are in the home, on the playgrounds in community centers, on street corners; at concerts and parties, in church, and at bible study. Themes can be present without overt acknowledgment or knowledge of their links to greater cultural systems and without official endorsement by society at large (Boykin and Allen 2002). Hence, they can be transmitted from generation to generation either intellectually and officially or unconsciously and tacitly.

Afrocultural Integrity and Communalism

The case for continuities between African and African American cultures can be made by comparing cultural research on various African groups with research on contemporary African American populations. We will offer such evidence for one Afrocultural theme, communalism, as a case in point; similar cases can be made for other Afrocultural themes (Boykin and Allen 2002).

Communalism denotes a commitment to social connectedness, where social bonds transcend individual privileges (Boykin 1986, 1983). This focus on social bonds has been observed in various African nations. For instance, the centrality of kinship networks and social bonding has been observed within the Wolof of Senegal and the Tallensi of Ghana (Fortes 1987; Rabain-Jamin 1994). Moreover, a social as opposed to an object basis for maternal responsiveness was observed among the !Kung of Botswana (Rabain-Jamin 1994). Further, a sense of community and group belongingness was salient within the Nso of Cameroon (Nsamenang and Lamb 1994), where shared responsibility was construed as a primary developmental goal. Similar references and observations have been made about populations of African Americans as well. This body of work points to observations of strong and elaborated kinship bonds, mutuality of support, a premium on social interdependence and collective responsibility, and identity tied to group affiliation (Young 1970; Nobles 1991; Hill 1997; Staples 1976; Malson 1983; Sudarkasa 1997; Aschenbrenner 1973; Stuckey 1987). Taken together, these observations show that although communalism is manifested differently across various African and African American communities, this basic theme remains central to the life experiences of all these groups.

It seems reasonable to infer that the cultivation of the Afrocultural realm has persisted among African Americans, especially those who because of economic circumstances have comparatively less access to mainstream themes. Afrocultural themes are appropriated early in development through participation in culturally structured contexts in the proximal experiences (home and community life) of African Americans. Given that they are so central to African American meaning systems, these themes come to significantly (but not exclusively) inform behaviors, values, and perceptions and to have developmental primacy and potency as they are linked to positive affect and significant others. Moreover, these Afrocultural themes come to characterize the site for the development and practice of emerging skills and accomplishments. So, as many African American children gain an understanding of the world, they do so primarily through the Afrocultural cultural-meaning systems provided within their proximal environments. We submit that this appropriation of Afrocultural themes has huge implications for how to approach these children in learning situations and thus for how to create resilient learning contexts.

Proactive Integrity and
African American Children's Task Performance

In our work, we have examined whether cultural themes like communalism serve as a form of social capital that is appropriated by many low-income African American children. If it is, we can capitalize on communalism to enhance learning and performance outcomes. The following empirical studies provide support for this claim.

Communalism does not usually figure prominently in public schools even when they serve low-income black children (Ellison, Boykin, and Towns 1997). Schools are more typically organized around the mainstream, or majority, cultural themes of competition and individualism (Katz 1985; Spence 1985). We propose that communalism is a theme often acquired early in these children's lives through home and neighborhood experiences and that it is developmentally primary and potent for black children as they enter school. In sum, this personally salient minority theme is at odds with the majority theme that prevails within most schools. In adopting a pedagogical strategy of proactive integrity, we endowed some of the learning and performance contexts of school with communalism, believing that doing so would increase positive attitudes toward the schooling experience and would enhance children's motivation and academic performance. The work we have done has tested these possibilities. Overall our research supports two general findings: (1) African American children prefer communalism as a learning context, and (2) African American children's performance is facilitated when they learn within a context of communalism.

Boykin (2001) describes a study that tested for ethnic differences in attitudes toward cooperative, competitive, and individualistic modes of school learning among fourth- and fifth-grade children in a southeastern U.S. community. The sample included roughly equal numbers of black and white children from low-income backgrounds who qualified for free or reduced-price lunch. These children attended the same schools and worked in the same classrooms. They were asked to fill out the Scales of Social Interdependence, an instrument that focuses on the three modes of school learning (Johnson and Norem-Hebeison 1979). Children evaluated a series of statements about how they liked to work in school. Items like "I like to work alone"; "I like to compete against other students"; or "I like to study in groups" represented tests of their commitment to individualism, competition, or cooperative/communalism respectively. The extent to which a communal orientation was a cultural theme within the home was also assessed.

The rank order of endorsements for the three learning orientations was the same for both groups: cooperation was preferred. However, the intensities of these rankings were different. While white students showed no difference in their ratings of the three learning orientations, black students were significantly more committed to cooperation than to competition or to individual work. Black students' rating of cooperation was also significantly higher than was the case for white students. Indeed black students' average ranking of the competition and individualism items fell significantly below the midpoint of the scale, indicating that they do not enjoy working in educational environments organized around these themes. The intensity of their responses can be construed as their outright rejection of these cultural themes. These preferences correlated highly with black children's perceptions of the extent to which they experience communalism within their homes, a finding that suggests both that they have appropriated this cultural theme through their home life and that they are psychologically prepared to exploit this value proactively when making the transition to school.

Using a slightly different methodology with black fourth-grade children from a low-income inner-city community located in a mid-western city, Miller (1997) found that, on average, the children perceived that people preferred to work or learn within their homes, a perception more consistent with a communal than with either an individual or a competitive theme. As with the children in the Boykin and Ellison (1995) study, the children in Miller's study preferred that the communal practices within their homes be transferred to the learning environment within the school. Unfortunately they did not believe the school endorsed their own cultural preferences. Indeed schools were not perceived as neutral with respect to proactive integrity. Black children thought they were likely to get into trouble or to be punished for engaging in activities consistent with communalism—for example, sharing ideas or helping their neighbors in the classroom.

These two examples reveal that low-income African American children more than their white counterparts prefer learning contexts that afford the opportunity to engage in communal exchange. Moreover, black children appear to believe that communalism is the context preferred by the significant people in their own homes. However, they are aware that communalism is not a valued cultural context in their school environment.

Other studies have examined whether communal learning leads to enhanced performance outcomes. Albury (1997) explored the question of whether black and white low-income children would perform differently on a vocabulary task after studying under conditions that promoted either communal interactions or individual study. The children were first given a list of twenty-five unfamiliar words to match with a definition. Once the baseline scores were determined, race-homogeneous groups of three children each were assigned to one of four study contexts. In the "individual criteria" context, students were told that they were to study alone and if they scored better than fifteen out of twenty-five correct on a posttest, they would receive a reward. In the "interpersonal competitive" context, children were told to study alone and the highest scorer of the three at posttest would receive a reward. In the third context, a traditional "cooperative-learning" manipulation was employed: children were told to study together and if their group was among the highest scorers at posttest, they would each receive a reward. The final context emphasized "communalism" in the absence of competition. Here children were given a talk about how they all came from the same neighborhood and how they needed to help one another so that each person could do well because what one does reflects on the group.

Children expressed culturally appropriate preferences for these types of conditions. White children rated the individual criteria favorably and communalism less favorably. The black children reversed the preferences. These group preferences mirrored performance. White children exhibited the greatest learning gains when they studied within the individual criteria context, with fewer gains realized in the interpersonal competitive context. White children's worst performance occurred in the communal study context. By contrast, black children showed the greatest learning gains when they studied in the communal context and the next highest gains in the cooperative context. In contrast to the white children, the black children's worst performance occurred in the individual criteria context. Further, the best performances by the black children and the best performances by the white children were essentially equal: in other words, studying in conditions that honor psychosocial integrity fosters equivalent performances across groups.

In another study, Coleman (1996) examined the influence of individual and communal contexts on creative problem solving in a sample of fourth-grade African American children from an inner-city low-income community. The task was made open-ended in an attempt to tap into divergent thinking. Children were tested individually and were asked to list as many examples as they could either of a good role model or of the things that would make one proud. Prior to this testing the children went through a learning, or practice, phase in which they were randomly assigned to either individual or communal learning. In the individual setting, children did one of the two tasks alone and were encouraged to do their best. In the communal setting three children at one time were encouraged to share and work together for the good of the group so that everyone could do his or her best. The experimenters impressed on them that this goal was important because they all came from the same community. The results for individual performance on the nonpracticed task revealed that children from both groups produced essentially the same number of exemplars on the test. But the quality of the examples was much better for those students who had been in the communal group. These children also reported putting more effort into their work and spending more time on task than did those who had been in the individual setting. These results do not demonstrate that children perform better in a group setting but only that they perform better in a solo setting after studying in a communal condition.

Coleman (1998) assessed the extent to which children exhibited advanced planning and monitoring during task performance, a measure called "metacognitive performance." The results duplicate those reported on less sophisticated learning tasks. Black low-income children (third and sixth grade) who had first worked at the task in a communal setting showed more metacognitive skill than those who had worked in a group study setting without communal prompting. They also showed more metacognitive skill than those who had worked in an individual setting. Similar enhanced performance outcomes were found for black children on math-estimation tasks that are not emphasized within the curriculum and that when taught generally prove to be difficult for young children (Hurley 1997, 1999).

In sum, this body of research demonstrates that providing low-income African American children's learning opportunities in a communal setting enhances their task performance. Such findings provide interesting possibilities for building resilient classrooms, classrooms that build on the proactive integrity of the African American cultural experience.

Some Concluding Comments

To be sure, the absence of such approaches in the education of African American children is not the sole reason so many of these children have experienced failure in school. Nor do we intend to imply that this approach is the only way to ensure effective learning and performance. There are as many routes to school failure as there are to school success. Children will learn well for a variety of reasons: to please adults, to please peers, because they get rewarded for doing so, because it makes them feel good about themselves, because they are afraid to fail, because they are well prepared and well motivated to succeed, and for a host of other reasons. Moreover, this line of research is not offered as evidence that black children cannot succeed in schools as they are presently constituted. Countless poor African American children have beaten the odds and done well via the majority culture's conventional approaches to schooling. However, all too many African American children continue to fail in our nation's schools. This outcome must be rectified.

Our work suggests that children are intellectually competent or have the cognitive and motivational potential to become so. Moreover, many of these children are intrinsically interested in performing school-relevant tasks. So we are led to conclude that academically valuable skills may go undetected or that opportunities for their development may go unrealized in the absence of appropriate facilitating contexts. Moreover, such facilitating contexts may lead some children to place greater value on school tasks and may lead them to more favorable attitudes toward and greater investment in school. Following the approaches validated in this line of research may even reduce negative opinions about many children's academic potential.

The central principle is that building on the cultural integrity that children bring with them to school does not imply that children must be taught in one certain way in order to learn. Indeed, the concept of psychosocial integrity implies that the proactive work cited above represents only one piece of the puzzle of African American children's school experiences. To be sure, the total school experience of black children is more complicated than the scope of the proactive integrity work. The complexities of the social order and of human psychological functioning and of cultural manifestations are much too daunting for any single cultural prescription. Yet the idea of proactive integrity does seem to provide an avenue for addressing some portion of the school problems faced by African American children. This research suggests that schools should provide increased diversity in the psychosocial themes that structure their contexts for learning and performance. In doing so, they would cast a wider net and capture the competencies and interests of a greater number of children. Increased diversity of cultural themes in the school setting will contribute materially to the cultivation of our children's potential and will reduce our tendency to solve the problems of our nation's schools by weeding out children.

Notes

Preparation of this chapter was supported by a grant from the U.S. Department of Education Office of Educational Research and Improvement (OERI) to the Center for Research on the Education of Children Placed at Risk (Grant R117D40005). The views expressed in this chapter are those of the authors. No OREI policy should be inferred.
1. Diversity encompasses race, ethnicity, national origin, language, socioeconomic status, religion, gender, sexual orientation, political ideology, theoretical approach, and the list can go on. In education, children from poor and minority backgrounds generally experience the most performance problems in the United States. So in this chapter the term *diversity* refers to those underrepresented minority groups who have historically exhibited the most disproportionate rates of academic failure.

References

Albury, A. 1997. "Social Orientation, Learning Condition and Learning Outcomes among Low-Income Black and White Grade School Children." Ph.D. diss., Howard University.

Ani, M. 1994. *Yurugu: An African-Centered Critique of European Cultural Thought and Behavior.* Trenton, N.J.: Africa World Press.

Aschenbrenner, J. 1973. "Extended Families among Black Americans." *Journal of Comparative Family Studies* 4:257–268.

Au, K., and A. Kawakami. 1994. "Cultural Congruence in Instruction." In *Teaching Diverse Populations: Formulating a Knowledge Base*, edited by E. Hollins, J. King, and W. Hayman. Albany: State University of New York Press.

Ausubel, D. 1966. "The Effect of Cultural Deprivation on Learning Patterns." In *The Disadvantaged Learner*, edited by S. Webster. San Francisco: Chandler.

Banks, J. C., and C. Banks, eds. 1995. *Handbook of Research on Multicultural Education*. New York: Macmillan.

Baratz, S. S., and J. C. Baratz. 1970. "Early Childhood Intervention: The Social Science Base of Institutional Racism." *Harvard Educational Review* 40:29–50.

Battle, S., and J. Rotter. 1963. "Children's Feelings of Personal Control as Related to Social Class and Ethnic Group." *Journal of Personality* 31:482–490.

Bereiter, C. M., and S. Engelmann. 1966. *Teaching Disadvantaged Children in Preschool*. Englewood Cliffs, N.J.: Prentice-Hall.

Berry, J. 1984. "Towards a Universal Psychology of Cognitive Competence." *International Journal of Psychology* 19:335–361.

Boykin, A. W. 1983. "The Academic Performance of Afro-American Children." In *Achievement and Achievement Motives*, edited by J. Spence. San Francisco: Freeman.

Boykin, A. W. 1986. "The Triple Quandary and the Schooling of Afro-American Children." In *The School Achievement of Minority Children*, edited by U. Neisser. Hillsdale, N.J.: Erlbaum.

Boykin, A. W. 1994. "Afro-cultural Expression and Its Implications for Schooling." In *Teaching Diverse Populations: Formulating a Knowledge Base*, edited by E. Hollins, J. King, and W. Hayman. Albany: State University of New York Press.

Boykin, A. W. 1996. "A Talent Development Approach to School Reform." Paper presented at the annual meeting of the American Educational Research Association, April, New York.

Boykin, A. W. 2000. "Talent Development, Fundamental Culture and School Reform: Implications for African Immersion Schools." In *Sankofa: Issues in African Centered Education*, edited by D. Pollard and C. Ajirotutu. Westport, Conn.: Greenwood Press.

Boykin, A. W. 2001. "The Challenges of Cultural Socialization in the Schooling of African American Elementary School Children: Exposing the Hidden Curriculum." In *Race and Education: The Roles of History and Society in Educating African American Students*, edited by W. Watkins, J. Lewis, and V. Chou. Boston: Allyn & Bacon.

Boykin, A. W., and B. A. Allen. 2000. "Beyond Deficit and Difference: Psychological Integrity in Developmental Research." In *Advances in Education*, edited by C. C. Yeakey. Greenwich, Conn.: JAI Press.

Boykin, A. W., and B. A. Allen. 2002. "Culture Matters in the Development and Schooling of African American Children." Unpublished manuscript.

Boykin, A. W., and C. Ellison. 1995. "The Multiple Ecologies of Black Youth Socialization: An Afrographic Analysis." In *African American Youth: Their Social and Economic Status in the United States*, edited by R. Taylor. Westport, Conn.: Praeger.

Bruner, J. S. 1966. "On Cognitive Growth." In *Studies in Cognitive Growth*, edited by J. S. Bruner, R. R. Olver, and P. M. Greenfield. New York: Wiley.

Coleman, K. 1996. "The Influence of a Communal Learning Context on African American Elementary Students' Creative Problem Solving." Master's thesis, Howard University.

Coleman, K. 1998. "The Influence of a Communal Learning Context on African American Elementary Students' Creative Problem Solving and Meta-cognition." Ph.D. diss., Howard University.

Davidson, H., and J. Greenberg. 1967. *School Achievers from a Deprived Background*. New York: Associated Educational Services.

Deutsch, M. 1965. "The Role of Social Class in Language Development and Cognition." *American Journal of Orthopsychiatry* 35:78–88.

Dixon, V. 1976. "World Views and Research Methodology." In *African Philosophy: Assumptions and Paradigms for Research on Black Persons*, edited by J. S. Bruner, R. R. Olver, and P. M. Greenfield. Los Angeles: Fanon Center.

Ellison, C., A. W. Boykin, and D. Towns. 1997. "Classroom Cultural Ecology." Technical Report, Howard University and Johns Hopkins University Centers for Research on the Education of Children Placed at-Risk.

Fordham, S., and J. Ogbu. 1986. "Black Students' School Success: Coping with the Burden of Acting White." *Urban Review* 18:176–206.

Fortes, M. 1987. *Religion, Morality and the Person: Essays on Tallensi Religion.* Cambridge: Cambridge University Press.

Gay, G. 1978. "Viewing the Pluralistic Classroom as a Cultural Microcosm." *Educational Research Quarterly* 2:45–59.

Gay, G., and R. Abrahams. 1972. "Black Culture in the Classroom." In *Language and Cultural Diversity in American Education*, edited by J. S. Bruner, R. R. Olver, and P. M. Greenfield. Englewood Cliffs, N.J.: Prentice-Hall.

Gordon, B. 1997. "Curriculum, Policy, and African American Cultural Knowledge: Challenges and Possibilities for the Year 2000 and Beyond." *Educational Policy* 11:227–242.

Greenfield, P. M. 1994. "Independence and Interdependence as Developmental Scripts: Implications for Theory, Research and Practice." In *Cross-Cultural Roots of Minority Child Development*, edited by P. M. Greenfield and R. Cocking. Hillsdale, N.J.: Erlbaum.

Greeno, J., and the Middle School Mathematics Through Application Group. 1997. "Theories and Practice of Thinking and Learning to Think." *American Journal of Education* 106:85–126.

Hale, J. E. 2001. "Culturally Appropriate Pedagogy." In *Race and Education: The Roles of History and Society in Educating African American Students*, edited by W. Watkins, J. Lewis, and V. Chou. Boston: Allyn & Bacon.

Harrell, J. 1980. "Psychological Factors in Hypertension: A Status Report." *Psychological Bulletin* 87:482–501.

Hill, R. 1997. *The Strength of Black Families.* Baltimore: Black Classic Press.

Hunt, J. McV. 1968. "The Psychological Basis for Preschool Cultural Enrichment Programs." In *Social Class, Race and Psychological Development*, edited by M. Deutsch, A. Jensen, and I. Katz. New York: Holt, Rinehart and Winston.

Hurley, E. 1997. "Communal vs Individual Learning of a Math Estimation Task: Communalism among African American Children and the Culture of Learning Contexts." Howard University.

Hurley, E. 1999. "Communal Group Learning and Group Process among African American and European American Students." Ph.D. diss., Howard University.

Johnson, D. W., and A. A. Norem-Hebeison. 1979. "A Measure of Cooperative, Competitive and Individualistic Attitudes." *Journal of Social Psychology* 109:77–82.

Jones, J. 1997. *Prejudice and Racism.* 2d ed. New York: McGraw-Hill.

Katz, I. 1973. "Alternatives to Personality Deficit Interpretation of Negro Underachievement." In *Psychology and Race*, edited by P. Watson. Chicago: Aldine.

Katz, J. 1985. "The Sociopolitical Nature of Counseling." *Counseling Psychologist* 13:615–624.

King, J. 1994. "The Purpose of Schooling for African American Children: Including Cultural Knowledge." In *Teaching Diverse Populations: Formulating a Knowledge Base*, edited by E. Hollins, J. King, and W. Hayman. Albany: State University of New York Press.

Ladson-Billings, G. 1994. "Who Will Teach Our Children: Preparing Teachers to Successfully Teach African American Students." In *Teaching Diverse Populations: Formu-*

lating a Knowledge Base, edited by E. Hollins, J. King, and W. Hayman. Albany: State University of New York Press.

Lee, C. 1994. "African-Centered Pedagogy: Complexities and Possibilities." In *Too Much Schooling Too Little Education*, edited by M. Shujaa. Trenton, N.J.: Africa World Press.

Malson, M. 1983. "The Social Support Systems of Black Families." In *Ties That Bind: Men's and Women's Social Networks*, edited by L. Lein and M. Sussman. Binghamton, N.Y.: Haworth Press.

Marans, A., and R. Lourie. 1967. "Hypotheses Regarding the Effects of Child-Rearing Patterns on the Disadvantaged Child." In *Disadvantaged Child*, vol. 1, edited by J. Hellmuth. New York: Brunner/Mazel.

Michaels, S. 1986. "Narrative Presentations: An Oral Preparation for Literacy with First Graders." In *The Social Construction of Literacy*, edited by J. Cook-Gumperz. Cambridge: Cambridge University Press.

Miller, O. 1997. "Cultural Influences on the Classroom Perceptions of African American Grade School Children." Master's thesis, Howard University.

Nobles, W. 1991. "African Philosophy: Foundations for Black Psychology." In *Black Psychology*, 3d ed., edited by R. Jones. Hampton, Va.: Cobb and Henry.

Nsamenang, A., and M. Lamb. 1994. "Socialization of Nso Children in the Bamenda Grassfields of Northwest Cameroon." In *Cross-Cultural Roots of Minority Child Development*, edited by P. M. Greenfield and R. Cocking. Hillsdale, N.J.: Erlbaum.

Ortner, S. 1984. "Theory in Anthropology since the Sixties." *Comparative Studies in Society and History* 26:126–166.

Pachter, L., and R. Harwood. 1996. "Culture, Child Behavior and Psychosocial Development." *Journal of Development and Behavioral Pediatrics* 17:191–198.

Perry, T., and L. Delpit, eds. 1998. *The Real Ebonics Debate: Power, Language, and the Education of African American Children*. Boston: Beacon Press.

Peters, A., and S. Boggs. 1986. "Interactional Routines as Cultural Influences upon Language Acquisition." In *Language Socialization across Cultures*, edited by B. Schieffelin and E. Ochs. Cambridge: Cambridge University Press.

Piestrup, A. 1973. "Black Dialect Interference and Accommodation of Reading Instruction in First Grade." *Language Behavior Research Laboratory Monographs* (University of California, Berkeley) 4.

Rabain-Jamin, J. 1994. "Language and Socialization of the Child in African Families Living in France." In *Cross-Cultural Roots of Minority Child Development*, edited by P. M. Greenfield and R. Cocking. Hillsdale, N.J.: Erlbaum.

Richards, D. 1989. *Let the Circle Be Unbroken: The Implications of African Spirituality in the Diaspora*. Trenton, N.J.: Red Sea Press.

Rogoff, B. 1990. *Apprenticeship in Thinking: Cognitive Development in Social Context*. New York: Oxford University Press.

Rogoff, B., and P. Chavajay. 1995. "What's Become of Research on the Cultural Basis of Cognitive Development?" *American Psychologist* 50:859–877.

Serpell, R., and A. W. Boykin. 1994. "Cultural Dimensions of Cognition: A Multiplex, Dynamic System of Constraints and Possibilities." In *Thinking and Problem Solving*, edited by R. Sternberg. New York: Academic Press.

Sheets, R. H., and G. Gay. 1996. "Student Perceptions of Disciplinary Conflict in Ethnically Diverse Classrooms." *NASSP Bulletin* 80:84–94.

Silverstein, B., and R. Krate. 1975. *Children of the Dark Ghetto*. New York: Praeger.

Spence, J. 1985. "Achievement American Style: The Rewards and Costs of Individualism." *American Psychologist* 40:1285–1295.

Staples, R. 1976. *An Introduction to Black Sociology*. New York: McGraw-Hill.

Steele, C. 1999. "Thin Ice: Stereotype Threat and Black College Students." *Atlantic Monthly*, August, 44–54.

Sternberg, R. J. 1986. *Intelligence Applied: Understanding and Increasing Your Intellectual Skills.* New York: Harcourt Brace Jovanovich.

Stewart, W. 1970. "School Desegregation: An Evaluation of Predictions Made in Brown vs. Board of Education." *Psychological Bulletin* 85:217–238.

Stuckey, S. 1987. *Slave Culture: Nationalist Theory and the Foundations of Black America.* New York: Oxford University Press.

Sudarkasa, N. 1997. "African American Families and Family Values." In *Black Families,* 3d ed, edited by H. McAdoo. Thousand Oaks, Calif.: Sage.

Super, C., and S. Harkness. 1986. "The Developmental Niche: A Conceptualization at the Interface of Child and Culture." *International Journal of Behavioral Development* 9:545–569.

Towns, D. 1998. "How Language Both Constructs and Is Constructed by Culture in the Classroom." Paper presented at the annual meeting of the American Educational Research Association, San Diego.

Tylor, E. 1871. *Primitive Culture.* London: Murray.

Williams, R. 1974. "Cognitive and Survival Learning of the Black Child." In *The Survival of Black Children and Youth,* edited by J. Chunn. Washington, D.C.: Nuclassics and Science.

Young, V. 1970. "Family and Childhood in a Southern Negro Community." *American Anthropologist* 72:269–288.

Chapter 7

"We Have These Rules Inside"

JUSTINE CASSELL

The Effects of Exercising Voice in a Children's Online Forum

I was earlier like an unlit lamp. Jr summit has lit a spark in me. So, now I spread the light around. I talk to my friends, read newspapers, do not take any injustice lying down.
—Pooja, India

THE DISCUSSION OF THE role of computational technology in children's development has become increasingly polarized. On the one hand we find a frantic push to provide computers and Internet access in all U.S. schools; this push is based on a belief that computer literacy will increasingly be required for success in the job market (Committee on Information Technology Literacy 1999). On the other hand, we find a frantic push-back to place a "moratorium" on children's access to computers (Cordes and Miller 2000); this push-back is based in part on a belief that the negative effects of computers on children have not been studied sufficiently. Clearly the answer lies at neither end of this spectrum; a careful review of existent studies shows a number of benefits, a handful of harmful effects, and a plethora of unknowns (Wartella, O'Keefe, and Scantlin 2000). History teaches us that whereas initial fears about movies or radio or television concerned the presence of the medium, it is the content of the medium—the message— that must be evaluated and improved. However, one difference between the computer and earlier media is that never before has a technology so effectively allowed people from around the world to congregate. Never before has a technology been so fundamentally bidirectional. With this particular technology, anybody can both consume and create the message. Although seemingly such a technology would be lauded for its ability to allow community, the contrary has been the case. Many believe, as do Hern and Chauk (1997), that the Internet is a technological innovation, akin to the automobile and television, that has the power to fundamentally undermine our already corrupted sense of community. Indeed, because communication on the Internet is at a distance and, in their view, without the possibility of face-to-face relationships, Hern and Chauk see it as being antagonistic to democracy as we have known it.

This chapter discusses an Internet-based, democratic, global learning community. The Junior Summit program was a $2.1 million project that brought together more than three thousand children, aged ten to sixteen, from 139 different countries, in an online forum that allowed the children to communicate with each other across languages on topics of international concern. This forum culminated in November 1998 in a six-day program at the Massachusetts Institute of Technology (Cambridge, Massachusetts), where one hundred of the children (from 54 countries) met with world leaders, heads of industry, and members of the international press to describe, get feedback on, and garner support for their ideas about how to use technology to improve children's lives. The children then returned to the online forum to discuss further how to implement the projects that they had designed and to amplify the voices of the Junior Summit by bringing in additional children from their respective communities. The community was democratic in the sense that the children chose the topics, organized themselves into work groups, elected delegates, and determined outcomes.

The remainder of this chapter first describes the philosophical and design underpinnings of the Junior Summit—the notions of voice, underdetermined design, designing to the lowest common denominator—then turns to the organization of the program, some outcomes to date, and the lessons we can learn in order to use the Internet and other communication technologies in the service of children's well-being.

Philosophy and Design of the Program

One of the principal concerns that emerges in contemplation of technological "progress" is that those whose stories have not been heard (girls and women, ethnolinguistic minorities, developing nations, children) may be even more silenced as technology advances. As a designer of new technology for children and as a developmental psychologist, I wished to ensure that the bidirectional promise of computers would be realized democratically and that technology would not become increasingly more U.S.-centric, English-centric, and geared to selling stuff to children, that it would rather invite children to give voice to their ideas.

My earlier work investigated computer games for girls including their design and implementation. I argued that designing games especially for girls risked ghettoizing girls as a population that needs special help in relation to technology. By contrast, I designed games for both boys and girls that encourage them to express aspects of self-identity that transcend stereotyped gender categories. My focus has been on what I term "feminist software" and how to apply it to the design of storytelling software for children. Modeled after feminist pedagogy (Lewis 1993), my design philosophy rested on five principles:

- Transfer design authority to the user
- Value subjective and experiential knowledge in computer use
- Allow use by many different kinds of users in different contexts
- Give the user a tool to express her voice and the truth of her existence
- Encourage collaboration among users

I argued that storytelling systems were the ideal genre for experimentation with this design philosophy and that, additionally, the ideal way for girls to learn about themselves and to construct their selves is through first-person storytelling and other kinds of participatory narratives. By "storytelling" I do not mean professional storytelling but an approach that gives girls the role of narrator and also allows them to choose whether to be the subject of the narration—that is, to give them voice. (See Chapter 5 for a discussion of narrative as central to creating a community of learners within the classroom.)

Some of the issues that face girls in the United States and elsewhere are similar to the issues faced by other children outside the mainstream—racial minorities, children from developing nations, children with disabilities. These children are at risk of not being taken into account in the design of technology, yet there is a danger of marginalizing their participation if we design technology only for them. For children who fit into these categories, empowerment, self-efficacy, and the notion of voice take on special importance. The term *voice* in narrative theory refers to an author speaking through a narrator or a character or speaking as herself. But popular books on adolescence, and much feminist theory, use the terms *voice, words,* and *language* metaphorically "to denote the public expression of a particular perspective on self and social life, the effort to represent one's own experience, rather than accepting the representations of more powerful others" (Gal 1991, 176).

The Junior Summit was to be an attempt to allow marginalized children to deploy their voices—to be heard in an essential way. The goal was to permit children of all sorts, from everywhere, to come to know their own experience as primary, to express themselves and tell their stories, to describe their version of how the world should be, and to learn to trust the value of their perceptions. The belief was that these opportunities would allow the growth of self-efficacy—the idea that children can have an effect on the world around them.

The Junior Summit focused on bringing children's voices to the table and giving them the means to be heard. The design included setting up computers and Internet connections for participants who needed them so that not just the "digerati" participated. In addition, moderators were prepared to help children reach beyond clichés to making claims and supporting them. Finally, the interaction among the children and their online space were designed in such a way that they were helped to respect one another's views during the summit and to increase their role on the world stage afterward.

In my work on girls and computer games, I had developed a philosophy called "underdetermined design"—designing just enough to make the system engaging, easy to learn, and intuitive. Users themselves determined how to use the system. That philosophy was essential to the implementation of the Junior Summit online forum, but it needed to be extended with a set of principles that I call "designing to the lowest common denominator." Whereas most websites for children feature as many bells and whistles as possible and appeal as much as possible to children's love for the novel and the technological, the Junior Summit was designed so that no feature was available to some children and not to others. All the children were equal participants whether they used an Apple IIC or a Pentium 4, whether they could support Flash plug-ins or just e-mail, whether they logged in from a dedicated T1 or used a 1200-band modem in the local Internet café. Underdetermined design puts all participants on an equal footing. And, in this simplified environment, the children's words became salient rather than the animation that adorned their personal web pages.

Implementation

Organizations have used communication technologies as diverse as the telegraph and television to bring children together. In autumn 1997, a handful of programs already in place either gathered children on the Internet or gathered children at an in-person summit to discuss the Internet. Though some of these programs were extremely impressive, a number of features common to most of them diminished the impact of children's own voices. In the following sections, we will see how Junior Summit differed from previous programs in the children who participated, the format of the online forum, the role of adults, how the issue of language was dealt with, the children's representation on the world stage, and how talk might lead to action.

PARTICIPANTS

Most of the previous programs targeted children who were already online. The goal of the Junior Summit was to accept a thousand participants who represented every country in the world: those who used a computer on a daily basis and those who didn't know what a computer was, those who struggled to exist on the margins of their society and those who received every benefit their society had to give. Junior Summit distributed entry forms in every way possible, trying to reach every child in every country. Here is an excerpt from the application:

> If you will be between 10 and 16 years old in November 1998 and would like to participate in the Junior Summit, you must submit an entry by March 31, 1998. We want to know how you see the state of children in your community and in the world, what changes you think can and should be brought about, and how these changes could be affected by the growth of the Internet and other new communication technologies. In your application you should do one or more of the following:
>
> - Suggest an important problem (either local or global) that you think children should take action on.
> - Describe the work that you have already done to change the world, and how you would like to expand that work.
> - Discuss how the Internet and other new communication technologies can change the roles that children play in the world.
>
> You can express your ideas in words, pictures, video, music, or any other medium (a web-site, a story). You can submit an entry as an individual or as a group.

Following the practice of UNESCO, which carries out 90 percent of its outreach in English, French, and Spanish, we sent out eighty thousand copies of the entry form in those three languages. Entry forms were sent to every ministry of education in the world, all UNESCO offices, offices of Education International in 300 countries, the 2,500 schools of the worldwide Associated Schools Project, the 850 members of the Association of Secondary School Principals, 300 offices of the Junior Achievement program, the headquarters of Education International, and many nongovernmental organizations (NGOs) and international conferences. Over a hundred educational websites around the world were linked to the Junior Summit website. In addition, entry forms were sent in response to requests submitted by fax, mail, and e-mail. Entries were received from more than eight thousand children in 139 countries, in thirty different languages and every medium imaginable. Because of a zealous local NGO, nearly four hundred entries were received from China. More surprisingly, more than thirty entries (from every child of appropriate age, as it turned out) were received from

Nieue, a country of eighteen hundred people—so small that the mailing address reads "Nieue, near New Zealand." With the help of international graduate students and faculty at MIT, one thousand entries from groups and individuals were chosen; the entries selected came from a total of 3,062 children between the ages of ten and sixteen, from 139 countries.

Examples of successful entries included a moving essay about female circumcision in Benin with documenting photos, taken by the thirteen-year-old applicant herself, that described how access to information about girls around the world could help local girls resist such treatment and how technology could help in other ways. Other successful entries included a video documenting the technological collaboration between an international school and a rural school for local children, both located in Tamil Nadu in Southern India, and a sketch demonstrating how the energy gleaned from walking could be used to power technology located in shoes. Despite worries about devising fair, equitable, nonethnocentric criteria for judging, passion turned out to be the key criterion. It was quite simple to distinguish passionate essays submitted by children who hoped to improve the world from the essays or drawings entered by children (or by adults behind the scene) who hoped simply to acquire a free computer. In only one case did we later become convinced that a parent had written the entry and was continuing to write the child's contributions online.

Although neither gender nor age was taken into account in the judging, successful entrants were roughly 55 percent girls and 45 percent boys, and their ages fell on a bell-shaped curve. The gender mix was particularly interesting given that other online forums for children reported greater numbers of boys than girls and that in 1997 computers and new technology were perceived as primarily masculine domains. We guessed that the even gender mix was due to including in the selection criteria our desire to have a mix of boys and girls and our explicit request on the entry form that the children's ideas about changing the world be their own. Forty percent of the participants chosen did not have computer fluency. The minority of accepted entries came from children working alone, but most represented the work of school classes or self-constituted groups.

FORMAT

In previous online forums for children, topics of discussion, rules, and interaction formats were chosen by adults and policed by adults. Our adult moderators were important in the development of the forum, but after the in-person Junior Summit, the adult moderators gradually reduced their own participation and left. Adult moderators were carefully trained to keep the discussion on track without directing the outcome, to make no decisions for the children, and to avoid influencing the direction of the discussion. A striking example came from the group that decided to work on the topic "bringing about peace." Early in the discussion, when the participants were introducing themselves, a worrisome debate developed between an Israeli and a Palestinian child. In this debate the conversation soon turned personal, and even threatening, with one of the children talking about avenging the death of his uncle. The moderator was at first frightened and then managed to hold fast to the desire to let the children find their voices. Within a day or so, the other children in the topic group joined the discussion; one of the children involved in the debate stepped back and suggested that their conversations concern only the present and future and not the past of their countries. A child from New Zealand summarized, "Ahxxx, did you see the importance of preconception in your life? You have to take your bad experience and not to take a revange [*sic*], but to take it to help other people. You have to fight because you don't want this to happen to other people. In summary, I want to say that you have to take it as an example to not do again. We don't wish your experience to anyone and this is why we have to work on peace. Bye."

This topic group subsequently suggested more concrete action projects than many of the other topic groups, had more communication among the members, and continued to work together longer after the in-person summit. This early chance to resolve conflict without adult intervention, to learn listening skills, and to use their voices to prevent harm to one another seems to have allowed this group to feel collectively and individually more self-efficacious and more inclined to act (Bandura 1997). As a Norwegian child from this group remarked, "We all are sharing one world and today's children are tomorrow's leaders. We have to start learning empathy and sympathy, not only in thinking, but also in handling."

The format of the online forum progressed from a structured exercise to a totally free exchange. The thousand participating children and teams spent their first week online in "homerooms" organized around region and language, where they participated in a guided exercise of initiation to the technology and the principles of the summit. After that, the children joined one or several of the twenty groups discussing topics that they themselves had proposed, or they suggested and implemented new ways of forming groups. Here are two examples of topics on which children chose to work:

- The use of computers to link disabled children to their peers and to educate children about the disabled. One fourteen-year-old girl in South Africa with cerebral palsy wrote, "The computer is in some ways my hands and feet and it even gives me wings to fly to other countries and far away places."
- Bridging the double gap between speakers of different languages and between the literate and illiterate in the world. One child from the

United States wrote that the computer could provide a natural link between pictures and words and sounds that would allow children both to learn to read and to learn other languages.

We designed the online interface so that it supported—encouraged even—these spontaneous forms of community. In order to respond to this demand, rather than playing the role of the "keepers of the forum," we implemented technology through which the children themselves could build new spaces. The online forum thus became a showcase for technologies that encourage and support a multilingual digital community. In particular, it allowed:

- Synchronous communication (real-time chat)
- Asynchronous communication (such as e-mail, mailing lists, threaded chat)
- Different discussions for different topics
- Intelligent and child-friendly archiving
- Multilingual communication (through automatic and human translation)
- Children's own website construction (for novice users)
- Sharing of photographs and other images
- Collaborative storytelling
- Voting (to allow children to elect the hundred delegates who came to Cambridge)
- A graphical time line to illustrate the current stage of the online forum
- A map to show who was logged in from each country at any one time

As we designed the online forum, we kept in mind that it was meant to support "deep chat" (sustained, content-rich discussion) and thinking before speaking rather than the shallow talk found in most chat groups.

After dividing into topic groups, the children worked on developing the twenty proposals to an action stage. The children were responsible for posting weekly updates to the publicly accessible Junior Summit website so that outsiders could view the progress of the forum. Next, each topic group voted for six children to serve as delegates to the in-person Cambridge summit. The organizers chose five out of those six children, with the goal of having an overall fair representation of region, age, gender, and language, and then made sure that all underrepresented countries also sent representatives. During the Cambridge summit week, the delegates were responsible for keeping in touch with their constituencies at home. After the summit, the final phase consisted of the children reuniting online to carry forward their projects with the support of the influential people they met at the Cambridge summit and taking advantage of the press that the summit had garnered.

ROLE OF ADULTS

Most previous Internet communities for children were classroom-based: teachers initiated participation and chose the participants, and involvement was organized through the schools. In the Junior Summit, children could apply individually or in teams or as school classes. But no adult participation was required or allowed. The decision to forbid adult participation (except for twenty moderators) was controversial. We believed that having powerful adults present might prevent children, especially from countries where children are supposed to be "seen and not heard," from finding their own voice and speaking out (Cassell and Ryokai 2001). In addition, children's moral reasoning and linguistic skills are more complex when they talk with peers than when they talk with adults (Kruger 1988). Moreover, parents, who were the likely participants if we allowed adults, differ greatly in their ability to help children to disclose or to use their voices (Fagot, Luks, and Poe 1995). We decided that the children should have the chance to reason and to talk on their own before presenting their thoughts to the adult world. Our decision to ban teachers and parents from the online forum was often challenged by adults but was as often supported by children. One child, from the United Arab Emirates, wrote to complain about an overzealous moderator: "She almost replies to every single message. Don't you think she should leave the kids there to give their opinions freely without stressing every single word they say? She's a grown-up after all, and with someone studying their every move believe me, kids won't be at their ease. I'm not saying she should stop giving comments she's doing a great job, but I personally believe she should ease off a bit."

With adults playing a minimal role, we found that children became their own moderator, as illustrated by the following interaction between two children who had just arrived in their topic groups:

HELP ME!!!!!
WHAT'S THIS TOPIC 11 EVERYONE IS REPLYING TO?!! AM I
ALSO SUPPOSED TO HAVE A TOPIC 11 TO REPLY TO??????
WELL, I DON'T!!!!!!!!! PLEASE CAN SOMEONE TELL ME
WHAT'S GOING ON!
THANKS
M
Hi M, It's Mo here, don't panic, we're just talking about war, and the
causes of it, and ideas for preventions and solutions, good to here [sic]
from you, I hope to get some of your ideas!!!!!!!!!!

As well, the children found ways to include others without altering the exclusive nature of their forum. For example, the online forum was not linked to the public Junior Summit website, so only participating children and moderators had access. However, children regularly posted updates about their work to the public Junior Summit site (www.jrsummit.net), where adults were welcome.

Our decision did not prevent parents and teachers from becoming involved. Because of a number of e-mails that we received from parents, we finally decided that it was important to run a parallel but strictly separate in-person summit for those parents who accompanied their children to Cambridge (roughly thirty parents). This program was run across campus from the children's program and lasted from 8 A.M. until 9 P.M., leaving no time for the parents to participate in the children's work.

LANGUAGE

All the previous Internet programs for children were conducted in English or, when there were several languages, children could participate only with other children who spoke the same language. We implemented a server running automatic translation into five languages (Chinese, English, French, Portuguese, Spanish). Children initially specified which of these languages they preferred and subsequently received messages in the original and in the chosen language. However, the state of machine translation is poor, and automatically translated messages gave only the gist of what the author of the message intended. Therefore, we set up a way for children in each group to specify which languages they were capable of reading and translating into which other languages. Thus, participants could also request human translation of any message they didn't understand from another participant. We even built a multilingual simultaneous chat system that worked along the same lines (now being used by other online programs for children).

Our primary goal in implementing language policies was to follow Bandura's advice on how to build communitywide efficacy for social change. Designers should create systems that enable or empower children, not systems that do what they are capable of doing (Bandura 1997). Thus, technical approaches were simply supports to the children's own translation work. We did not meet our goal of providing equal access to speakers of all languages. The automatic translation setup was imperfect, even for getting the gist of a message, and child translators were often too busy replying to messages to translate for other participants. The sad result was that English speakers were more likely to contribute than speakers of other languages, and a Spanish-speaking group coalesced in a separate room. In the future, establishing a rotating board of translators might be a more successful approach.

PARTICIPANTS AND PARTICIPATION AT IN-PERSON PROGRAM

Previous Internet programs for children were either Internet-only or, if they did bring the children together in the physical world, the sessions were directed by and toward adult organizers. To represent children's ideas on the world stage and to support bringing their ideas to fruition, we decided that the online forum would culminate in a week-long in-person summit where representatives of each topic group could hone their ideas through intense interaction with each other and with experts in new technology. They could then present those ideas to the press and to governmental and industry officials.

This goal led us to structure the in-person Cambridge summit to include a combination of general sessions, press briefings given by the children and attended by child reporters from around the world, many small group meetings, and immersion workshops, during which participants had the opportunity to design, explore, and create using the new technologies for children that the Media Lab at MIT is famous for (music, filmmaking, storytelling, manipulatives). As we planned it, the week would culminate in a Friday morning session at which the participants would deliver their final proposals to one another and decide which proposals should be delivered to the general assembly on the last day. That afternoon they would hold a videoconference with the United Nations General Assembly in New York City. On Saturday, at a half-day assembly convened at MIT, children could present their impassioned proposals to attendees including press from around the world, ministers of technology, industry executives, and digital notables. The nine hundred online forum participants who did not come to Cambridge could participate in many events through online activities linking them to their representatives and through special two-way pager systems at the conference that allowed the representatives to check in with their work groups at home.

These were our plans. The children themselves had other ideas. In fact, on the evening the children arrived, at their welcome reception, I showed up to find that the children had kicked out our staff members and were staffing the check-in desk themselves, handing out name badges and welcome packets. After dinner, I led a discussion about rules that we would adhere to—respect for one another, no wandering off to explore Boston, cooperation and not competition. I had hardly jotted down the first point on a huge whiteboard when a fourteen-year-old Indian girl stood up to say, "We have these rules inside. We don't need this written down." The others clamored their agreement, and I sat down.

A little after the end of the activities on the evening of the first day of the summit, I received similar e-mails from two participants. One of them read:

> I need to let you know about the task group I'm in—the "Kid's Bank" which went, to be honest, terribly today. I feel awful about it and I need to tell you before I can sleep. Basically what we did: Had lectures—a student/teacher relationship, everyone falling asleep, no interaction between us kids in the least. . . . There was some lady who had her laptop computer and was making "mission statements" and almost telling us how we should do our project. None of us kids were able to connect to each other or even discuss—everyone was half asleep and most were disinterested in the topic. The adults were taking complete control over it and didn't just leave it up to us to work on like it would have worked just fine as—if not much better. The list goes on . . . I feel like screaming. I think we have to change this whole organization.

As with the fight online, my first reaction was panic: our carefully crafted summit was going down the tubes before the end of the first day. But I managed to remind myself once again that I had promised these children that their voices would be heard, and that included listening to their ideas about process as well as content. We turned over the second day's plenary meeting to the delegates, and they began to make changes. In fact, after a half-day of meetings with one another and with us, the summit returned to the activities that we had planned but with important changes. The quietest children and the children who spoke languages that only they and their interpreters understood sat at the front of the room, where they were more likely to make a contribution. The children began to design an overarching organization to coordinate all their action plans, and they met to work on that idea. And, at their request, adults no longer stood at the front of the room, if they were in the room at all.

On the last day of the in-person summit, the children stood up in front of an audience of two thousand, including ministers of technology, members of the press, chief executive officers of Fortune 500 companies, and gave presentations that knocked their socks off. Two presentations in particular, on child labor and on disability, left not a dry eye in the house. One of the children participating described the disability presentation as follows: "What we tried to do is to tell people stories and through these stories make them listen."

ACTION

Previous forums had been for the most part discussions among children that remained at the level of "just talk." The Junior Summit was intended to bring children together and give them the means to come up with and to bring to fruition radical ideas to change the world for children. Already during the online forum, we had examples of children bringing ideas home and implementing them. One child in India began a program in which she collected "only a single fistful of grain" from each of the families in her neighborhood and then, with the help of the other children in her school, set up a storehouse in a local vacant building so that poor families could get the grain to feed their families. Another team of two children in Malta was able to interview the president of Malta and the minister of education to ask them about Maltese policies toward educational technology.

During the week in Cambridge, a number of additional projects got off the ground. Child laborers were concerned to share their stories by publishing photoessays illustrating their lives. From this idea was born the *Junior Journal,* an online newspaper written and edited by Junior Summit participants. The first issue was published during the week of the in-person summit; a visiting Reuters news crew wasn't allowed to take pictures or interview the children until they agreed to donate an unlimited Reuters news feed. At the end of the week, software was put in place to allow the children to publish from home. They could submit, revise, and edit without any of them being in the same room. They also requested a mechanism to allow a rotating editorship so that participants could get the chance to be both journalist and editor. Remarkably, the *Junior Journal* continues today. Currently in its thirtieth edition (an edition that sports fifty stories and photos from thirty-two different countries), the journal won the prestigious international Global Junior Challenge award in Rome in 2000.

Another project born during the in-person summit was Nation1, a vehicle for realizing the desire for an overarching organization within which participants could pursue their action projects. On the fifth day of the in-person summit, the children passed out a press release entitled *A Nation1 Declaration.* It read:

> Young people of the world, entering the age of communication without barriers, you are already part of an emerging nation, Nation1. Join us there.
>
> Nation1 is a global nation made of young minds. It is created, governed, and sustained by the young. It is a place where adults may not enter unless invited, and may not stay if asked to leave.
>
> We believe that Nation1 has always existed. There has always been a universal culture of young humanity, but only now are the means arising for us to make common cause, using technology to bring all of us closer. Together we can harness the natural virtues of youth: tolerance, energy, playfulness, hope, and a willingness to share.
>
> Kids from all over the world have much in common, despite cultural and national differences. Nation1 is a place to combine the strength of our similarities with the genius of our differences and create a strong bond between people physically separated by distance and national borders. Through integration, we can gain knowledge, support, and friends, and authority in the "real" world.

Because of press coverage on the last day of the Cambridge summit, the children who were spearheading the Nation1 effort received more than five hundred requests for information in the following week. Nation1 has continued to grow in numbers by opening its website to non-Junior Summit children.

At the time of this writing, two Junior Summit participants are employed full-time in a Nation1 office in New York. They have set up a foundation, been successful at raising funds, and are forming alliances with other nonprofit organizations for children in the hope that together they can maintain an umbrella organization to support children. Clearly they have transformed our thinking about children's understanding of the world and their social motives and organizational competencies for affecting the world. Despite these quite extraordinary accomplishments, the children report feeling frustrated by how little has been accomplished since the summit ended. Without the support of and interchanges within a vast and varied collective, some other kind of forum may be required to maintain collective efficacy. In other words, during the online forum, the children were receiving constant feedback from others, feedback that allowed them to know that their voices counted. Without that demonstration of collectively empowered voice, more individual action is required. Six months after the in-person summit ended, one of the children wrote:

> When you're one person working on a dream, you can get hung up, wondering if there are people who care if you succeed, if you will ever make it happen, and sometimes you lose motivation along the way. Besides that, one person has a difficult time making a huge impact on their own. Through Junior Summit, we were 3,000 children working together. Even when we split off into our separate interests there could be twenty of us working together, and we knew that in the long run all of us, despite our different focuses, were working on the same project— making the world a better place.

Outcomes and Lasting Contribution

Evaluating a program with such large scope is a formidable challenge. My own interests were evaluating the technology and interface design principles as well as evaluating the effects of the Junior Summit on children's lives. Some of the effects of the interface and format decisions have been documented above: the positive effect of allowing the children to resolve their own conflicts and, on the negative side, the not completely successful attempt to deal with a multiplicity of languages. Like speakers of languages other than English, those children who had no prior experience whatsoever with computers and the Internet found themselves handicapped, but less so than we had anticipated. They were less likely to continue with the online forum, but they were more likely to persevere if they were members of a team. A small school in rural India had three teams accepted to the Junior Summit none of whose members were computer literate. Two children from the school were elected delegates of two separate topic groups. Three years later, these teams of children were still active.

Although preliminary studies found that the Internet was associated with increased loneliness and depression (Kraut et al. 1998), self-reports from Junior Summit participants three years after the summit ended revealed children who were anything but depressed. A teacher from Spain wrote several months after the in-person summit that the way the summit was conducted led her students to "feel empowered to act as leaders, as world wide ambassadors of digital culture. They regard school with new eyes, as a GLOBAL place where people may meet people easily, where they can learn and voice their opinions about the world that surrounds them. A place where they may feel loved, heard, taken into consideration, where technology is (for the first time in history) a powerful tool that they employ better than adults."

Three years after the summit's supposed conclusion, the children refused to consider the project ended. They continued to use the online forum, to communicate with one another, and to take part in their Junior Summit work. One Junior Summit participant gave a speech at the White House on New Year's Eve 2000 as a part of a roundtable about voices of the new millennium. Several others traveled from India, Jamaica, Australia, France, and the United States to the Hague Appeal for Peace to meet with Kofi Annan, secretary general of the United Nations, in May 2000. Still others gave workshops about the Junior Summit at the NGO I*EARN's conference in Beijing, China, in 2000. In October 2000 one of the summit participants won the $5,000 Global Youth Peace & Tolerance Award, presented at the United Nations. Another child won the American Community Schools International Peace Prize in 1999. In January 2001, the children obtained grant money to continue their work on Nation1.

Conclusion

Organizing such a global community for children entails not only educationally relevant and empowering technical and design work but also fundraising, footwork, policy analysis, education, and the occasional late-night pizza run when the participants don't like the food planned for them. In my case, I have continued as advisor, cheerleader, agent, fundraiser, and technical staff. Most important, I continue to try to ensure that the children's voices are heard and that in using their voices they can develop the belief that they can control the world around them and their own destinies. We know that those reporting low levels of voice in a given context also report low self-esteem (Harter 1997). The question is whether high levels of voice in one context can transfer to other contexts.

One child from Brazil wrote, "We think we have matured in this project, it has made us feel more secure about ourselves. It hasn't changed us!!!"

Although the Junior Summit officially ended in 1998, its effects continue to spread—the projects the children devised have become more widely known: the *Junior Journal* online newspaper, Nation1, delegations to the Hague Appeal for Peace and to the Olympics. The Houghton Mifflin publishing firm committed to run some images of the Junior Summit in a new edition of a high school history textbook to illustrate "the large scale meeting of young minds, and the global dimension of technological developments"![1] Finally, the harm wrought by a thoughtless digital divide is better understood today than it was when plans for the Junior Summit began.

Amy Aidman, research director at the Washington-based Center for Media Education, gave public testimony to the Democracy Online National Task Force that included reference to the Junior Summit's democratic basis: "When a teen from Greece can get a response to a question from one of the great thinkers of the world—and the great thinkers can have access to the questions of promising young people in other parts of the world, I think we are seeing the Internet's potential as a tool for the future of democracy expanded in the best sense."[2]

Notes

Thanks to David Berg, Isolde Birdthistle, Steve Buka, and Mary Beth O'Hagan for assisting with the design of an evaluation of the Junior Summit; to Mia Keinanen, Anindita Basu, Lira Nikolovska, and Jennifer Smith for assisting with gathering and coding data; to Dona Tversky for bravely diving into coding and designing a follow-up study; and to Sandy Calvert and Ellen Wartella for conversations and comments that improved the manuscript. I am indebted to Pam Smith of Merrill Lynch for a research grant to study the Junior Summit, as well as to the other generous sponsors of the MIT Media Lab. Most of all, thanks to the 3,062 Junior Summit participants who have illuminated my vision of what it means to be a child and a citizen of the world. They have made my life immeasurably better.

1. E-mail dated 30 May 2001 from Zoe Kovel at the photo-research department of McDougal Littell Press.
2. E-mail dated 10 April 2000 from Amy Aidman.

References

Bandura, A., ed. 1997. *Self-Efficacy: The Exercise of Control*. New York: Freeman.

Cassell, J., and K. Ryokai. 2001. "Making Space for Voice Technologies to Support Children's Fantasy and Storytelling." *Personal Technologies* 5 (3): 203–224.

Committee on Information Technology Literacy. 1999. *Being Fluent with Information Technology*. Washington, D.C.: National Research Council.

Cordes, C., and E. Miller. 2000. *Fool's Gold: A Critical Look at Computers in Childhood*. Washington, D.C.: Alliance for Childhood.

Fagot, B., K. Luks, and J. Poe. 1995. "Parental Influences on Children's Willingness to Disclose." In *Disclosure Processes in Children and Adolescents*, edited by K. J. Rotenberg. Cambridge: Cambridge University Press.

Gal, S. 1991. "Between Speech and Silence." In *Gender at the Crossroads of Knowledge:*

Feminist Anthropology in the Postmodern Era, edited by M. di Leonardo. Berkeley: University of California Press.

Harter, S. 1997. "The Personal Self in Social Context: Barriers to Authenticity." In *Self and Identity: Fundamental Issues*, edited by R. Ashmore and L. Jussim. New York: Oxford University Press.

Hern, M., and S. Chauk. 1997. "The Internet, Democracy and Community: Another Big Lie." *Journal of Family Life* 3 (4): 36–39.

Kraut, R., M Patterson, V. Lundmark, S. Kiesler, T. Mukophadhyay, and W. Scherlis. 1998. "Internet Paradox: A Social Technology That Reduces Social Involvement and Psychological Well-Being?" *American Psychologist* 53 (9): 1017–1031.

Kruger, A. C. 1988. "The Effect of Peer and Adult-Child Transactive Discussions on Moral Reasoning." Paper presented at the Conference on Human Development, Charleston, S.C.

Lewis, M. 1993. *Without a Word: Teaching beyond Women's Silence*. New York: Routledge Kegan Paul.

Wartella, E., B. O'Keefe, and R. Scantlin. 2000. *Children and Interactive Media*. New York: Markle Foundation.

Part III

Voice and Agency within Families

Chapter 8

Advertising and Marketing to Children in the United States

ENOLA G. AIRD

Rᴀᴅɪᴏ, ᴛᴇʟᴇᴠɪsɪᴏɴ, ᴡᴇʙsɪᴛᴇs, video games, toys, music videos, computer games, clothing, magazines, billboards, ads on neighborhood streets, at bus stops, in buses, in classrooms, in community centers, in malls, in doctors' offices, at supermarket checkouts, in elevators, in movie theaters, in airports, at ATM machines, and more. At home, at school, at play, and at work, children today march through their lives to a steady drumbeat of advertising and marketing.

From the moment they wake up in the morning until the minute they lay their heads on their pillows at night, most children in the United States are exposed, through a wide variety of media, to a stream of marketing messages urging on them an ever-growing number of products and services produced by business entities that include the largest corporate conglomerates and that together constitute the largest consumer economy in the world.

Since the early 1980s, children have become a major target for businesses seeking to maximize the sales of their goods and services. In the words of James McNeal, a leading authority on the children's market, children "represent more market potential than any other demographic segment" (1999, 17). They have increasing amounts of disposable income. They exert a growing influence over the purchasing decisions of their parents. And if they are, in McNeal's words, "nurtured as future consumers" (17), they can be a source of a lifetime of sales for aggressive corporations and advertising and marketing agencies.

To tap into the lucrative markets of children and youth, a growing number of advertisers and marketers are using the tools of psychology and other behavioral sciences to understand children's emotional vulnerabilities and to craft their campaigns to maximum effect. They are exploiting advertising and marketing opportunities nearly everywhere children can be found and employing every available media technology.

The basic strategy for many advertisers today is to grow consumers from childhood. As one marketing executive has described it, "All these people understand something that is very basic and logical, that if you own this child at an early age, you can own this child for years to come. . . . Companies are saying, 'Hey, I want to own the kid younger and younger and younger'" (Michael Searles, cited in Harris 1989, A1).

This chapter examines a major commonality for children in the United States today: the increasing commercialization of childhood. It identifies a number of the advertising and marketing practices designed to grow consumers from childhood and explores some of the effects of these practices on children's lives. It considers what the pressure to consume is doing to children in our society and how today's brand of consumerism might be affecting the development of children's agency and voice, which Richard Unsworth and Peter Pufall describe in the Introduction as their ability to help shape their world and to articulate their hopes, wishes, and fulfillments.

Agency and Voice

Children are born with great curiosity and a fundamental drive to explore, make sense of, and master their environment. Children's drive to find out, capacity to figure things out, and need for mastery are "facilitated by the extent to which their environments provide opportunities and supports for growth" (Shonkoff and Phillips 2000, 27). Children are thus active participants in their own development throughout childhood. They are agents in the sense that as they explore, they construct a set of beliefs and values in regard to themselves and the world around them, and they act on those beliefs and values. As they acquire the skills of language, they also develop the ability to communicate, to tell their stories, to give voice to their own beliefs and values instead of simply accepting those imposed on them by others.

The focus in this book on children's agency and voice is, at bottom, animated by a respect for the dignity and integrity of children as persons. This point of view recognizes every child's need and right, at every age and at all stages of development, to be given room to learn, make sense of the world, grow, and become. It also recognizes the responsibility of mothers, fathers, and other adults to build the kinds of relationships with children and create the kinds of conditions that facilitate their growth and the development of their agency and voice.

A fundamental respect for persons arises from an understanding of human beings as free, self-determining, and possessing a basic drive to question in order to know and understand. Through the lens of respect for persons, children are ends in themselves entitled to respect and dignity for who they are. Children are not means to other ends. They are subjects to be valued, not objects to be controlled or used. This orientation to the human person requires that children be accorded the space and the breathing room to develop and unfold.

Unfortunately, a growing number of companies in search of new markets and maximum sales are leaving children too little room, too little space, within which to grow and develop their own identities. Driven by a determination to promote consumerism, these companies are guilty of what might be called "marketing authoritarianism."

Childhood in a Consumer-Driven Culture

Most of the civilian workforce in the United States is engaged, directly or indirectly, in producing consumer goods and services. Advertising, marketing, promotions, and related activities are the tasks of the multi-billion-dollar industries that support and promote the sales of the goods and services produced. Commercial media are key partners in the business of selling, with advertising and marketing driving much of the programming created by the media.

Marketing to children has become big business. A record number of children with unprecedented purchasing power have given rise to the vibrant new career of children's marketing experts, who provide a wide range of services designed to help businesses fully exploit the children's market. Children have become critical segments of the consumer market. Young people ages four to twelve spent almost $27 billion of their own money in 1998. In the same year, they directly influenced over $187 billion in parental purchases and indirectly influenced at least $300 billion more (McNeal 1999).

Children in the United States today live in a media-saturated environment. A study of children's media use by the Henry J. Kaiser Family Foundation revealed that a typical child in the United States is exposed to almost five and a half hours of media each day outside of school (Rideout et al. 1999). On average, children between the ages of two and seven spend three and a half hours a day absorbed in a variety of media. Children above the age of eight are exposed to almost six and three quarter hours of various media a day. Much of children's media use, according to the Kaiser study, is unsupervised.

Media are hand in glove with advertising and marketing. The average child in the United States is exposed to more than twenty thousand ads each year on television alone, even more if he or she goes online (American Academy of Pediatrics 2001). The number of television and cable channels targeting children and youth has grown dramatically, and websites focusing on children and teens are a staple of the Internet world.

In media programs targeted at children across the age spectrum, from early childhood to the teen years, the lines between commercials and program content are so regularly blurred that corporate advertisers can constantly promote the sales of their products and services.[1] Using the power of marketing alliances and synergies through licensing and merchandising, television shows, movies, music, clothes, toys, food, and other products reinforce each other and provide multimedia opportunities to generate sales and keep corporate brands and logos front and center in the minds and psyches of young consumers at all times (Schlosser 2002).

According to *Kidscreen,* a newsletter "about reaching children through entertainment, . . . there have never been more ways in the culture to support marketing toward kids, and there have never been more outlets to study how to speak to them. That makes the competition for kids' attention significantly greater, forcing advertisers to work harder to get inside kids' heads" (Kirchdoeffer 1999). What is the meaning for today's children of this competition to get inside their heads?

The Pervasiveness of Marketing

The philosophy that seems to drive marketing these days is this: target children early and constantly in order to become part of the everyday experience of their lives (Consumer Union 1995). The goals for a growing number of corporations are to market to children at every age and developmental level and to reach children everywhere they can be found. An executive at General Mills, one of the nation's largest advertisers, described the strategy this way: "When it comes to targeting kid consumers, we at General Mills follow the Procter & Gamble model of 'cradle to grave.' . . . We believe in getting them early and having them for life" (Wayne Chilicki, cited in Ruskin 1999).

What is new about this explosion in marketing to children is that it is no longer limited to traditional children's products such as toys, and companies are now using extraordinarily powerful media tools aimed at manipulating children. Children are now seen as potential adult customers with whom corporations should be building relationships throughout childhood and adolescence and into and throughout adulthood. Consequently, car companies, clothing stores, financial-service institutions, and a wide range of other companies producing products and services traditionally marketed to adults are aggressively vying for the attention and lifetime loyalties of young consumers using every available technology and the potent tools of psychology and other behavioral sciences. Of particular concern are current industry trends targeting preschoolers and preteens, the increase in marketing in schools, and the use of psychology and other behavioral sciences to scrutinize and manipulate children.

THE LITTLEST CONSUMERS

For much of the history of advertising and marketing, people trying to sell products and services aimed at children, especially babies and toddlers, have assumed that they have to tailor their marketing appeals to parents, especially mothers. That assumption is now being challenged. For McNeal (1999), one of the marketing experts responsible for the surge in interest in the children's demographic, babies are "consumer cadets" and "born to be consumers." The goal of advertisers, as he describes it, should be to "bond with" and "maintain a permanent relationship with children" (13, 18, 32, 37, 202).

Buoyed by this change in attitude toward the exploitation of the children's market, advertisers have increasingly been aiming their appeals directly at children—at younger and younger ages. Talking about the zero to three demographic, Paul Kurnit, president of one of the leading marketing agencies specializing in the children's market, observed that "traditionally, it's been a parent target, but we're going to see that change in a big way. . . . We've been seeing it in programming [*Barney, Teletubbies*]; it's just a matter of time before we see it in advertising as well" (cited in Kirchdoeffer 1999).

Teletubbies, the first television program broadcast in the United States to be targeted at children as young as twelve months, has given rise to serious objections from pediatricians and mental health experts. Notwithstanding the fact that the American Academy of Pediatrics (2000) "strongly opposes programming that targets children younger than age 2, which may also be designed to market products," the producers of the show and its distributor, the Public Broadcasting System, have marketed it as suitable for children as young as one and have allowed the characters in the show to be licensed and merchandised and used as a vehicle for promoting the sales of Burger King and McDonald's products.

Marketing experts nowadays trumpet the phenomenon of KGOY, shorthand for "kids getting older younger." Arguing that two-year-olds today are as "sophisticated" as, say, four-year-olds were ten years ago and citing evidence that children as young as twelve months can identify brands and make brand associations, a growing number of corporate advertisers and marketers are exploring ways to market to the youngest ages—including babies and toddlers, children at the most impressionable stage of life. According to media analyst Douglass Rushkoff, "Today the most intensely targeted demographic is the baby—the future consumer. . . . By seeding their products and images early, the marketers can do more than just develop brand recognition; they can literally cultivate a demographic's sensibilities as they are formed. . . . This indicates a long-term coercive strategy" (1999, 196–197).

TARGETING TWEENS

Nine- to thirteen-year-olds, in middle school and in the early years of high school, have been named "tweens" by the marketers because they are between childhood and adolescence. They are isolated as a separate marketing segment that is both lucrative and vulnerable; their spending is projected to reach almost $41 billion in 2005.[2] They are tweens in another respect: they exert significant influence over parental purchases, and they influence their younger brothers' and sisters' purchasing decisions. As one marketer puts it, "We look to the older kids to help us bring the younger kids along" (Cyma Zarghami, cited in Hall 2001, 76).

Leading youth marketing firms operate on the assumption that tweens are impressionable and are in search of the things that will give structure to their lives by providing acceptance by their peers. They have a strong need to know what is "in," whether in clothing, music, electronic paraphernalia, or other "gear." To find a way to take advantage of these developmental needs, advertisers who focus their efforts on young people scour the writing and research of child-development scholars and the reports of studies of youth centers, sports competitons, and other places where the young pick up their essential signals.

Tween-focused entertainment media, including Disney and Fox Family, give advertisers their platform. Increasingly, they are so tied to the advertising they carry that it becomes hard to tell where the advertising ends and the programming begins.[3] These media serve as the Pied Pipers, with the advertisers providing the tune, and both benefit.

Among the leading marketing approaches to the tween demographic are these: (1) treat tweens as though they are older than they are; (2) promote images (and role models such as Britney Spears, Christina Aguilera, Jennifer Lopez, Destiny's Child) that encourage tween girls to dress and act "sexy"; (3) promote an image for boys that is vulgar and "in your face" and encourages disrespect and rebelliousness. Douglass Rushkoff, writer and narrator of "Merchants of Cool," a Public Broadcasting Service *Frontline* report on marketing to youth, vividly describes the extent to which market research on tweens and teens shapes ads on programs that in turn help shape tweens and teens. As Rushkoff puts it, "It's one closed feedback loop. . . . Kids' culture and media culture are now one and the same, and it becomes impossible to tell which came first—the anger or the marketing of anger" (Public Broadcasting Service 2001).

ALONG SCHOOL CORRIDORS

According to the General Accounting Office (2000), an agency of Congress, "In-school marketing has become a growing industry. Some marketing professionals are increasingly targeting children in school." According to Lifetime Learning Systems (cited in Sheehan 1999), the nation's largest producer of corporate-sponsored, custom-made learning materials, "School is the ideal time to influence attitudes, build long-term loyalties, introduce new products, test market, promote sampling and trial usage, and above all—to generate immediate sales."

The increase in the number of vending machines and snack bars in schools across the country has become a widely discussed and worrisome issue that has prompted considerable attention from the media and other groups. Magazine-format television shows (like 60 *Minutes*), Sunday supplements in newspapers, school boards, and government agencies have all raised serious questions about this increasingly widespread practice. The fundamental question is straightforward: Can children be effectively taught about the essentials of good nutrition and healthy food choices when the schools themselves install commercially owned vending machines and snack bars that offer foods with low nutritional value? The lesson in the classroom has a hard time competing with the reality in the cafeteria.

Channel One is a commercial satellite network that provides television sets to about twelve thousand schools across the country to deliver ten minutes of news and two minutes of ads to approximately eight million middle, junior, and high school children each day. According to the Center for Commercial-Free Public Education (1998), "Channel One's daily broadcasts are twelve minutes long. However, only 20 percent of airtime is devoted to coverage of 'recent political, economic, social, and cultural stories.' The remaining 80 percent is spent on advertising, ads, sports, weather, natural disasters, features, and Channel One promotions." Channel One often broadcasts ads for candy, snack foods, and soda, and other commercials that, according to the newsletter of the American Academy of Pediatrics, "encourage materialism and market products that in many cases can contribute to eating disorders, obesity, poor nutrition, inappropriate behaviors and poor self-esteem" (Reid and Gedisman 2000).

The Role of Psychology and Other Behavioral Sciences

Experts in child development are key players on most marketing teams. Psychologists and others who understand the various theories of child development are regularly retained by corporations and advertising and marketing agencies to share their knowledge about children's growth and development and to study children's habits, assess their psychological and emotional states and vulnerabilities, and apply their insights to the creation of advertising and marketing campaigns that get through to children. Child-development experts spend a great deal of time observing, studying, and analyzing children in order to inform the development of marketing campaigns. They are assigned the task of finding out about children's tastes, habits, hopes and dreams, fears and anxieties and figuring out how to use this raw material to sell products.

Kidscreen described the industry practice this way (Kirchdoeffer 1999, 41):

> Progressive agencies meet with kids on a regular basis to find out the relevant brand insight for new products and concepts. Beyond tradi-tional focus groups, methods employed include "friendship pairs" in which kids talk to each other about products, . . . playlabs to observe kids' play patterns with products, and CAPs (Child and Parent Studies), . . . which evaluate the "nag factor" (the influence kids have in purchasing a product) by determining if the information communicated to a child enables them to convince the parent to make a purchase.

In September 1999, sixty psychologists wrote to the American Psychologi-cal Association (APA) stating that "the use of psychological insight and meth-odology to bypass parents and influence the behavior and desires of children" constitutes a "crisis for the profession of psychology." The authors concluded that "regrettably a large gap has arisen between the APA's mission [to 'work to miti-gate the causes of human suffering' and to 'help the public in developing in-formed judgments'] and the drift of the profession into helping corporations influence children for the purpose of selling products to them. . . . Today these practices are reaching epidemic levels, and with a complicity on the part of the psychological profession that exceeds that of the past. The result is an enormous advertising and marketing onslaught that comprises, arguably, the largest single psychological project ever undertaken" (Commercial Alert 1999).

Mounting Concerns

A growing number of parents, health care professionals, scholars, educators, ad-vocates, and young people themselves are concerned that current marketing trends are exerting an increasingly negative influence on children and how they live (Mothers' Council 2001). Advocates worry that the all-encompassing mar-keting approaches from which children cannot easily escape are causing them harm, especially in the areas of health, behavior and values, and education.

HEALTH

Eating habits established in childhood tend to last into adulthood. Advertise-ments that promote the consumption of fast foods, snacks, processed foods, and foods high in sugar, calories, and fat, and low in nutritional content are marketed in a wide variety of media and in media specifically targeted at children.

Childhood obesity has become a major public health problem. Studies suggest a significant link between increased television use and obesity, "the most prevalent nutritional disease among children in the United States" (American Academy of Pediatrics 1995, 295). Fast foods are a major contributor to obesity, which in turn contributes to a number of other diseases, such as diabetes, certain cancers, and heart disease.

A study by the Canadian Heart and Stroke Foundation found that the current life-styles of tweens "could put them on the fast track for developing heart disease and stroke as early as in their 30s." The study found that the "majority of children in this age group are not eating nearly enough fruit and vegetables" ("Tweens Could Be Headed for Trouble" 2002).

BEHAVIOR AND VALUES

McNeal (1992) classified seven major categories of children's nagging. From "pleading" nagging to "pity" nagging, he described the many tactics children use to get what they want. He also laid the foundation for a new marketing specialty in the art of nagging as well as for important industry research papers, such as "The Art of Fine Whining" (Ruskin 1999), and books, such as *Why We Buy: The Science of Shopping* (Underhill 1999). This research helps marketers design appeals to children in ways that will enhance their nagging potential and maximize the chances that parents will be worn down and buy whatever their children may want.

Attempts to maximize children's nagging potential can create family conflict. According to Kunkel (2001), several studies confirm that "frequent purchase requests associated with children's advertising exposure may place strain on parent-child interaction at times, an issue of consequence largely because of the sheer volume of commercials viewed by most children" (384). Beyond creating strain within the family, Kanner and Kasser (2000) believe the current marketing climate contributes "to the formation of a shallow 'consumer identity' that is obsessed with instant gratification and material wealth. . . . From our clinical work we know that when adults chronically deceive and manipulate . . . child[ren], it erodes the youngsters' ability to trust others and feel secure in the world. We would expect the falsehoods and distortions in commercials to have a similar effect."

EDUCATION

And what is marketing in schools doing to the education of children? The answer is not fully known. There has been relatively little research on the effects of the explosion of in-school marketing on the children who are compelled by education laws to sit still for marketers who seek to sell their products during the school day.

But some parents and students worry that the educational mission is undermined by advertising that takes children's time away from their studies while substituting the values of commerce for the values of learning. They are concerned as well that marketing in a school lends the school's imprimatur to the notion that selling is always good, that no place is off limits. Some students see their education being subverted by corporate promotional materials made to look like educational resources.

Others, such as the two students at an Ohio school who were forced to spend a day in a juvenile detention center because they refused to watch Channel One, wonder how school-business deals that require them to listen to and watch corporate marketing messages during school hours prepare them for citizenship (Commercial Alert 2000). Nell Geiser, a high school student in Boulder, Colorado, puts it this way, "We are a captive audience to whatever . . . corporate sponsors want to throw at us. And when those sponsors can make sure we drink only Coke or only Pepsi for thirteen years of school because they have an exclusive deal with our district, their investment pays off through a lifetime of brand loyalty. This is about exploiting under-funded schools and violating the fundamental purpose of educational institutions, which is to prepare students to be active citizens, not passive consumers."[4]

Implications for Children's Agency and Voice and for Parenting

Too many corporations today see children as means to their own ends: to increased sales, a better bottom line, lifetime brand loyalty. The basic view underlying many of the trends in marketing today is that a children's value and worth are found in their capacity to spend money and buy things. The increasingly coercive strategies being pursued by advertisers and marketers seek to convince children that their worth resides in their capacity to spend and buy. Marketers are all too willing to subordinate children's health, well-being, character, and educational development to their goal of selling products and services.

To the extent that current trends in marketing and advertising seek to direct children toward assuming a "consumer identity," they run afoul of the fundamental respect for persons and must be stopped. Aggressive marketing strategies that seek to maximize the chances that children will nag their parents for specific products should be of particular concern when they are focused on babies and toddlers, who are just beginning to develop the critical capacity for self-control and regulation of their emotions. Strategies that seek to shape the attitudes and values of tweens toward more and more adult behaviors and materialistic values are problematic because nine- to thirteen-year-olds are struggling to find their own identity, separate from their parents, and find a place for themselves.[5] They are also beginning to show an interest in the opposite sex. It is during these years that self-determining capabilities emerge most fully, a time that marks the beginning of an autonomous sense of self for many children. Marketing to tweens taps into children's need for models of self and supplies compelling and often harmful images of how children should behave, dress, eat, and what they should believe and value.

Today's advertising and marketing onslaught presents important challenges for mothers and fathers. Will we insist on the elbow room, the breathing space, necessary for the development of our children's agency and voice? In light of today's marketing trends, parents are called on to respond on two fronts: on the home front and in the public square. As economist Juliet Schor has observed, the "first step toward transforming America's consumer culture is to understand it better" (1998, 24). Parents can play a critical role by helping their children understand the strategies and tactics used by advertisers and marketers, and they should prepare their children to deal with our hyper consumer culture by encouraging them to think critically and independently and by arming them with the tools of media and marketing literacy.[6]

Parents should also prepare their children for resistance by joining with young people to insist on a comprehensive national response to excesses in advertising and marketing to children. To begin, parents should press for federal funding for research into the psychosocial and health consequences of marketing to children and a Federal Trade Commission fact-finding inquiry into corporate marketing practices aimed at children. Any such research initiative or fact-finding inquiry must include an effort to listen to the voices of children and understand their perceptions. Mothers, fathers, and other adults should encourage and support the efforts of young anticommercialization advocates, such as Nell Geiser, and work in collaboration with young people through intergenerational groups such as the Coalition to Stop the Commercial Exploitation of Children.

The principle of respect for persons demands that children be given room to develop a sense of themselves free of the ever-encroaching messages of marketing. Marketing and advertising are not objectionable in and of themselves. But when they seek to impose the will of the advertisers on children, as is the case with today's all-encompassing marketing strategies for creating "lifelong consumers," they must be challenged. These harmful marketing trends must be reversed.

Notes

1. See, for example, Carlsson-Paige and Levin 1999, which discusses the ways in which children's television programs have been used to market toys such as GI Joe, Teenage Mutant Ninja Turtles, and Power Rangers.

2. "The US Tweens Market Packaged Facts," cited in the promotional brochure for the Institute for International Research's "Consumer Kids Presents the Fifth Annual Targeting Tweens Conference: Marketing to The InbeTween Stages of Youth," July 29–30, 2002. Available at www.iirusa.com/tweens.
3. To note one example: Disney Channel's original prime-time movie, "The Luck of the Irish," featured Irish teen artist Samantha Mumba, who performed the song "What's It Gonna Be." The movie, coupled with a Disney Channel concert special, led to a dramatic increase in sales of her CD.
4. Remarks of Nell Geiser, Summit on the Commercialization of Childhood: How Marketing Harms Children, sponsored by the Coalition to Stop the Commercial Exploitation of Children, New York City, September 10, 2001.
5. Poverty combined with materialistic values can heighten feelings of low self-esteem and low social status among children, as noted by Karen Gray in Chapter 9.
6. For a wide range of media-literacy resources see www.medialit.org/Catalog/alphaindex.

References

American Academy of Pediatrics. 1995. "Children, Adolescents, and Advertising." Policy Statement RE 9504." *Pediatrics* 95 (2): 295.

American Academy of Pediatrics. 2000. *AAP Addresses TV Programming for Children under Age 2*. www.aap.org/advocacy/archives/juntele.html

American Academy of Pediatrics. 2001. *Television and the Family*. www.medem.org

Carlsson-Paige, N., and D. Levin. 1999. "The War-Toy Connection." *Christian Science Monitor*, 5 October, 9.

Center for Commercial-Free Public Education. 1998. *Facts about Channel One*. www.commercialfree.org/channelone.html

Commercial Alert. 1999. *Letter from Various Psychologists to Richard Suinn, President of the American Psychological Association*, 30 September. www.commercialalert.org/psychology

Commercial Alert. 2000. *Governor Taft Urged Not to Punish Children Who Decline to Watch Channel One or TV in School*," 18 October. www.essential.org/pipermail/commercialalert/2000/000040.html

Consumers Union. 1995. *Selling America's Kids: Commercial Pressures on Kids in the '90's*. Yonkers, N.Y.: Consumers Union.

General Accounting Office. 2000. *Report No. GAO/HEHS 00–156*. www.gao.gov

Hall, L. 2001. "Cable Nets Catch the Tween Spirit: Programmers Target a Surging Audience Segment." *Multichannel News*, November, 76.

Harris, R. 1989. "Children Who Dress for Success." *Los Angeles Times*, 12 November, A1.

Kanner, A., and T. Kasser. 2000. *Stuffing Our Kids: Should Psychologists Help Advertisers Manipulate Children?* www.commercialalert.org/psychology/stuffingourkids.html

Kirchdoeffer, E. 1999. "Keeping Up with Today's Kids." *Kidscreen on Line*, January, 41. www.kidscreen.com/articles/ks24101.asp

Kunkel, D. 2001. "Children and Television Advertising." In *Handbook of Children and the Media*, edited by D. Singer and J. Singer. Thousand Oaks, Calif.: Sage.

McNeal, J. U. 1992. *Kids as Customers: A Handbook of Marketing to Children*. New York: Lexington Books.

McNeal, J. U. 1999. *The Kids' Market: Myths and Realities*. Ithaca, N.Y.: Paramount Market Publishing.

Mothers' Council. 2001. *Watch Out for Children: A Mothers' Statement to Advertisers*. New York: Institute for American Values.

Public Broadcasting Service. 2001. "Synopsis." *Frontline: Merchants of Cool*. www.pbs.org/frontline/shows/cool

Reid, L., and A. Gedisman. 2000. "Required TV Program in Schools Encourages Poor Lifestyle Choices." *AAP News*, November). www.aap.org

Rideout, V., U. Foehr, D. Roberts, and M. Brodie.1999. *Executive Summary, Kids & Media @ the New Millennium: A Comprehensive National Analysis of Children's Media Use*. Menlo Park, Calif.: Henry J. Kaiser Family Foundation.

Rushkoff, D. 1999. *Coercion: Why We Listen to What "They" Say*. New York: Riverhead Books.

Ruskin, G. 1999. "Why They Whine: How Corporations Prey on Children." *Mothering Magazine*, no. 97 (November/ December).

Schlosser, E. 2002. *Fast Food Nation: The Dark Side of the All-American Meal*. New York: Harper Perennial.

Schor, J. 1998. *The Overspent American: Why We Want What We Don't Need*. New York: Harper Perennial.

Sheehan, J. 1999. "Why I Said No to Coca Cola." *Rethinking Schools* 14 (4). www.rethinkingschools.org

Shonkoff, J., and D. Phillips, eds. 2000. *From Neurons to Neighborhoods: The Science of Early Childhood Development*. Washington, D.C.: National Academy Press.

"Tweens Could Be Headed for Trouble Says Heart and Stroke Foundation's Report Card." 2002. *Canada Newswire* (Toronto), 5 February.

Underhill, P. 1999. *Why We Buy: The Science of Shopping*. New York: Simon & Schuster.

Chapter 9

Children's Lives in and out of Poverty

KAREN A. GRAY

In 1997, ALMOST 20 percent of children in the United States lived below the poverty level; 10 percent of children in two-parent families and 49 percent of children in female-headed families were poor. Proportionally, more of these children were of color (Federal Interagency Forum on Child and Family Statistics 2001), and children of female-headed families were more likely to have longer periods of being poor (Kennedy, Jung, and Orland 1986).

Most of the research on childhood poverty is quantitative, and of the few qualitative studies almost none examine poverty from the perspective of the children themselves. Even when children are asked about living in poverty, they may be asked to deal with it as if it were a hypothetical condition. For example, one researcher asked children from low-income families to speculate on what poverty might be like by asking them to comment on fictional situations rather than asking them directly about their own experiences (Weinger 2000). Although "there is growing evidence that children's perceptions of work and family-related experiences exert considerable influence on their behavior" (McLoyd et al. 1994, 567), little in the literature examines how children say they experience poverty or what they think about it (Toomey and Christie 1990). The emphasis on quantitative analyses is related to the fact that funding sources emphasize gathering reliable statistics that bear on the outcomes of living in or out of poverty.

Quantitative research continues to be important. However, this approach runs the risk of leaving unanalyzed the assumption that living in poverty entails a certain kind of childhood, usually one of deficits. Therefore, interviews with children probing their experience of living in poverty are equally important. We need research that goes "beyond conventional reviews of the research linking poverty to negative child outcomes" and looks "at the meaning of poverty in the life of a child" (Garbarino 1998, 110). Interviews with children and their families help us to explore the meaning of being poor. Asking children to talk about their experiences within their family and their perceptions of deficits and strengths allows us to test our attributing to them a life of deficits.

The purpose of this chapter is to briefly review child-development research that is germane to children's experiences of self and poverty. More important, my research explores the views of children who have experienced poverty but who no longer live in poverty. The chapter begins with three brief literature reviews that sketch the framework within which the current research was carried out. Results from a qualitative study examining children's views of their lives in poverty are then presented. I conclude with policy and program recommendations.

Research Reviews

The first review describes the development of children's self-esteem, social status, and social acceptance. The second sets out the possible effects of poverty on children's esteem and social status. The last review looks at childhood from a social-constructionist perspective and challenges the assumption that childhoods spent in poverty are of a single kind.

SOCIAL STATUS, SOCIAL ACCEPTANCE, AND SELF-ESTEEM

The research reviewed here provides a framework within which to pose questions about the potential effects of poverty. In these studies, income was not an explicit variable; therefore, the questions raised have to be accepted as speculations about the impact of poverty on social acceptance and social status as well as on self-esteem.

Social status, as it is expressed in measures of popularity, is "associated with sociability and low levels of aggression and withdrawal" (Newcomb, Bukowski, and Pattee 1993, cited in Underwood and Hurley 1999, 240). Social acceptance sustains psychological adjustment. By contrast, peer rejection may be related to problems such as dropping out of school and delinquency (as shown, for example, in Parker and Asher 1993). Although literature on the role that physical attractiveness plays in gaining peer status is limited (see Hartup 1983 for a review), these studies have invariably demonstrated that facial and general physical attractiveness are important in peer acceptance (Evans and Eder 1993; Kennedy

1990). As one would expect within U.S. society, fashionable clothes or at least good clothes also contribute to children's popularity (Coleman 1980). The children in these studies were most likely not poor; for instance, the children in Kennedy's sample were students at a university lab school. Even if they were poor, family income was not factored into the analyses, and so we do not know the extent to which clothing could play a part in marginalizing poor children. However, it is probable that "clothes make the child" and that children whose parents are unable to afford new clothes are at risk of rejection by their peers. Although this probability is not documented in the research literature, ample popular literature supports it. In addition, some researchers have hypothesized that economically disadvantaged youth, lacking other legitimate avenues to success, use clothes as a preemptive indicator (Burton, Obeidallah, and Allison 1996).

If social acceptance is the social status children seek, conformity is the means by which they believe they will be accepted. Conformity is at its height in early adolescence (Berndt 1979), when youth want to look and dress like their peers and have similar possessions. They do not want to be different; to be included requires being like everybody else. If they wear worn clothes that were in fashion five years ago, they stick out and run the risk of being socially excluded. Beyond clothes, a child without a bike or a VCR may be perceived as different by peers who own such goods, and the child may be left behind as the others roam the neighborhood on their bikes or invite each other over to watch a movie.

For all children, social acceptance by peers is as critical to who they are as it is to the comfort gained from belonging. Crick and Dodge (1994) hypothesized that the way children interpret the manner in which peers respond to them influences their self-perception. If children interpret (or misinterpret) peers' smiles to mean that peers like them, they perceive themselves to be accepted or even worthy of friendship.

How one perceives oneself with respect to others affects whether one holds oneself in high or low esteem. Positive self-esteem is critical for psychological well-being (Harter 1985). Just as there is a link between clothing, material goods, and social status, there is a likely link between material goods and self-esteem. Material goods "often serve the critical function of being symbolic extensions of the real self" (Jackson 1979, 139). Even though, for many Americans, you are what you own, the importance that children place on material goods is rarely discussed in the child-psychology literature. Success in school also affects self-esteem (for a review, see Eccles et al. 1999). Hence life experiences that keep children away from school or that diminish their opportunities to learn when there create a risk of failure and damaged self-esteem. In the end, children whose self-esteem suffers in either the academic or social domains often report symptoms of depression, social isolation, anger, and aggression (Parkhurst and Asher 1992).

HYPOTHESIZED EFFECTS OF POVERTY ON STATUS AND ESTEEM

The literature on children in poverty is abundant, though limited historically—most of the work has been done in the last few decades. Scholars from various disciplines have studied children's physical health, education, academic achievement, and a variety of behavioral attributes as outcomes of lives lived in poverty. Nevertheless, "the effects of economic deprivation are not well understood" and the results of studies are sometimes conflicting (Duncan, Brooks-Gunn, and Klebanov 1994, 297). And, conflicting or not, they are usually quite disheartening.

Much less is known about the impact of poverty on children's subjective, or personal, views of their lives. The outcome literature on self-esteem and social status is limited. Evidence derived from current research indicates that children living in low-income households may be more likely to report low self-esteem than those living above the poverty line. Some children in persistent or even intermittent poverty are more likely to report problems with peers and of school conduct than children whose families have higher incomes (Bolger et al. 1995). Ultimately, as Garbarino (1998) speculated, one of the stresses for poor children in the United States is realizing that their circumstances do not meet societal standards and they are therefore different. Children recognize that status is not just about what they have but also very much about what they don't have. In short, the prevailing scholarly and popular view is that children living in poverty become acculturated to experiences of deficits, to occupying a status lower than that of the majority.

A SOCIAL CONSTRUCTIONIST PERSPECTIVE ON CHILD DEVELOPMENT

The assumption that a childhood lived in financial poverty is experienced exclusively as a childhood of deficits has not gone unchallenged. Social constructionists and other scholars increasingly challenge the view that the process of development is simply a tug of war between nature and nurture (see Chapter 4). These scholars are moving away from seeing development as the individual's resolution of psychic crises and away from the study of a decontextualized inner self. Instead they are urging social and behavioral scientists to view development in the context of relationships (Gergen 1994). The contextualized self is constructed through its actions within historical time (as Jack Meacham points out in Chapter 4).

Relationships are the means by which we construct our views of ourselves, the context within which we create self-perceptions. Our personal stories are co-constructed within relationships (Gergen 1994); they "are not merely a way of telling someone (or oneself) about one's life; they are the means by which identities may be fashioned" (Rosenwald and Ochberg, cited in Gergen 1994, 193). Our self-narratives develop within local social contexts. They are the products of our actions (or interactions) and conversations (or dialogues) with significant others (Anderson 1997). We craft our stories most often with family and friends, and with family and friends most of us become who we are.

The process of development is no different for poor children. The context is. They usually live in low-income neighborhoods and go to school with other poor children. Their direct experience of the lives of others generally validates the lives they lead. They do not witness daily how living within higher income neighborhoods would affect them. Instead, they have only indirect experiences of those lives. Information-age children watch television with plenty of sitcoms whose characters are either wealthy or middle class. Few if any sitcoms are about children who are poor, and in the portrayals that do exist the children on television are not living in the poverty these children know. Advertising on television and elsewhere whets their appetites. Marketing is democratic: it is directed at all children, and it is designed to increase their desire to acquire and to consume (as Enola Aird demonstrates in Chapter 8). Though they are told that they should want what the marketplace is selling, their economic condition prevents them from experiencing the good life that all children deserve. They are also experiencing stigma. In a country where four-fifths of one's peers appear to live the good life, it seems inevitable that poor children will view themselves as stigmatized and will construct a negative image of themselves—in short, that they will inevitably live out the deficit model of poverty.

Children's and Mothers' Stories

My interviews of the graduates of Project QUEST and their children do not sustain the notion that a childhood of poverty is part of an inescapable cycle. Project QUEST is an innovative, community-based job-training program initiated by two Industrial Areas Foundation organizations in San Antonio, Texas. It offers a holistic approach to job training in that it understands that job-training programs for the disadvantaged are long-term efforts; it therefore supports training with offers of college tuition, books and other supplies needed for college, childcare, transportation, counseling, and emergency assistance. Outcome research by Osterman and Lautsch (1996) indicates that this program successfully guides its graduates, including welfare recipients, to living-wage jobs. It thus differs from most job-training programs, which focus simply on training for any job, regardless of whether one is available and whether it pays a living wage. (For a further description of Project QUEST, see Osterman and Lautsch 1996.)

METHOD: LISTENING

Twenty women participated in the study; all of them had attended Project QUEST and were at the time of the study employed or working on a bachelor's degree. As well, eighteen of their children participated. In this study I employed an in-depth case-study approach, the only way to study truly disadvantaged people (Sjoberg et al. 1991). I interviewed the women and their children sometimes together, sometimes separately (the decision was made by the family). I then analyzed the interviews for their generic and specific properties, as is consistent with the collective case approach (Denzin and Lincoln 1994).

I conducted the interviews at least a year after the mothers had graduated from QUEST. Hence, the study provides a retrospective account of their lives. The older teenagers reflected back to early adolescence and childhood. The younger teenagers reflected on a childhood not so far removed in time. (All names are aliases.)

In all cases it was clear that the children's views of themselves and their families' circumstances were constructed within relationships, both with respect to family systems and with respect to peer relationships and friendships. The social-constructionist assumption about childhood appeared to be both logical and potentially clarifying.

CHILDREN'S AWARENESS OF THEIR POVERTY

I've heard many baby boomers and older people say, "I didn't know we were poor when I was a child." When one of my clinical supervisors was a child, she lived in the basement of the school she attended because her father was the janitor. She didn't realize her family was poor until she went to college. Garbarino (1998) offers similar accounts about himself and others: "A priest told his childhood story of spending a day at school putting together 'poor baskets' for Christmas, only to be shocked the next day when one was delivered to his house. . . . I myself never realized we were poor until my father had to sell our car to buy groceries" (1998, 112).

However, perhaps because of generational differences or the information age or the particular children in this study, half the children I interviewed knew very well that they were poor and how much their families struggled. Although they may not have known that their families received public assistance, they were aware of how tenuous their financial status was before their mothers enrolled in QUEST. They usually became aware of their situation in one of two ways. Sometimes the mother was frank with her children about being poor. For example, Bob's mother told her children, "We don't have money, guys. We're poor." Other children compared themselves with others. Luis's mother said her children were aware of how little money they had, and she illustrated her point with this story: "As I'm getting to school, my son told [*sic*] me his shoes; I was surprised to notice there were holes on his shoes. I asked my son, 'How come you never mentioned it?' and he said, 'Mom, I noticed you're going through a hard time. There's not enough money,' . . . and it made me feel like I wanted to cry. As opposed to children asking, 'Mom I need this and I need this.'"

Although all the families suffered economic distress, several of the mothers told me they felt that their children didn't really do without either because a family member or friend helped out with purchases or because mothers were able to find free or cheap goods and recreation or entertainment. This might be the reason some children did not understand the extent to which their family had been financially strapped until after their mothers completed the program and for the first time were financially independent.

PERCEPTIONS OF THE AVAILABILITY OF MATERIAL AND NONMATERIAL GOODS

Most of the children were aware of goods that they did not have and the enter-tainment that they could not enjoy. Fifteen children spoke of "things" (to use the children's word) they didn't have prior to QUEST or "things" they received after the family completed the program. These "things" were both material goods, such as clothing, and nonmaterial goods, including activities like going to the movies or having birthday parties. One could not comfortably categorize these "things" as necessities. An exception was Luis, who mentioned essentials like · shoes, a remark that indicated his family still has few "extras." His mother was the only woman in this study who did not finish college and who still receives food stamps.

Because she was cut off from her family, John's mother relied on friends. John knew that these friends could be counted on when the family lacked ne-cessities such as food. A friend provided their kitchen table and chairs and res-cued a dresser from the dump and refinished it for John. The family still owns this furniture.

Thirteen-year-old Cindy was grateful for the attention the father of her mother's boyfriend paid to her, such as taking her to the circus. Although it was only a few times a year, she appreciated the public entertainment because he paid for it. In addition to knowing that her family was supported by friends and relatives, she knew that the family was on public assistance but did not under-stand what that meant. "It was kind of weird": her mother couldn't buy her toys even though her mother "worked all the time." Cindy didn't understand that one could be employed and still be poor.

This struggle to understand the fullness of their hard times in the face of contradictory evidence led to mothers' and children's shared uncertainty about their poverty that neither addressed directly. Thirteen-year-old Sarah recalled,

"Well, my mom didn't have a lot of money, so we couldn't do a lot of things with each other or with anyone else." Prior to the interview, Sarah's mother told me that Sarah might downplay how difficult it was for her: "She's hard like a rock too. I think she hides a lot. She was telling me last night that she didn't have hard times. . . . I think she did." There is no deciding between these two accounts of Sarah's experience of poverty.

However, it was clear that parents' constructions included their understanding that their children were denied when they lived in poverty. Luis's mother spoke of how she was now able to enjoy the things most middle-class Americans take for granted, such as a telephone. In contrast to her son, she thought they now enjoyed more than basic necessities. She said, "Before I couldn't afford things they needed. And now . . . [we are able to] go out to the movies, to go out to eat; so it made a big change in our lives. Now I can afford other things that I couldn't before . . . before no cable, no telephone, and now I'm able to have, I would say more luxuries. . . . I'm able to give my children an allowance that I wasn't able [to] before."

Eleven-year-old James also spoke about the changes in his family's life once his mother was employed: "After she graduated, . . . I guess we got more money or something because of the job. And then we got to get more stuff for Christmas and my birthday and stuff. . . . We usually have my birthday at my grandmother's, but see now I'm going to have it at Chuck E. Cheese's."

James and some of the others spoke of the goods only as introducing pleasure into their family life, but they did not suggest that this change transformed their sense of self. Indeed, many spoke not of the things they did not have but of the things they could not do together. Some, like James, did not suggest that life was without pleasure while they lived in poverty but rather that they now experienced pleasure in other and more varied ways.

In summary, children's reactions to "going without" varied. It was difficult for several children to understand why they couldn't have some of the belongings their friends had. Not owning certain possessions or relying on public assistance were embarrassing for a few of the children and quite worrisome for others. Their coping devices for dealing with poverty ranged from not asking mother for new shoes to replace outworn ones to expecting mother to use any means necessary to get money for designer jeans to focusing more on what they did have rather than what they didn't. Like Mark, whom Eileen Lindner describes in Chapter 3, some of the children in this study tried to avoid hurting their mothers by not disclosing their own struggles. It may be that mother and child engage in a mutual pretense in which the mother acts as if she can afford more than she can and the child pretends that her needs are being met even though they are not. This pretense may not imply a denial of their material reality as much as it demonstrates respect for each other's feelings.

SOCIAL STATUS, SOCIAL ACCEPTANCE, AND SELF-ESTEEM

Though most of the children did not link having "things" with social status or self-esteem, four children specifically did so. However, even these children's constructions of self were based not only on material possessions but also on the heroic efforts of their mothers when they lived in poverty and the opportunities to function as a family that followed when they were no longer poor. Twenty-year-old Cleo explained that when she was in junior high, her mother "used to give blood to buy my clothes. Like go donate blood two or three times a week . . . because I would have to have like a pair of jeans in order to be socially acceptable." For Cleo, being popular with her peers was important, and she felt clothes were a means by which she could achieve popularity. Cleo appeared to be struggling to reconcile or integrate two compelling values: a socially imposed sense that clothes make the person, and the personal realization that her mother was willing to do extraordinary things to meet her daughter's needs.

Stacey, like Cleo, gave an account of this struggle between values coming from outside the home and from within herself. She remembered being unhappy in junior high because she did not have the material possessions her friends had. Eventually, she "kind of let go of what other people had and what I didn't have." Because Stacey's mother was unable to go to such extremes as Cleo's mother did, Stacey went without goods that she wanted. To compensate, she decided to focus instead on her more enduring personal attributes and her success in school.

Not that the children did not appreciate what having "things" meant once they finally had them. Some children admitted that their perceptions of themselves were enhanced when they could dress like those who were not living in poverty did. Possessions were interwoven with feelings about self. These changes were important because they helped make the children feel "normal," more like their peers. Seventeen-year-old Stacey said, "Now we do get a lot more things than we did when [my mother] was in school. . . . I think we're better now than where we were." Her mother added, "I think they feel better now, like where we were living they didn't want to bring their friends over. Now they have no problem. Things like that. They're a lot more comfortable in their surroundings than they were."

For eight years fourteen-year-old Rose, her brothers, and her mother had to live with her grandmother and endure her maternal aunts' and uncles' constant urgings to move out. She mentioned how this experience shaped her self-perception: "I'm happier that I don't have to live with someone that doesn't really want me there. When we were living at my grandmother's, . . . that made me feel bad about myself, like the way they did that. But now I feel better about myself that we have our own house and everything now."

During his mother's interview, thirteen-year-old John became quite emotional. He recalled how not having certain possessions affected his feelings of self-worth and how his family became "better" people—more like his friends—once his mother had a living-wage job. He interrupted his mother and said:

> It was kind of hard not being able to be who I wanted to be, not always having what I wanted and lots of stuff. [After Project QUEST], . . . we were able to see [my mother] a lot more. I was able to do stuff with her, talked to her more. I was able to go and get stuff that I needed. We were able to be a better family [crying], be like the people that my friends would like, always there for them. . . . [It] made me feel a lot better.

After his tears subsided, he added:

> We got a lot more stuff. . . . We moved and came here. We got this house, and we got a truck. We got a new car just recently. [His mother then reminded him that he got his own room.] I got, specifically, my privacy. [Before] I had to share everything with everybody. . . . I never really had time to like be in the room by myself, just sit there and do my work, and homework or projects that I have to do or some schoolwork. Sit there, just draw by myself, just think about all the blessings I have.

Like Rose, John was keenly aware of the personal significance of a space of one's own. It was important to him that he no longer had to share a room with his sister. The privacy meant he could focus on what was important to him, including the opportunity to do his schoolwork. In addition, he was happy that his mother now had a career that was satisfying, and he was pleased that the family saw more of each other. He explicitly equated money with normalcy.

A final story illustrates that these families in poverty constructed a sense of self and others through the complex relationships of their lives. More to the point, it reveals the mistake of construing poverty as a one-dimensional variable when trying to understand the relationship between poverty and feelings about self. When I arrived at Frida's home, she apologized, saying that her eleven-year-old daughter was at a science contest and would not be able to speak to me. Although her daughter was excited about the contest, she was disappointed that she would not be interviewed and had asked her mother to show me a project she had done for school. The poster was of her family's history as migrant workers in Minnesota. There was a photo of a little girl in a dress on a tractor with her maternal grandfather and another much older photo of family members posed in front of a boxcar.

The poster was not exclusively a documentation of her family tree; it was a powerful statement of the pride the daughter felt for her extended family. Her lineage was that of hard workers. According to Frida, her daughter was not ashamed of coming from a family of migrant workers, even though they were poor, but she was ashamed of her recent life of poverty in San Antonio. Perhaps she found something romantic about farms and the North, which she visited for a few summers, that she did not find in her neighborhood in San Antonio. Perhaps she understood that being poor was not stigmatized in the same way being in poverty and on welfare was. Furthermore, Frida said that even though her daughter's friends were not well-off financially, they at least got new clothes, albeit cheap clothes from discount stores. Frida's daughter and her other children "stood out" in their thrift-store clothes. According to Frida:

> She was embarrassed. She didn't like to go into the stores where her friends were going to see her give them food stamps. And if she got some clothes, she'd say they were from her cousin, anyone else, but they would be from the thrifty store. But she was not embarrassed at all to say that she'd go to Minnesota to work in the fields. Like she'd be embarrassed because everyone else would have like, back then it was a Little Mermaid backpack. And she couldn't have that. And just little things like [my children's] teeth would hurt. But I didn't have the money to get them fixed, or just little basic stuff that everyone else had. Everyone else had a VCR. We didn't have a VCR. "Why can so and so have a bike and I can't?"

Frida said her children now love to have friends visit their beautiful house, something they hated doing in their subsidized apartment. In addition they now have pets, which they could not previously afford. Like having friends over, having a pet helped bring feelings of normalcy. She recounted that "before they couldn't have a dog. I said, 'I can barely feed you! What do you mean you want a dog or a cat' because, I mean, to me, $5 for dog food or cat food was like oh my god; that could be ten Ramen noodles. So now they have a dog, cat, fish, and a turtle."

Frida was pregnant again and was happy that now she could afford to "do it right." In her previous pregnancies, even something as inexpensive as a diaper bag was a luxury she could not afford. Now, "it's kind of exciting because now I can do it right. . . . My oldest slept in a drawer kind of thing. And I'm like, now I get to buy a crib. I get to do stuff the right way. I mean even a diaper holder. Oh I wanted a diaper holder so bad! Just one with that hook on the side. And then [I tried] to make one out of a towel with a clothespin." Clearly, Frida regretted that she hadn't been able to give her children material comforts when they were babies. Now that she was pregnant again, she was determined that life was going to be different for this baby. Although she was only a few months along in her pregnancy, she'd already furnished the baby's room with new furniture, which she proudly showed me.

A few children went to great lengths to make it clear to me that they had certain possessions or that they were doing well in school. It was as if they were trying to assure me how normal or even extraordinary they were and that neither living in poverty nor having a low income had left its mark. For instance, when Sarah and her mother walked me to my car, Sarah noticed my Camry. It was thirteen years old and the original color was indeterminate after ten years in the Phoenix sun. Sarah poked fun at it and wanted to make sure that I noticed their new, beautiful Camry. Also, Luis wanted me to know that he had a bike and that he did very well on the ACT.

In a study of children's views of their working parents, time together with their parents did not top the children's wish list. Instead, income did; 23 percent wanted their parents to make more money (Galinsky 1999). Although the author surmised that the children hoped having more money would reduce the stress and fatigue their parents received from working, it is also possible the children knew about family finances and knew that an increase in earnings could have other positive impacts on their lives. Because the study did not let children describe their life experiences, we are left to speculate.

Many children realized that not having certain possessions affected their self-esteem; for instance, one child said he "couldn't be who I wanted to be." Mothers also mentioned the importance of material possessions for children's self-esteem. Some children spoke of how much better they felt when their mothers became wage-reliant. Both mothers and children spoke of the shame they felt for receiving public assistance. Wearing old clothes and having few material possessions likely increased the probability of peer rejection or avoidance. Indeed within such a social climate it is likely that behavioral and psychological problems will increase, and thus the lack of certain material goods presents poor children with yet another obstacle to success.

Although these interviews contained accounts of the deficits of poverty, they also contained stories of strengths and resilience. These families constructed strong networks of kin. None of the families reported ever being without food; mothers were resourceful enough that their children did not go hungry. The children admired their mothers' fortitude and long hours of work. None of the children or mothers regretted the mother's return to school. The children said it was difficult to see so much less of their mother while she was at school or studying, but they said such sacrifices were worth the outcomes of a higher income, a happier mother, and more time together as a family. They spoke openly of what they lost in order to make such gains, perhaps to remind themselves of why they made such large sacrifices. Most of the children were proud of their mothers' accomplishments, and several held their mothers up as role models.

Conclusions: Policy and Program Recommendations

Policymakers, child advocates, and program developers rely on their beliefs about children to guide their decision making (Gergen, Gloger-Tippelt, and Berkowitz 1990). Their beliefs are usually based on personal experience as well as research. However, the available research often provides only some indices of children's experiences. It almost never involves children's voices; children are rarely asked to share their constructions of the reality of their lives.

Retrospective accounts of being a child in poverty reveal both living without and living with those who care. These stories help address "the glaring need for clearer and more understandable indicators of the adverse conditions associated with poverty" (Ramey 1995, 262) as well as the coping mechanisms families create. This knowledge will strengthen our efforts to reform policy.

The themes in the stories in this study were resilience and vulnerability. Public policy, carefully developed, can both enhance resilience and reduce deficits. Policies and programs aimed at helping children adjust to poverty cannot. Both public policy and public programs should be aimed at helping children get off welfare and leave poverty, and one demonstrable way to meet this goal is through helping their families achieve economic security.

Most of the families in this study attributed their move from public assistance to financial independence to three factors: the particular formula of help designed in Project QUEST, the support of family and friends, and their own hard work. For most of these families, QUEST was more than a way off public assistance and a road to reliance on wages. It provided opportunities for psychological change. Children believed that their lives changed after their mothers' graduation from college because their mothers were happier and able to spend more time with the family and because the increased family income meant they could purchase certain of the material goods that helped raise their self-esteem. Ironically, listening to the children directed our attention as much toward the lives of their mothers as toward their own. These children offer a compelling justification for holistic job-training programs.

Unfortunately, the Personal Responsibility and Work Opportunity Reconciliation Act of 1996 (PRWORA) and past welfare-reform policies were designed with little knowledge of how women leave poverty. Most job-training programs have not been designed to provide the kind of training required if people are to develop enduring skills and hold living-wage jobs. "Work-first" programs tend to have foreshortened horizons; they get women into any job and off public assistance quickly, without thought for long-term consequences. Many of these jobs require few skills and consequently lead at best to a step up, not to a career ladder. Even with some possibility of advancement, these jobs often offer "terminally" low-wages (Harris, 1993). Work-first programs disregard research specifying the necessary role of postsecondary education if families are going to achieve wage-reliant financial independence. Further, research on the results of PRWORA indicates that welfare policies that increase employment but do not increase the income realized on welfare have few positive effects on children (Morris 2002).

In her review of the literature on the effects of postsecondary education, Dann-Messier (2001) reported that such education increases a woman's years in the workforce and decreases the probability that she will live in poverty. In addition, postsecondary education improves a woman's self-esteem and increases her children's educational aspirations, as the families in this study confirmed. With a living-wage job, women are likely to leave poverty permanently. Mothers in this study would agree that if policymakers truly want to help women stay off public assistance, they need to consider postsecondary education as fulfilling a work requirement. Women could then receive public assistance while going to school. The families in this study also described the importance of friends and family in helping them reach wage reliance. These families had informal, yet strong, networks of support in addition to their program support. As James Spilsbury and Jill Korbin suggest in Chapter 11, children's input would be helpful in designing programs that develop or improve support networks of family and friends.

Several children in this study spoke of being embarrassed about receiving public assistance. The way to rid us of the stigma attached to public assistance would be to change from income-tested programs to universal programs, such as health care. Such programs do a much better job of reducing poverty too (Huston 1995). Shifting at least some of our need-tested programs to universal programs might save us money in the long run by reducing expenditures for prisons, special education, and medical care (Huston 1995).

Most researchers agree with Huston that "changing macroeconomic conditions, increases in single-mother families, and declining government transfers were major contributors to the increases in children's poverty in the last 20 years" (1995, 307). Although the first two factors are difficult to change, especially in the short term, the third, providing income sufficient to train family members for stable employment, is a relatively quick means to combat children's poverty.

To expect that poor families will be able to beat the odds on their own is unrealistic (Gadsen 1995) and, according to the families in this study, nearly impossible. Well-designed policies, based on research findings that include children's voices, are necessary to help families on the path out of poverty.

Note
I am grateful to Peter Pufall, Richard Unsworth, Laura Lein, and Julie Miller-Cribbs for their helpful comments.

References

Anderson, H. 1997. *Conversation, Language, and Possibilities: A Postmodern Approach to Therapy*. New York: Basic Books.

Berndt, T. J. 1979. "Developmental Changes in Conformity to Peers and Parents." *Developmental Psychology* 15:608–616.

Bolger, K. E., C. J. Patterson, W. W. Thompson, and J. B. Kupersmidt. 1995. "Psychosocial Adjustment among Children Experiencing Persistent and Intermittent Family Economic Hardship." *Child Development* 66:1107–1129.

Burton, L. M., D. A. Obeidallah, and K. Allison. 1996. "Ethnographic Insights on Social Context and Adolescent Development among Inner-City African American Teens." In *Ethnography and Human Development: Context and Meaning in Social Inquiry*, edited by R. Jessor, A. Colby, and R. A. Shweder. Chicago: University of Chicago Press.

Coleman, J. C. 1980. "Friendship and the Peer Group in Adolescence." In *Handbook of Adolescent Psychology*, edited by J. Adelson. New York: Wiley.

Crick, N. R., and K. A. Dodge. 1994. "A Review and Reformulation of Social Information-Processing Mechanisms in Children's Social Adjustment." *Psychological Bulletin* 115:74–101.

Dann-Messier, B. 2001. *Levers for Change: Educational Opportunity Centers and Welfare Reform*. National TRIO Clearinghouse. Retrieved from http://trioprograms.org/clearinghouse/shared/outlookjournal.pdf on 17 May 2002.

Denzin, N. K., and Y. S. Lincoln. 1994. "Strategies of Inquiry." In *Handbook of Qualitative Research*, edited by N. K. Denzin and Y. S. Lincoln. Thousand Oaks, Calif.: Sage.

Duncan, G. J., J. Brooks-Gunn, and P. K. Klebanov. 1994. "Economic Deprivation and Early Childhood Development." *Child Development* 65:296–318.

Eccles, J. S., R. Roeser, A. Wigfield, and C. Freedman-Doan. 1999. "Academic and Motivational Pathways through Middle Childhood." In *Child Psychology: A Handbook of Contemporary Issues*, edited by L. Balter and C. S. Tamis-Lemonda. Philadelphia: Psychology Press.

Evans, C., and D. Eder. 1993. "No Exit: Processes of Social Isolation in the Middle School." *Journal of Contemporary Ethnography* 22:139–170.

Federal Interagency Forum on Child and Family Statistics. 2001. *Indicators of Children's Well-Being. America's Children: Key National Indicators of Well-Being*. Retrieved from http://www.childstats.gov/ac2001/pdf/econ.pdf on 20 May 2002.

Gadsen, V. L. 1995. "Literacy and Poverty: Intergenerational Issues within African American Families." In *Children of Poverty: Research, Health, and Policy Issues*, edited by H. E. Fitzgerald, B. M. Lester, and B. Zuckerman. New York: Garland.

Galinsky, E. 1999. *Ask the Children: What America's Children Really Think about Working Parents*. New York: Morrow.

Garbarino, J. 1998. "The Stress of Being a Poor Child in America." *Child and Adolescent Psychiatric Clinics of North America* 7 (1): 105–119.

Gergen, K. J. 1994. *Realities and Relationships: Soundings in Social Construction*. Cambridge: Harvard University Press.

Gergen, K. J., G. Gloger-Tippelt, and P. Berkowitz. 1990. "The Cultural Construction of the Developing Child." In *Everyday Understanding: Social and Scientific Implications*, edited by G. Semin and K. J. Gergen. London: Sage.

Harris, K. M. 1993. "Work and Welfare among Single Mothers in Poverty." *American Journal of Sociology* 99 (2): 317–352.

Harter, S. 1985. "Competence as a Dimension of Self Evaluation: Toward a Comprehensive Model of Self-Worth." In *The Development of the Self*, edited by R. L. Leahy. New York: Academic Press.

Hartup, W. H. 1983. "Peer Relations." In *Handbook of Child Psychology*, 4th ed., edited by P. H. Musson and E. M. Hetherington. New York: Wiley.

Huston, A. C. 1995. "Policies for Children: Social Obligation, Not Handout." In *Children of Poverty: Research, Health, and Policy Issues,* edited by H. E. Fitzgerald, B. M. Lester, and B. Zuckerman. New York: Garland.

Jackson, R. L. 1979. "Material Good Need Fulfillment as a Correlate of Self-Esteem." *Journal of Social Psychology* 108 (1): 139–140.

Kennedy, J. H. 1990. "Determinants of Peer Social Status: Contributions of Physical Appearance, Reputation, and Behavior." *Journal of Youth and Adolescence* 19 (3): 233–244.

Kennedy, M. M., R. K. Jung, and M. E. Orland. 1986. "Poverty, Achievement and the Distribution of Compensatory Education Services: An Interim Report." In *The National Assessment of Chapter 1.* Washington, D.C.: Office of Educational Research and Improvement, U.S. Department of Education.

McLoyd, V. C., T. E. Jayaratne, R. Ceballo, and J. Borquez. 1994. "Unemployment and Work Interruption among African American Single Mothers: Effects on Parenting and Adolescent Socio-emotional Functioning." *Child Development* 65:562–589.

Morris, P. A. 2002. "The Effects of Welfare Reform Policies on Children." *Social Policy Report* 15 (1): 4–19.

Osterman, P., and B. Lautsch. 1996. *Project QUEST: A Report to the Ford Foundation.* New York: Ford Foundation.

Parker, J. G., and S. R. Asher. 1993. "Friendship and Friendship Quality in Middle Childhood: Links between Peer Group Acceptance and Feelings of Loneliness and Social Dissatisfaction." *Developmental Psychology* 29:611–621.

Parkhurst, J. T., and S. R. Asher. 1992. "Peer Rejection in Middle School: Subgroup Differences in Behavior, Loneliness, and Interpersonal Concerns." *Developmental Psychology* 28:231–241.

Ramey, C. T. 1995. "Setting Research Priorities for Poverty Children at Risk for Advance Outcomes." In *Children of Poverty: Research, Health, and Policy Issues,* edited by H. E. Fitzgerald, B. M. Lester, and B. Zuckerman. New York: Garland.

Sjoberg, G., N. William, T. Vaughan, and A. Sjoberg. 1991. "The Case Study Approach in Social Research: Basic Methodological Issues." In *A Case for the Case Study,* edited by J. Feagin, T. Orum, and G. Sjoberg. Chapel Hill: University of North Carolina Press.

Toomey, B. G., and D. J. Christie. 1990. "Social Stressors in Childhood: Poverty, Discrimination, and Catastrophic Events." In *Childhood Stress,* edited by L. E. Arnold. New York: Wiley.

Underwood, M. K., and J. C. Hurley. 1999. "Emotion Regulation in Peer Relationships during Middle Childhood." In *Child Psychology: A Handbook of Contemporary Issues,* edited by L. Balter and C. S. Tamis-Lemonda. Philadelphia: Psychology Press.

Weinger, S. 2000. "Children's Perceptions of Class Differences: Worries and Self-Perceptions." *Journal of Poverty* 4 (3): 9–117.

Chapter 10   Children of Divorce

JAN PRYOR
ROBERT E. EMERY

CHILDREN'S VOICES, AS THEY talk about families and what they mean, are being increasingly heard as it is realized that they have something both important and unique to say. Several factors have contributed to an increasing sensitivity to their voices. One is a radical change in views of childhood, most recently articulated by sociologists of childhood (see for example Archard 1993; James and Richards 1999). Allied with this change is a focus on the history of childhood by historians and historiographers who have illuminated the radically different and changing ways in which children and childhood have been constructed (Cunningham 1995; de Mause 1974). The twentieth century was, indeed, characterized as the century of the child, to the extent that some children became "emotionally priceless" to their parents (see, for example, Beck and Beck-Gernsheim 1995; Cunningham 1995). Today, adults no longer have children in order to provide for them in their old age; on the contrary, children are significant economic liabilities. This status is offset by their psychological value. They are sources of emotional sustenance to their parents, priceless beyond tangible measure; in this sense, parents are as dependent on their children as children are on them. "Sons and daughters are supposed to help the parents achieve their goal of being spontaneous, sensual, uninhibited and creative personalities. It is not the parents raising their children but conversely the children raising their parents. In the truest sense of the word, sons and daughters embody their parents' ego-ideal" (Bopp 1984, 70, cited in Beck and Beck-Gernsheim 1995, 107).

In Chapter 14, Alice Hearst points out that a further impetus for taking children seriously is the recognition of their legal rights—for example through the United Nations Convention on the Rights of the Child (CRC). If, as this convention insists, children have the right to participate in decisions affecting their lives, then we must listen seriously to them and take their views into account when making decisions on their behalf. Although the CRC has not been ratified by the United States, it has been by almost all other countries, and it is having a fundamental influence on how children and their rights are viewed.

Paradoxically, when families undergo change, children are rarely given the chance to tell adults what they think and feel about these major issues in their lives (Dunn et al. 2001; Neugebauer 1989; Smith et al. 1997). We tend to make decisions for children with too little consideration of their point of view, assuming that especially young children do not have views or that, if they do, there are good reasons why their voices are better not heard. The received view is that children are not able to say anything sensible until about the age of twelve. And although the majority of states have statutes requiring the consideration of children's views in deciding what their best interests are at divorce (as Barbara Woodhouse points out in Chapter 13), they need to be of "sufficient age and capacity to reason so as to form an intelligent preference" (Jones 1984).

We can detect the irony in this position when we consider the power that children's voices have in the day-to-day lives of families. Children are encouraged to be articulate, to express opinions on everything from bedroom décor to world events, and to be independent. Families have become, by and large, democratic units allowing considerable participation by all members. Yet when it comes to questions of family change, we often deny children rights to express their opinions. Why? Part of the answer may lie in the powerful emotions that swirl around when families break up. Adults commonly experience guilt, anger, grief, and rejection, and they are aware of the potential impact of their divorce on their children. To ask children what they are feeling, then, is to run the risk of feeling rejected should they express a desire to live with the other parent and of guilt should they speak of their distress and bewilderment. It is then often easier not to ask.

Another reason may be the widely held "caretaker" view of children, the view that they should be allowed to be children and should be protected from grown-up issues. Allied with this view is the belief that they are incapable of understanding adult issues and that even if they are not included in discussions they will not be unduly affected by what is happening in the family. Parents do not want to "trouble" their children with the information that is vivid and available to them at the time of parental separation.

Acknowledging that children do have feelings and views about family change, enabling their voices to be heard, does not amount to conferring decision-making powers and responsibilities on them. As we shall see later in the chapter, children often do not want to make decisions about adult matters, even when they are deeply affected by them. In our zeal for recognizing the rights of children we may overinterpret their desire to have a voice in family matters.

A particular tension leads to a confusion of approaches to the voices of children. The view that children should be protected and not bothered with issues related to family change and its accompanying disruption runs counter to the increasing recognition of children's rights and desires to be heard. As Cunningham says: "The peculiarity of the late twentieth century, and the root cause of much present confusion and *angst* about childhood, is that a public discourse that argues that children are persons with rights to a degree of autonomy is at odds with the remnants of the romantic view that the right of a child is to be a child" (1995, 190).

The current debate about children's voices and their rights and abilities to hold opinions takes place in the wider context of ongoing arguments about the effects of divorce on children. Judith Wallerstein, for example, has consistently taken the position that divorce is almost always bad for children (in Wallerstein and Kelly 1980, for example). The more generally conservative position on families exemplified by her and by writers such as Popenoe (1996) leads to calls for a return to fault divorce and for women and men to revert to more traditional family roles. In contrast, some writers view the demise of the family as a timely reprieve from the constraints on nuclear families imposed by rigid gender roles and the belief that children are always better off living with two biological parents (for example, Stacey 1990). Another example of this viewpoint is the headline in a prominent U.K. newspaper that greeted a report on the impact of divorce on children: "Divorce—the Great Liberator" (Toynbee 1998). Sadly many of these arguments, although they purport to be focused on the well-being of children, turn out to support the rights of men or the rights of women rather than the protection and nurturing of children. The perceptions of children in this context, then, are of particular interest.

Throughout this chapter, we use the phrase *hearing children's voices* (and variations) to indicate the middle ground between ignoring children's opinions, at one extreme, and, at the opposite extreme, burdening children with the responsibility for making major decisions about matters such as who they want to live with following a separation. Our point, and our goal, is that parents should hear children's viewpoints and the emotions they convey. Further, we believe that children's needs and preferences should be paramount in the mind of parents as they negotiate the often dangerous waters of postdivorce family life. Still, the parents, not the children, have the responsibility for making major decisions. For example, we would expect parents to listen to children's voices in relation to relocation, but we would not expect parents who are at odds about the move to agree, as a compromise, with the child's preference.

Parental responsibility and children's autonomy can be kept in balance as children's decision-making power matures during adolescence. If a fifteen-year-old wishes to move to the other parent's home, we believe parents should honor this preference, if not always, then almost always. Honoring a preference means that parents respect their children's will while at the same time maintaining responsibility for the decision. Parental authority can be preserved, including the authority to rethink the change at a later time if necessary, and children are not forced to choose one while rejecting the other parent.

Children's Views of Families

What do children say about families and family transitions? In this section we focus on children's voices in relation to these issues, drawing on research from the United States, the United Kingdom, Australia, and New Zealand.

Because divorce encompasses structural change in children's families and households, it is valuable to consider first how children see families in general as a prelude to illuminating their understanding of divorce and other transitions, such as stepfamily formation. Several approaches have been taken to hearing children's views about families. One is simply to ask them to define what family means to them and then to identify themes and commonalities. Another is to present groupings of individuals in vignettes or pictures (or both) and to ask children whether they think the groups constitute a family. In this way both traditional and nontraditional groupings can be judged. An extension of this exercise is to ask children to explain why or why not a particular group is a family. Although these situations are hypothetical, children's lived experiences will likely have a bearing on their responses.

Several conclusions emerge from studies that have used these approaches. First, for children and adolescents an overarching and dominant feature of a family is an atmosphere of love, support, and mutual caring. "A family is loving people. Families are for telling people secrets and they care about you" (quoted in Morrow 1998, 23). This theme dominates in children's definitions of families and takes precedence over other factors such as co-residence, blood relationships, and legal status (Anyan 2002).

A second feature is the remarkable diversity of family structures that are endorsed by children as families. Although the traditional tableau of married parents and children living together is almost universally seen as a family, so too are children living with single parents, cohabiting parents, and gay parents, and relatives living in other households. Table 10.1 shows the percentages of children at several ages who endorse various household types as families. Children, then, are remarkably pragmatic about family structures, perhaps because they experience the diverse forms that family takes as they visit friends and walk their neighborhoods.

A third aspect of children's views of families is the varied way they describe family at different ages. From a structural perspective, adolescents have increasingly complex and encompassing perspectives and experiences and are more

Table 10.1. Percentages of Children and Young People Endorsing Household Types as Family at Different Ages

Household type	6-year-olds	10-year-olds	17-year-olds	21-year-olds
Nuclear	90	100	99.6	100
Solo mother and children	55	80	92.6	95
Unmarried parents and children	20	40	88.4	
Sole father and children	45	75	86.6	95
Grandparents	60	85	86	100
Aunt, uncle, and cousins	45	80	83	85
Two women and child			80	
Two parents without love	15	55	64.3	70
Nonresidential father and children	5	50	62.8	85
Couple, no children	45	70	62.1	85
Nonresidential mother and children	10	75	56.3	90

NOTE: In the studies, not all children were asked to judge all the household types. Hence, some cells are empty.

SOURCES: Anyan 2002; Gilby and Pedersen 1982; O'Brien, Alldred, and Jones 1996.

likely than younger children to endorse a wide range of groupings. Ninety percent of the young children endorse the nuclear family as prototypical. For them family implies co-residence, the presence of two parents, children, and blood relationships as defining qualities. Young adults do not have a prototypical image of family; rather they endorse a broad range of adult-child configurations. For young adults, two parents and co-residence are less important than they are for young children (Gilby and Pedersen 1982). Young children, too, are more likely to use concrete descriptions of families as people who do things for you, whereas adolescents more often mention affective and psychological aspects of families (Morrow 1998).

An important aspect of children's perspectives on families, and one central to the theme of this book, is that they do not see themselves as passive recipients of care and love. Rather, they consider themselves to be active agents within their families, full members who care about their parents and who are pro-active in negotiating and determining the nature of family relationships. Indeed many of them see themselves as the center of the family and as major achievements on the part of their parents (Allatt 1996). One young person suggested that "families are for giving me stuff. . . . Loving, caring for me, *and for giving things back to*" (quoted in Morrow 1998, 23, emphasis added). They have a concept of democratic parenting, which involves balancing care and protection with respect and participation.

For children, then, families are loving, dynamic, diverse groupings of people. Although they almost universally accept the traditional nuclear structure of heterosexual married parents living with biological children, they also regard a wide range of other groupings as valid families. Above all, in the opinions of children, families should be loving and mutually supportive with children as active participants in building and maintaining relationships.

Children's Views of Family Change

How do children feel when their own family undergoes change? Given the almost universal emphasis on love and support, we might assume that their concerns would focus on threats to love and support posed by divorce. Beloved parents depart, and others may enter their day-to-day world. When they have no control over the decisions, it is natural to expect them to be stressed as their agency is eroded and their contribution to the state of the family is denied. Another possible consequence of their belief in their own agency is that they may, albeit without objective foundation, blame themselves for the disruption. We know that young children, in particular, are prone to blame themselves for their parents' separation.

Some difficulties are inherent in talking to children about their parents' divorce. If they are interviewed close to the time that it happens, they may repress or disguise their true feelings both to the interviewer and to themselves. However, talking to them some time afterward runs the risk that their memories about their feelings will be inaccurate. Some investigators have chosen a neutral way of asking children how they feel by using vignettes and stories about fictitious families (for example, Plunkett and Kalter 1984; Pryor 2001; Anyan 2002). Others have questioned them directly about their own experiences. A study in Australia followed the same group of children over ten years (Burns and Dunlop 1999), and Wallerstein and her colleagues interviewed a clinical sample of children at several intervals after their parents' divorces (Wallerstein and Kelly 1980). These studies enable us to track changes in feelings over time.

How do children understand divorce? Although the practical aspects of their parents' divorce are all too apparent to children, what divorce means to them is less obvious. Few studies have examined this question, but from that literature (Kalter and Plunkett 1984; Kurdek and Siesky 1980) we know that their understanding approximates the explanations typically offered by adults. Children see divorce as a psychological and emotional issue between parents that leads to incompatibility and an inability to "get along."

How do they feel about their parents separating? It should come as no surprise, given the diversity of situations children find themselves in, that they describe a wide range of responses to parents' separation. Not only do children vary individually, but they can also hold conflicting feelings within themselves. So although it is probably safe to say that no child is unaffected and that most find the experience distressing, beyond that it is not safe to generalize about children overall. In an early study of Australian children, Amato (1987b) found that 44 percent reported negative responses and 38 percent reported neutral or positive reactions to their parents' divorce. Negative comments included feelings of being pulled both ways: "I felt really sad, really upset. I felt like I was a rag doll being pulled by both arms because they both wanted me" (fifteen-year-old girl) (614). Positive comments often reflected relief: "When Dad was happy he was nice, but sometimes he got mad and then he got pretty mean. It was pretty quiet when he was gone, and after that I got used to it. I was relieved that he wouldn't belt any of us and smack us or do anything bad to us" (nine-year-old girl) (614). Notably, though, in this group 48 percent said they did not know how they felt. In a New Zealand group interviewed in the 1990s, 33 percent said they felt negative, 23 percent had mixed feelings, and 44 percent were neutral or positive (Smith et al. 1997).

Mixed reactions were also evident in an Australian sample of children and adolescents followed over ten years by Burns and Dunlop (1999). The predominant response was sadness, followed by shock and disbelief. Paradoxically, levels of anger and relief were at similar levels in these young people. Likewise, they had similar levels of feeling glad about the separation and of wanting their parents to reunite.

The fact that so many children indicate either mixed feelings or that they do not know what their feelings are suggests that finding their voice in the face of family disruption may not be as easy as we would assume. The implications of this finding are discussed later.

Some evidence indicates that children long for the reconciliation of their parents, although what they say depends on whether they have experienced the divorce of their own parents or are talking about the divorce of hypothetical parents. Kurdek and Siesky (1980) asked children whose parents had divorced whether they thought their parents would live together again; only 3 percent thought so. Does this answer reflect their wishes or their realistic assessment of the chances of reconciliation? We can't be certain, but in Amato's (1987a) Australian study few children and adolescents whose parents had divorced wished their parents would get back together. On the other side, when children think about the hopes of hypothetical children, over 95 percent expect the hypothetical children to wish their parents would unite (Plunkett and Kalter 1984).

Whom do children blame for their parents' divorce? In Plunkett and Kalter's vignette study (1984), one third of the children said the child was to blame.

But only 5 percent of children who had experienced divorce and who were asked directly in Kurdek and Siesky's study (1980) considered that the child was the cause of the separation. It is thus not safe to assume that children will feel responsible for their parents' separation. Generally, younger children and those whose parents have recently separated are the most likely to blame themselves (Wallerstein and Kelly 1980). A nine-year-old interviewed by one of us (Pryor) thought she was to blame because she had gone into the hospital two weeks before her parents parted and her mother had stayed in the hospital with her. It was not until she watched a children's television program about divorce that she realized her parents' separation was not her fault. In short, children seem to be most vulnerable when their cognitive and emotional agency is less well developed and shortly after their perceived central position within the family constellation has been destroyed.

Sometimes children describe positive aspects of parental separation. Alongside the understandable relief that accompanies a reduction in conflict and tension, children describe an enhanced sense of competence and increased feelings of psychological growth, maturity, and independence (Amato 1987a, Kurdek and Sinclair 1986; Pritchard 1998; Reinhard 1977; Rosen 1977). Adolescents describe a closer relationship with their mothers (Arditti 1999; Kurdek and Sinclair 1986). One of Amato's interviewees said that "Mum and I have a very good relationship, I reckon. And I don't think that would've been—not that it wouldn't have been good—but the relationship that's there now wouldn't have been possible. And Mum's more happy and Dad's more happy" (Amato 1987a, 619). Young people who were eighteen or older when their parents separated also found that they developed a better understanding of their fathers and, in some cases, became close to them for the first time (Pryor 1999).

When children talk about the worst aspects of their parents' separation, they are most likely to say they miss the parent who has moved away from home. For some a parent leaving home triggers the fear that the other parent may leave as well. Wallerstein and Kelly (1980) found that younger children, in particular, fear that if one parent has "abandoned" them, then the other might as well. Most express longing for more contact with the departed father (Dunn et al. 2001; Smith et al. 1997) and if he is unreliable in maintaining contact, the loss appears to be compounded. Interestingly, even though divorced children rank the loss of a parent as most distressing, children in intact families are more likely than those who have experienced separation to think the divorce is accompanied by feelings of abandonment and betrayal in children (Plunkett and Kalter 1984).

Children frequently describe the denigration of one parent by the other as among their worst experiences after a divorce (Rosen 1977). Being asked to carry messages and to report about the activities of the other parent is distressing and damaging for children who try to love both parents—as most children do. One young woman said that "I wanted to see my father but pretended not to because of loyalty to my mother. I knew how she felt, and I didn't want to hurt her" (quoted in Rosen 1977, 26).

Clearly it would be foolish to generalize about children's responses to their parents' separation because children vary widely in their responses and feelings. Yet within those varied experiences may be a resourcefulness that emerges when we set the views of children from intact and divorced families side by side. Plunkett and Kalter have concluded that "kids do have conscious [beliefs] . . . that divorce is pain and trouble" (1984, 621). But children who have experienced divorce are more realistic and optimistic than those who have not. Plunkett and Kalter go on to report that children in intact families were more likely than those in divorced families to see children in vignettes as feeling abandoned and surprised. They were also less likely to see children who experienced divorce as actively helping out at home, wanting to do better at school, and looking forward to having time alone with each parent. In other words, children anticipate the worst should their parents separate, but those who experience a separation find that they cope better than they might have thought.

Whom do children turn to for support and information? At the time of separation, households are typically chaotic as parents wrestle with distress, anger, and guilt. Children are in the middle of the resulting confusion, and few parents find it easy to muster sufficient resources to talk calmly with them. As a result, few children are aware beforehand that their parents are going to separate; only about one quarter of them are told beforehand (Neugebauer 1989; Smith et al. 1997). Similarly, not many are given an explanation for what is happening. About a quarter say they know the reason for the separation (Neugebauer 1989; Wallerstein and Kelly 1980), but in a large U.K. sample only 5 percent thought they understood fully, 23 percent received no explanation, and 45 percent were given a blunt explanation with no elaboration (Dunn et al. 2001). One English child said that "we were sat down, and mum more or less announced to us that [our father had] gone and that he wasn't coming back this time. . . . I was very bitter about that. In one day, my safe secure little world went to pieces" (quoted in Gorrell Barnes et al. 1998, 57). Some parents find it simply too distressing and difficult to talk to their children. Others believe that it is inappropriate to bother children with the details of adult problems. Either way, children are more often than not left confused and uninformed as their world changes around them.

Whom, then, do they turn to for support? A considerable number of children say that they cope alone (Neugebauer 1989; Smith et al. 1997; Wallerstein and Kelly 1980). For those who do confide in someone, the people they most frequently turn to are grandparents and other relatives (Dunn et al. 2001). Though the role of grandparents in children's lives in general is understudied, their importance at times of family change is becoming increasingly apparent. In groups of U.S. college students from intact, lone-parent, and stepfamily homes who were asked how close they felt to grandparents, those in stepfamilies reported the closest relationships and those in intact families the least close relationships (Kennedy and Kennedy 1993). Thus the salience of grandparents in children's lives varies, becoming more significant during times of family transition. Cherlin and Furstenberg (1986) have described grandparents as having a latent function for children that becomes active involvement when required, either because children solicit their care or because grandparents perceive a new role in the face of divorce or both.

The role of friends is also important, though variable. In the U.K. study by Dunn and colleagues (2001), friends were the second most-often nominated by children as people they turn to (ahead of mothers). Yet children, and perhaps especially boys, are ambivalent about talking to friends. A New Zealand teenage boy said that "I just said that Mum and Dad are separating and we went off and played cricket or something." Another said, "I don't know if they really gave a shit[;] . . . they asked, and I took it quite hard really you know, and they didn't really give a shit when I told them" (quoted in Smith et al. 1997, 29). Younger children are less likely than older ones to talk to friends. There may be several explanations for these findings. Children may find it difficult to talk about painful experiences and so do not talk about their parents' separation. The separation may, however, be less salient in their day-to-day activities with friends unless they visit each other's houses. Adolescents may find it more difficult to be secretive about home situations and may, too, be more inclined to discuss personal matters with friends. Or children may not talk with their friends about divorce because it has become much more common and children are less likely now than in the 1970s to fear being stigmatized by it. As one young person said recently to an acquaintance, "Are your parents together or are they normal?"

It is not safe to assume that children want to talk to anyone. Some young people found being active, doing things, was more helpful than talking (Wade and Smart 2002). Distractions such as going to the movies or doing things with friends were as useful for coping as was confiding in other people. More broadly, it may be that the best way for parents to help children adjust to the many changes of postdivorce family life is not just to talk but to do: to manage their conflicts effectively or at least apart from the children; to reestablish or establish for the first time authoritative parent-child relationships; to find rhythms in their new lives that offer children stability and predictability; to manage finances as well as possible; and, always, to keep the children's needs foremost in mind.

How do children's feelings and responses change over time? As we have seen, children's feelings about divorce, and their responses to it at the time it happens, are varied but usually involve some distress. We know that about two years after a separation, families tend to stabilize, and both adults and children are functioning at about the same level as those from intact families. How do their feelings change? Amato asked his Australian sample in the 1980s to report retrospectively how they felt at the time of divorce and how they felt in the present. There was at best a weak relationship between their feelings at the two times. The most common pattern was nonnegative responses at both times (51 percent of the sample). Among those who were eight to nine years old at the time of the divorce, the time since separation seemed to reduce the level of negative feelings; for others the levels of feelings were similar regardless of the time since separation. One 16-year-old said, "I don't think I'd have it any other way really. I've grown accustomed to it—just doesn't worry me. Speak about it freely" (1987a, 619).

Children's feelings change over time. Burns and Dunlop (1999) asked children whose ages ranged from thirteen to sixteen years at the time of their first interview to express their feelings on a scale from 1 to 4 with the higher numbers representing stronger feelings. They interviewed them at the time of the divorce and then three years later and ten years later. After three years their feelings of sadness, disbelief, shock, self-blame, refusal to accept the divorce, and a desire for parents to reunite declined sharply and significantly (Figure 10.1). By contrast, their feelings of gladness and relief had increased. At ten years, feelings of gladness and relief predominated with anger at one parent remaining fairly high (about one quarter of the sample).

At the ten-year mark children were asked to give retrospective accounts about how they felt at the time of the divorce, and these retrospective accounts were compared with what they had said at the time (see Figure 10.2). The findings were striking: young people significantly overestimated the negative feelings they had in comparison with what they had reported at the time; in particular, they remembered their feelings of sadness, anger, disbelief, self-blame, rejection, shock, and a desire for the reunion of their parents as worse than they had expressed them at the time. As young adults they may have felt they were "over the divorce" and so overestimated distress. Alternatively, they may have repressed their true feelings at the time and acknowledged them only later. Or perhaps the children readjusted their standards, and, like children from intact families, they came to believe the personal pain of divorce to be more than it is for most. The issue is not deciding which account is accurate; the issue is respecting the voice we hear so that we can engage children of divorce as they currently understand and feel the experience.

Although the majority of children who have experienced divorce appear to recover from sadness and distress and to function well, feelings of regret and loss persist (Laumann-Billings and Emery 2000). They report continuing feel-

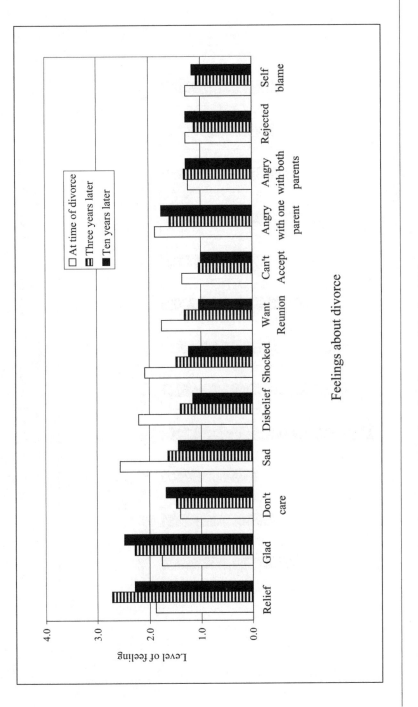

Figure 10.1. Children's feelings about divorce over time. Data from Burns and Dunlop 1999.

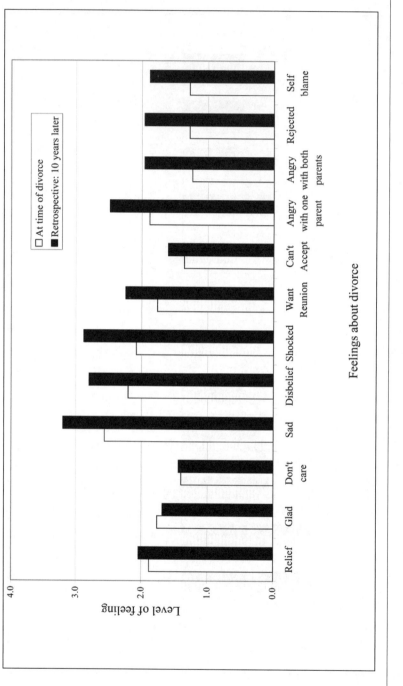

Figure 10.2. Children's immediate and retrospective feelings about divorce. Data from Burns and Dunlop 1999.

ings of loss and of anger toward their fathers, and they see their lives as having been changed by divorce despite believing that their parents' divorces were right for their families. In comparison with their peers whose parents have not divorced, they believe they had harder childhoods and wish that their fathers had spent more time with them.

Although joint legal custody is now comparatively common, joint physical custody remains less so. We have no good national data on joint physical custody in the United States, but educated estimates indicate that only a small minority of divorced families, perhaps 5 to 10 percent, raise their children in joint physical custody (Emery 1999). In the 1990s in the United States, most children of divorced parents lived with their mothers; fathers headed only 14 percent of lone-parent families (Rawlings and Saluter 1996). Frequency and regularity of contact varies, and accurate estimates are difficult to obtain. Figures differ depending on the informant (father or mother), and because frequency declines over time, these estimates differ according to the time that has elapsed since the divorce. Estimates suggest that one quarter to one third of children see their fathers once a week (Seltzer 1998) and up to half lose all contact with their fathers by ten years after a divorce (Seltzer 1991). It is of interest to note that a study of distress among young people from divorced families found the highest levels of pain among those who saw their fathers one to three times a month. Children who saw their fathers weekly or only several times a year both reported fewer feelings of loss (Laumann-Billings and Emery 2000).

Because the every-other-weekend standard persists as the norm, the possibility should be carefully considered that this level of contact is just enough to keep the father-child relationship emotionally alive, yet not enough to keep it emotionally secure. Frequency of contact in itself does not appear to be linked directly with well-being; however the closeness of the relationship and high levels of involved parenting by fathers are associated with low levels of externalizing and internalizing behavior and with good academic performance (Amato and Gilbreth 1999).

Does Listening to Children Matter?

Children's voices and perspectives are increasingly in the spotlight, as the writing of this book attests. The spotlight is especially strong in relation to families and divorce because legislation and other influences have encouraged children's participation in decisions made about them. There appears to be general agreement that their involvement is a good development, but do we have evidence that it matters in measurable ways?

In a British retrospective study of children and adults who had experienced parental divorce (Walczak and Burns 1984), four groups were discerned: those who had been harmed overall, those who had benefited, those for whom the divorce had little effect, and those for whom the effects were mixed. Those who felt harmed said that their parents had not talked with them at the time. According to the authors, in these cases the relationship between parent and child was likely to deteriorate independent of its quality before separation. Good relationships eroded and poor ones got worse, and in both cases they appeared to do so because parents made little effort to explain the divorce and expressed limited sensitivity to the child's personal feelings at the time. Those children who benefited described good relationships with both parents. These children felt they had been listened to as decisions were made. In adulthood they felt well-adjusted and resilient. In addition, children who attributed control during the period of divorce to an unknown source were most likely to manifest high levels of anxiety, depression, and conduct disorders (Kim, Sandler, and Tein 1997). Walczak and Burns suggest that "understanding why events occur, rather than believing in an internal locus of control, is the dimension that buffers stress in children of divorce" (1984, 153).

When they are asked, children express a longing to see more of their nonresident parents. It is not surprising, then, that most say that equal time with both parents is their first choice (Derevensky and Deschamps 1997; Kurdek and Sinclair 1986; Pryor 2001). Younger children are more likely than adolescents to want to spend equal time with both parents. Older children's lives may be more complicated, and they may view moving sports gear and musical instruments from house to house and maintaining relationships with friends while living in two houses particularly challenging. Of the children who lived in coparenting situations, those who had been consulted about the arrangements being made showed the best adjustment to the situation (Dunn et al. 2001).

However, not all children want full involvement in decision making about living arrangements. Young children, in particular, often say they want their parents to decide (Brannen, Heptinstall, and Bhopal 1999; Smart and Neale 1999). Others want to take full responsibility for these decisions. Most, however, say that parents and children should make decisions about living arrangements together. One young person put it this way: "I think there are some decisions you should make for yourself, . . . but sometimes there are decisions you can't make on your own; you need to like either get your friends involved, or your teachers or your parents, or your family" (quoted in Morrow 1998, 24). Listening to children's views about living arrangements, then, and taking into account their desire to be informed and consulted are supported by both common sense and research findings.

Conclusions

There is no doubt that children have voices to be heard, voices that describe their experiences and express their views of families. Neither is there any doubt that they are agents in their families in the contextualist sense described by Jack Meacham in Chapter 4. Children construct and interpret events within families and are active in creating their own identities as family members. Moreover, what they are telling us about families and family change does not necessarily coincide with what parents and clinicians assume to be in their best interests. The received views of adults including parents, clinicians, and writers are in many instances not substantiated by the words of children.

Children have a remarkably pragmatic, rather than political, perspective on families; it reflects the real world in which they live. And their views of families do not necessarily reflect media or idealized portrayals. They do not consider structure, biological relationship, or legalities as paramount; rather, for them the presence of love and support among family members matters most. In addition, they see themselves as active participants and shapers within their families.

Yet voice and agency become complex when we consider them in the context of family change. Events occur that are manifestly beyond the control of children, yet concern them intimately. And, commonly, adults screen children's voices from these events, interpreting for them in the belief that they are protecting them from adult issues. In turn, children themselves are often confused. Even when their voices are enabled, they are not always sure what they want to say or whether they want to say anything at all. The possibility of being held responsible for the consequences, should their voices be heeded, may be frightening and overpowering.

How, then, might we empower children appropriately when family transitions occur? The child's right to be heard is paramount if he or she wants to exercise that right. In the context of family change, a child's voice may express confusion, bewilderment, distress, or the desire not to be required to articulate feelings. In practice, skill and sensitivity are called for on the part of parents and other adults in enabling children to decide whether they want their voice to be heard and, if so, how it might best be heard and heeded. For some children simply being asked sympathetically whether they want to be involved and being given the opportunity to abstain from involvement will go a considerable way toward honoring their voice. Others desire appropriate information, the opportunity to express feelings without fear of hurt or reprisal, and understanding of their confused feelings.

Children's agency, their participation in the reconstruction of families and relationships, is even more complex. Children often seem to understand that responsibility is the corollary of rights. Young children especially are clear that they do not want to be responsible for major decisions at these times. It may be, then, that adults are well advised to provide a scaffolding structure for children within which they are enabled to foster, maintain, and abstain from relationships as far as possible. In practice, when divorce occurs, adults should nurture relationships with nonresident parents, not insist on close relationships with new partners, and, importantly, create and maintain an atmosphere free of animosity within which children can exercise agency in creating their own relationship network and identity.

When a separation occurs, children do not want to be protected from all information, and they seem to benefit from knowing. They want to be told what is happening and to be given the opportunity to be heard and to be involved at levels both comfortable and appropriate for them. Children do not "get over" a divorce. Most function well as adults despite retaining painful feelings about the divorce. By listening to their voices and enabling their agency within limits that work for them and for their families, we both diminish their vulnerability and enhance their resilience.

References

Allatt, P. 1996. "Conceptualizing Parenting from the Standpoint of Children: Relationship and Transition in the Life Course." In *Children in Families. Research and Policy*, edited by J. Brannen and M. O'Brien. Falmer, U.K.: Falmer Press.

Amato, P. R. 1987a. *Children in Australian Families: The Growth of Competence*. Upper Saddle River, N.J.: Prentice-Hall.

Amato, P. R. 1987b. "Family Processes in One-Parent, Stepparent, and Intact Families: The Child's Point of View." *Journal of Marriage and the Family* 49:327–337.

Amato, P. R., and J. G. Gilbreth. 1999. "Nonresident Fathers and Children's Well-Being: A Meta-Analysis." *Journal of Marriage and the Family* 61 (August): 557–573.

Anyan, S. 2002. "What Is a Family? Adolescents' Perceptions." *Childhood & Society* 16: 1–12.

Archard, D. 1993. *Children: Rights and Childhood*. New York: Routledge.

Arditti, J. A. 1999. "Parental Divorce and Young Adults' Intimate Relationships: Toward a New Paradigm." *Marriage & Family Review* 29 (1): 3555.

Beck, U., and E. Beck-Gernsheim. 1995. *The Normal Chaos of Love*. Cambridge: Polity Press.

Brannen, J., E. Heptinstall, and K. Bhopal. 1999. *Connecting Children: Care and Family Life in Later Childhood*. London: Routledge Falmer.

Burns, A., and R. Dunlop. 1999. "'How Did You Feel about It?' Children's Feelings about Their Parents' Divorce at the Time and Three and Ten Years Later." *Journal of Divorce and Remarriage* 31 (3/4): 19–36.

Cherlin, A. J., and F. F. Furstenberg. 1986. *The New American Grandparent: A Place in the Family, a Life Apart*. New York: Basic Books.

Cunningham, H. 1995. *Children and Childhood in Western Society since 1500*. New York: Longman.

de Mause, L., ed. 1974. *The History of Childhood*. New York: Psychohistory Press.

Derevensky, J. L., and L. Deschamps. 1997. "Young Adults from Divorced and Intact Families: Perceptions about Preferred Custodial Arrangements." *Journal of Divorce and Remarriage* 27 (1/2): 105–122.

Dunn, J., L. C. Davies, T. G. O'Connor, and W. Sturgess. 2001. "Family Lives and Friendships: The Perspectives of Children in Step-, Single-Parent and Nonstep Families." *Journal of Family Psychology* 15 (2): 272–287.

Emery, R. E. 1999. *Marriage, Divorce and Children's Adjustment.* 2d ed. London: Sage.

Gilby, R. L., and D. R Pedersen. 1982. "The Development of the Child's Concept of Family." *Canadian Journal of Behavioral Sciences* 14:111–121.

Gorrell Barnes, G., P. Thompson, G. Daniel, and N. Burchardt. 1998. *Growing Up in Stepfamilies.* Oxford: Clarendon Press.

James, A. L., and M.P.M. Richards. 1999. "Sociological Perspectives, Family Policy, Family Law and Children: Adult Thinking and Sociological Tinkering." *Journal of Social Welfare and Family Law* 21 (1): 23–39.

Jones, C. J. 1984. "Judicial Questioning of Children in Custody and Visitation Proceedings." *Family Law Quarterly* 18:43–91.

Kalter, N., and J. W. Plunkett. 1984. "Children's Perceptions of the Causes and Consequences of Divorce." *Journal of the American Academy of Child & Adolescent Psychiatry* 23 (3): 326–334.

Kennedy, G. E., and C. E. Kennedy. 1993. "Grandparents: A Special Resource for Children in Stepfamilies." *Journal of Divorce and Remarriage* 19 (3/4): 45–68.

Kim, L. S., I. N. Sandler, and J-Y Tein. 1997. "Locus of Control as a Stress Moderator and Mediator in Children of Divorce." *Journal of Abnormal Child Psychology* 25 (2): 145–155.

Kurdek, L. A., and A. E. Siesky. 1980. "Children's Perceptions of Their Parents' Divorce." *Journal of Divorce* 3 (4): 339–378.

Kurdek, L. A., and R. J. Sinclair. 1986. "Adolescents' Views on Issues Related to Divorce." *Journal of Adolescent Research* 1 (4): 373–387.

Laumann-Billings, L., and R. E. Emery. 2000. "Distress among Young Adults from Divorced Families." *Journal of Family Psychology* 14:671–687.

Morrow, V. 1998. "Understanding Families: Children's Perspectives." London: National Children's Bureau.

Neugebauer, R. 1989. "Divorce, Custody and Visitation: The Child's Point of View." *Journal of Divorce* 12 (2–3): 153–168.

O'Brien, M., P. Alldred, and P. Jones. 1996. "Children's Constructions of Family and Kinship." In *Children in Families: Research and Policy*, edited by J. Brannen and M. O'Brien. Falmer, U.K.: Falmer Press.

Plunkett, J. W., and N. Kalter. 1984. "Children's Beliefs about Reactions to Parental Divorce." *Journal of the American Academy of Child & Adolescent Psychiatry* 23 (5): 616–621.

Popenoe, D. 1996. *Life without Father.* New York: Martin Kessler Books.

Pritchard, R. 1998. *When Parents Part. How Children Adapt.* London: Penguin Books.

Pryor, J. 1999. "Waiting until They Leave Home. The Experiences of Young Adults Whose Parents Separate." *Journal of Divorce & Remarriage* 32 (1/2): 47–61.

Pryor, J. 2001. "Adolescent Attitudes to Living Arrangements after Divorce." *Child and Family Law Quarterly* 13 (2): 1–13.

Rawlings, S., and A. Saluter. 1996. *Household and Family Characteristics: March 1994.* Washington, D.C.: U.S. Department of Commerce.

Reinhard, D. W. 1977. "The Reaction of Adolescent Boys and Girls to the Divorce of Their Parents." *Journal of Clinical Child Psychology* 6:21–23.

Rosen, R. 1977. "Children of Divorce: What They Feel about Access and Other Aspects of the Divorce Experience." *Journal of Clinical Child Psychology* 6 (Summer): 24–27.

Seltzer, J. A. 1991. "Relationships between Fathers and Children Who Live Apart: The Father's Role after Separation." *Journal of Marriage and the Family* 53:79–101.

Seltzer, J. A. 1998. "Fathers by Law: Effects of Joint Legal Custody on Nonresident Fathers' Involvement with Children." *Demography* 35 (2): 135–146.

Smart, C., and B. Neale. 1999. *Family Fragments?* London: Polity Press.

Smith, A. B., N. J. Taylor, M. Gollop, M. Gaffney, M. Gold, and M. Heneghan. 1997. *Access and Other Post-separation Issues.* Dunedin, N.Z.: Children's Issues Centre, University of Otago.

Stacey, J. 1990. *Brave New Families.* New York: Basic Books.

Toynbee, P. 1998. "Divorce—the Great Liberator." *The Observer* (London), 24 June.

Wade, A., and C. Smart. 2002. *Facing Family Change. Children's Circumstances, Strategies and Resources.* Leeds, U.K.: Centre for Research on Family, Kinship & Childhood, University of Leeds.

Walczak, Y., and S. Burns. 1984. *Divorce: The Child's Point of View.* New York: Harper & Row.

Wallerstein, J. S., and J. B. Kelly. 1980. *Surviving the Breakup: How Children and Parents Cope with Divorce.* New York: Basic Books.

Part IV

Voice and Agency in Neighborhoods and Sports

Chapter 11

JAMES C. SPILSBURY
JILL E. KORBIN

Negotiating the Dance

Social Capital from the Perspective of Neighborhood Children and Adults

As we were visiting households in one of the study neighborhoods in order to recruit participants, we heard the crash of a bicycle on pavement. Two young girls (9–10 years of age) were bicycling, and one of them had fallen over in the street. The girl sat next to her bicycle and cried. We started to walk towards her and as we neared the site, we were joined by three adults: two men who while driving their vehicles down the street, saw the girl lying in the street, pulled over, got out of their cars and walked over. Soon after, an elderly woman who happened to be walking down the sidewalk, saw the accident and came over to the girl. The three adults asked the girl if she were OK. She said nothing but continued to cry. She appeared to have a large scrape on one leg. The men offered to help her get up. She continued crying. One of the men suggested he could take her home and asked where she lived. She kept crying. The elderly woman said "I'll ride with you so you aren't alone," but to no avail. The girl's companion told us that she lived about two blocks up the street. At this point, the girl got up, picked up her bicycle and, crying, slowly walked the bike down the street in the direction of her house. Her friend rode out in front of her. The man who offered to take her home got into his vehicle and along with the elderly woman on foot, followed the girl as she slowly made her way down the street to her home. We watched them go down the street, like a strange sort of parade. (July 9, 1996)

This episode, recorded in ethnographic field notes during a study of the impact of neighborhood conditions on child well-being, is the cautionary tale with which we begin. A child is in need of help. Numerous adults stop to offer such help. Thus, one expects the picture-perfect scenario of a child in need assisted by vigilant adult neighbors. However, instead of gratefully accepting help, the child refuses. Why? Was she in violation of parental rules regarding her play in the neighborhood? Did she fear that acceptance of assistance would lead to parental awareness of the "transgression"? Was she simply embarrassed by the fall and the subsequent sudden attention of several adults? Had she been taught to be wary of strangers? Or did her behavior have any number of other possible explanations?

In recent decades, researchers have made several attempts to conceptualize and explicitly describe the social cohesion among residents that influences the quality of life in a neighborhood. In particular, research has been concerned with the qualities of the adult social networks that are needed to enhance child well-being. This perspective assumes that the presence of adults who will intervene both to correct and to assist children—frequently viewed as manifestations of neighborhood social capital or collective efficacy—is critical to understanding neighborhood quality of life for children and families and indices of child well-being. Interestingly, children's perspectives are rarely part of the equation. Usually the tacit assumption is that children will respond positively to manifestations of social capital or collective efficacy; that children will accept an offer of assistance when help is needed seems to be more or less taken for granted. However, as we reconceptualize and reconsider children's agency, episodes such as this one, where children do not act as we expect, deserve our attention. Just as we do not conceptualize children as passive recipients of socialization, neither can we assume, a priori, that their responses to offers of assistance will be divorced from a consideration of children's agency within the context in which assistance is offered.

In this chapter, we describe the workings of social capital or collective efficacy in urban neighborhoods of Cleveland, Ohio, from the point of view of both adults and children. Our research revealed that adults and children respond in a range of ways to a help-offering/help-seeking situation; children's acceptance of assistance cannot be assumed, even in neighborhoods where adults indicate that social capital may be present and operating. Far from being picture perfect, the help-seeking process is probably best conceptualized as a negotiation between child and potential adult helpers.

Background

Coleman (1988) conceptualized social capital as the resources for action inherent in social networks. According to Coleman, forms of social capital include obligations and exchanges (that is, reciprocities), enforced standards, and shared norms held by members of a social network. Although subsequent definitions of social capital vary, most revolve around the notion of "social networks, the reciprocities that arise from them, and the value of these for achieving mutual goals" (Schuller, Baron, and Field 2000, 1). Sampson, Morenoff, and Earls (1999) elaborated on the concept, viewing social capital as "the resource potential of personal and organizational networks" (635) that gives rise to "collective efficacy," or adults' shared expectations and mutual engagement to support and control children. As concepts such as social capital have been explored and debated (see, for instance, Earls and Carlson 2001; Fine 1999; Morrow 1999; Portes 1998), these social resources have been viewed as a quality of adult social networks that may provide benefits to adults and children. In other words, regardless of the precise formulation, it is the reciprocities, enforced standards, or shared expectations among adults that are thought to produce better conditions for children. Interestingly, the articulation between children and neighborhood social capital as well as children's role in the process remain largely unexplored (Morrow 1999).

Children's help-seeking behavior has received notable attention in the social science literature. However, research on the subject has gravitated either toward assistance with schoolwork in academic settings (for example, McKessar and Thomas 1978; Nelson-LeGall, DeCooke, and Jones 1989; Townsend, Manley, and Tuck 1991) or toward obtaining clinical/health services (for example, Lewis et al. 1977; Rudolf et al. 1992; Saunders et al. 1994; Srebnik, Cauce, and Baydar 1996; Stephenson 1983), with less attention focused on problems occurring in a neighborhood context (for example, Barnett, Sinisi, and Jaet 1990; Bryant 1985; Harman, Armsworth, and Henderson 1989; Westcott and Davies 1995).

Collectively, this body of research indicates that (1) children generally turn to members of their social networks for assistance, and (2) the specific targets of children's help seeking are selected on the basis of various factors including the individuals' perceived ability to handle the problem at hand, their willingness to help, their accessibility, and the kindness and understanding they show to the children. The growing body of research on children's social networks (see Belle 1989; Nestmann and Hurrelmann 1994) indicates that as children develop, their networks expand to include a greater proportion of non-kin members, such as peers, and non-kin adults, as well as teachers, neighbors, and coaches (Belle 1989; Feiring and Lewis 1989, 1991a, 1991b; Garbarino, Stott, and the Faculty of the Erikson Institute 1989). Such expansion of social networks may increase the options for children seeking help. But do children perceive neighborhoods as sources for help when they need assistance? Answering this question was one of the goals of our research on children in Cleveland neighborhoods.

Methods

This chapter draws on two data sets: one a subsample from a large study of four hundred parents' perceptions of neighborhood in twenty census tracts of Cleveland, Ohio, a Midwest industrial city of approximately a half million residents, and one from a study of sixty children's perceptions of neighborhood in five neighborhoods drawn from the original twenty tracts. The two studies are briefly described below (for an expanded discussion, see Coulton, Korbin, and Su 1999; Korbin and Coulton 1997; Spilsbury 2002).

ADULT STUDY

To generate the sample in the original study of parents, a two-stage strategy was employed, with neighborhood units selected first and respondents then selected from within those neighborhoods. Neighborhoods were selected on the basis of a set of structural characteristics that predicted a range of adverse child outcomes from maltreatment to teen pregnancy (Coulton et al. 1995). Based on these profiles, a stratified sample of twenty census tracts was drawn. A census-defined block group was randomly selected from each census tract as the neighborhood unit. Streets within each block group were then randomly ordered and an address randomly chosen on each street. Beginning with this address, every third household was contacted, which was the interval deemed necessary to obtain the required twenty households with children. To be eligible for the study, households had to have at least one child under eighteen and at least one parent or guardian living in the home. Informed consent was obtained from all study participants.

Here, we focus on the parental data obtained from the five neighborhoods where we subsequently collected data from children. The subsample of one hundred adults living in these five neighborhoods was largely female (88 percent) with a mean age of 34.1 years. The sample consisted primarily of European Americans (71 percent), with a smaller representation of African Americans (15 percent) and Hispanic/Latinos (11 percent), who were primarily Puerto Rican, and Native Americans (3 percent). The high percentage of European Americans within the five neighborhoods reflected Cleveland's extremely high level of racial segregation (Farley and Frey 1994; Massey and Denton 1993). Participants had lived an average of 9.1 years in their neighborhoods. However, their length of residence varied widely, from one month to forty-five years. On average, participants' households included 2.5 children under eighteen. Fifty-five percent of the sample were married, just under two-thirds of the sample had completed high school or its equivalent, and nearly two-thirds were employed at least part time. Over half the sample (56.7 percent) reported a total household income less than $20,001, while 13 percent reported an income greater than $40,000.

As part of the structured interview about neighborhood conditions, adult participants were asked to rate from 1 ("not at all likely") to 10 ("very likely") the likelihood of residents (1) helping a child who was wandering the neighborhood alone, and (2) helping a child who had fallen off a bicycle. Sixty-two adults randomly selected from the original sample of four hundred parents were asked to describe in an open-ended manner what neighbors would do if they saw a child wandering around the neighborhood. Responses were post-coded based on themes emerging from the narrative responses.

CHILD STUDY

The sample of sixty children between the ages of seven and eleven years was recruited from five of the twenty census tracts included in the adult study. Nearly three-quarters of the sample, forty-four children, were recruited from systematic door-to-door visits to all households in the study neighborhoods, and an additional sixteen children were recruited through flyers, public meetings, and referral by previous participants. These two recruitment strategies did not yield differences in demographic characteristics. To be eligible for the study, children had to be seven to eleven years old; had to have resided in the neighborhood for at least two months; and had to spend at least 50 percent of their time at home. Only one child per household participated. If two eligible children lived in the household, the one with the most recent birthday was selected. Informed consent was obtained first from parents and then assent was obtained from the children.

The sample consisted of thirty-seven boys and twenty-three girls with a median age of nine years. The median number of children in each household (including the participant) was three, and over two-thirds of the families consisted of a parent living with a spouse or partner. The median length of family residence in the current house was five years. Forty-one of the children (68.3 percent) were European American, with smaller numbers of Hispanic (n=7; 11.7 percent), African American (n=6, 10 percent), and mixed ethnicity (n=6, 10 percent).

Children's perceptions of neighborhood quality, social support, and help-seeking behavior were gathered using a modified version of Bryant's (1985) "neighborhood walk," in which the child led James Spilsbury on a walking tour of the neighborhood. Child interviews were audio-recorded and transcribed.

During the neighborhood walk, children were presented with three scenarios a seven-to-eleven-year-old child might encounter in the neighborhood: (1) being accosted by a bully; (2) being seriously injured after falling down or falling off a bicycle; (3) having parents argue heatedly. For each scenario, children were asked a series of open-ended questions to elicit their narrative responses. During the discussion of each scenario, children were also asked what they would do if an adult they didn't know saw that they needed help, approached them, and offered to help. Moreover, the children were also asked to imagine a fourth scenario, in which a child was wandering around the neighborhood, and were asked what they thought neighbors would do. Children's responses to all the scenarios were post-coded according to themes that emerged from content analysis of the responses. The child study was not designed to parallel the adult study. However, two of the scenarios were presented to both adults and children—a child involved in a bicycle accident and a child wandering around the neighborhood. We now turn to the similarities and differences between adults' and children's responses.

Adult Perspectives on Providing Help to Children

The hundred adults participating in the structured interview in the five neighborhoods where we also conducted the child study thought it likely that neighbors would intervene should a child be found wandering around the neighborhood or if a child fell off a bicycle: in both scenarios the median response of the likelihood of intervention was 8 on the 10-point scale (10 equaled "'very likely"). These findings suggest that the adults we interviewed shared the expectation that neighborhood residents would offer assistance to children in need, which is considered an indicator of social capital or collective efficacy.

In-depth interviews of sixty-two adults provided a more textured account of how their perceptions of the children, their own responsibilities, and their risks modified their expectations of neighbors providing help to children.[1] Forty-nine (79 percent) of the adults indicated that neighbors would approach the child, ascertain whether the child were lost, and, if so, take action to get the child home.[2] These actions included calling the child's parents, talking with other neighborhood children or adults to try to locate the child's home, and calling authorities, especially if the child didn't know whom to call or where to be taken. Ten of these adults described how neighbors would bring the child into their own homes as they attempted to identify the child. One thirty-seven-year-old woman said, "Oh, I think somebody would scoop him up. Yeah, something like that, you know, oh yeah we'd scoop him up and call the police. That's happened. One time a child wandered out of a house. The mother was in the house sleeping. We scooped him up out of the street." Some adults elaborated that neighbors would be concerned about making the child feel safe and comfortable. As one forty-four-year-old woman explained, "We'd probably find out where the child lives, or is he visiting or is he lost, um, do what we could. A child is a child. If he don't live in the neighborhood, and he's lost, maybe we can get a hold of the parent. Maybe he's hungry and thirsty and needs somethin' to eat."

At the same time, twelve adults (19.4 percent) indicated that some neighbors would not do anything to help a wandering, potentially lost child. Most of these respondents explained that children were out and unsupervised frequently enough in their neighborhoods that such a child would be unremarkable. Further, they said that because of the high resident turnover the presence of unknown children in the neighborhood was a usual, rather than an unusual, occurrence. Six adults (9.7 percent) said that residents would not intervene directly with the child but would call the police or other civil authorities. Some adults, then, apparently viewed intervention with children as a public agency's responsibility rather than an individual responsibility. A thirty-seven-year-old woman remarked, "I think pretty much any of them [neighbors], if it was a little one, they would probably call the police . . . if they see the child wandering." Only two of the twelve adults who stated that some neighbors would not intervene attributed this inaction to the neighbors' indifference to the child's situation.

Some of our previous work in these same neighborhoods suggested that adults do not intervene in children's misbehavior because they fear that children and their parents will retaliate (Korbin and Coulton 1997). Interestingly, here, in response to a child in need, two adults (3.2 percent) offered this same reasoning—that fear of retaliation would keep neighbors from helping. One of them, a twenty-seven-year-old woman, said:

> [Neighbors would be] scared that, you know, something bad is going to
> happen if you approach a child. You don't know what the situation is,
> you know? If that child approached me and asked for help, I would help,
> but unless they just looked like they were hurt or something, I wouldn't
> say nothing because I see a lot of kids, you know, that I don't know, just
> walking around sometimes by themselves or in groups, and I don't know
> the situation, you know?

Even some of the adults who reported that neighbors would intervene raised the fear that the parents might misconstrue the effort as an attempt to kidnap or otherwise harm the boy or girl. One thirty-four-year-old woman's comments exemplified this fear. She thought the neighbors would be scared: "They don't know whose child it is [and] maybe the mother was comin' back, or you never know if they've [parents] just dropped them, or maybe the mother would come and see them talking and maybe they think that you are a stranger. You understand what I mean?"

Such fear apparently led to strategic adjustments in the way adults approached or offered to help children. For example, some participants described how they would purposefully engage the assistance of other adult neighbors, who could attest to the fact that the child was unharmed:

And if they were lost, I would ask them where they do live, and um, or maybe have to call the police and try to get some assistance. I wouldn't try to really do it on my own 'cause I wouldn't want to have no kidnapping charge on me. (thirty-two-year-old woman)

What I would do? I would let another neighbor know that I'm gonna call for this child so that there would be two persons to witness that nothing really went on. (thirty-eight-year-old woman)

Finally, adults did not perceive all children as equally needy or dangerous. Some adults offered the opinion that younger children or children who specifically sought help were more likely to receive help from neighborhood adults.

In summary, adults participating in the study judged that overall neighbors were likely to offer some form of intervention or to assist in some way a wandering child or a child in a bicycle accident. To be sure, respondents reported that not all neighbors would assist for reasons ranging from indifference to the child's plight to fear of repercussions.

Children's Perspectives on Receiving Help from Adults

In several respects, children's narrative responses to the scenarios presented resembled those of adults. However, one noteworthy disconnect between adults' and children's responses emerged.

SIMILARITIES BETWEEN ADULTS' AND CHILDREN'S PERSPECTIVES
In the cases of a bicycle accident and of a lost child, most of the sixty children (n=53, 88.3 percent) indicated that at least one neighbor would offer assistance. Moreover, children, as did their adult counterparts, reported that some neighbors would not help, and the children were sensitive to the same issues that adults reported would stand in their way of helping. Fourteen children (23.3 percent) indicated that some neighbors would be indifferent or unkind:

> SPILSBURY (S): Can you think of some neighbors who would help a boy if
>   they thought he were lost?
> CHILD (C): No.
> S: Do you have any idea about why the neighbors wouldn't help the boy?
> C: Mean. They're mean. (ten-year-old boy)

> A few neighbors wouldn't help because they don't care about kids.
> They'd just let him wander. (eight-year-old boy)

> S: Who would help the lost boy?
> C: Frank and Harold would. So would George. John and Mary wouldn't
>   because they're mean. (seven-year-old boy)

Children and adults also shared the view that some neighbors would be afraid of helping children, especially children they did not know well. Five children (8.3 percent) reported that adults feared verbal abuse, false accusations, and even bodily harm, as illustrated by these responses:

> c: They like don't know who she is, and like, um, they wouldn't know like what she would do, like if she's a good person or a bad person.
> s: So they don't know what she might do?
> c: Yeah.
> s: Huh. What kinds of things might they be afraid she'd do if she's a bad person? Do you know?
> c: Um, maybe hurt 'em, or tell her parents a lie and maybe they'll do something about it. (eleven-year-old girl)

> If they [neighbors] knew him [lost child] like really good, they would help him[;] . . . actually they might not 'cause on the news, they might have seen people, like kids my age, carrying guns and they don't know if he is carrying a gun or not. (ten-year-old boy)

Moreover, in regard to the lost child, children responded similarly to adults when they said that seeing a wandering children in the neighborhood was such a frequent occurrence that it was unremarkable:

> You always see four- or five-year-olds around here, walking around. (eleven-year-old boy)

> Everybody always wandering around on like bikes or something[;] . . . you never know if they're lost or anything, but usually they're not. (nine-year-old boy)

Children agreed with adults in predicting that younger children were more likely to receive assistance from adults, as illustrated by this interview with an eleven-year-old girl:

> c: It depends how old the kid was.
> s: So what if it was someone your age? Would people help?
> c: Yeah [but] like fifteen [years old] maybe not.
> s: Why wouldn't they help somebody older?
> c: Because [pause] like [pause] I don't know.
> s: Are they afraid of older kids?
> c: I, in my opinion yeah, a little.

A ten-year-old boy offered a similar explanation:

> Yeah [neighbors would help] . . . if it were some like little kid . . . like eight or ten or something.

A DISCONNECT BETWEEN ADULTS' AND CHILDREN'S PERSPECTIVES

When adults' and children's views disconnect, they do so around children's willingness to accept assistance. Adults largely presumed that children who need help will want help and will accept it. Adults' discussion of the lost-child scenario contained no mention of the possibility that a child in need would refuse an offer of adult assistance, even if the offer were made by an unknown adult. In contrast, some of the children voiced hesitancy, concern, and even offered specific strategies to avoid receiving help from adults in such situations.

Interviews with children revealed that this hesitancy or concern did not arise from a general belief that asking for or receiving help was in and of itself inappropriate. In fact, almost all the children (n=56, 93.3 percent) indicated that asking for help was, in principle, a good strategy. The following responses were typical:

> You should ask for help whenever you need it . . . because if you really need help and nobody tries to help you, you're on your own. (nine-year-old boy)

> If you need help, you need it! (ten-year-old girl)

> Yeah, I think you should ask for help when you need it because [if] you need help, you should get help because you know, you're not, you're just gonna, if you don't let anyone help you, you'll just be stuck wherever you are. (eleven-year-old girl)

> If you need help and you just leave [keep] it in, then it's just going to get worser. (ten-year-old boy)

Yet, while they supported help seeking as a general principle, children expressed some reticence and concern about asking for and accepting help. For example, two (3.3 percent) of the children's responses to the lost-child scenario reflected the need for caution if an adult offered assistance, especially an adult the child didn't know. A ten-year-old girl explained:

> s: What would neighbors do [if they saw a girl wandering around the neighborhood]?
> c: I would usually go get my parents, and my parents would help them find their home. Unless they're like me, that don't like strangers. [Then she'd] just say, "Go. Bye."
> s: Do you think that neighbors around here if they saw this girl looking like she was lost or something, . . . what would they do in that case?
> c: Um, they probably would ask like, "Are you lost?" or something [like] "Can I help you?" And they would probably tell her where her street is, but I don't really think that they would walk her home.

s: Why would they not walk her home?

c: I don't know. Maybe the girl just doesn't like strangers or something.

One seven-year-old boy described how he would surreptitiously watch the interaction between adult neighbors and child, apparently to make sure nothing bad happened:

s: What would neighbors do?

c: I would help him.

s: Would other people in the neighborhood help him or would they not help or what would they do?

c: Uh . . . if somebody, if he asks somebody, if somebody says, "Yes, [I'll help]," I'll just be right there peeking to see what's gonna happen.

Children's concerns about their own safety during the help-seeking process arose not only in response to the wandering child and bicycle scenarios but at various points throughout the interview; they described several strategies they would use to maintain personal safety while obtaining help, which have been reported elsewhere (Spilsbury 2002). A primary strategy was to accept help only from known persons. If that failed, children explained that they would try to accept assistance only from those whom the child deemed safe or at least "safer" based on an assessment of personal appearance or other obvious characteristics. For example, women were considered safer than men, and women with children, preferably with a stroller, were viewed as particularly safe choices. Characteristics such as sloppy clothing, unkempt hair, tattoos, and having a gruff voice signaled potential danger. Children also described limiting the types of assistance, such as asking the unknown adult only to call their parents. Some children, though, viewed unknown adults as categorically unsafe and indicated that they would refuse assistance no matter what.

We found that the scenario in which children were most likely to be seriously injured—falling off a bicycle and being unable to get up or walk—was highly illustrative of the range of ways children might respond to a help-offering/help-seeking situation. Nearly one-third of the children (n=19, 31.7 percent) revealed that in such a situation they would accept help from a neighborhood adult they didn't know, sometimes emphatically so. A ten-year-old boy declared, "Say like I was in pain, then, you know, I would let anybody help me. Say like a dog, a talking dog, offered to lick me. I'd let him."

Yet, in this scenario, which involved potentially serious injury, twelve children (20.7 percent) said they would refuse outright an offer of assistance from a neighborhood adult they didn't know, and another twenty-two children (36.7 percent) expressed clear reservations about accepting help. For example:

I wouldn't let [them] help because I don't know them. They may try to trick you so they can take you. (nine-year-old girl)

c: I wouldn't let them help me.
s: How come?
c: They probably take me to their house, kill me. (eight-year-old boy)

I'd say no . . . because I don't know them. You don't know if they're going to hurt you even worse [than you already are], or you don't know if they're going to try to kidnap you or anything. (nine-year-old girl)

These responses to a help-offering/help-accepting scenario illustrate considerable variability, and, therefore, they suggest that a specific response can never be automatically assumed.

Negotiation and the Dance

The responses of both children and adults allow us to paint a picture of a negotiation, a dance. A "positive" outcome depends not only on adult provision of help, which is rooted in social capital and collective efficacy, but also on children's agency. Neighborhood adults expressed willingness to help children, but they also raised concerns that their offers of help would be misconstrued as threatening to a child. Similarly, neighborhood children recognized that they might sometimes need help and that adults would give it, but they also expressed concern that letting adults help might compromise their safety. Children also recognized that some adult neighbors' fear of possible repercussions might preclude them from offering assistance.

The dancers circle, cautiously assessing each other. As some children indicate, accurately sizing up your "dance partner" is critical:

They [adults] could look really nice and everything, but turn around and be like a kidnapper or something. . . . If they looked bad . . . they could be really nice, because I've met plenty of people that look like they're kidnappers but they're really nice. (ten-year-old boy)

They can like take you. They can act like they are your friend or something; . . . sometimes robbers can act like they're cops, dress up like them. (eight-year-old girl)

Adults, likewise, dance cautiously:

A lot of things come into play here. You don't know what's wrong. You don't know why that child is lost. (forty-one-year-old woman)

They [children] make comments [like] "What are you doing out here?" A lot of times they'll come back with a smart aleck "Yeah, so?" [or] "I'm from up the street." [Their language is] especially profane. (thirty-year-old woman)

This image is at odds with the picture that most adults take for granted, in which children need and seek, adults offer and provide, and children accept, with their well-being enhanced. Less often are these adult-child interactions viewed as negotiations, in which both adults and children weigh risks and benefits and in which both parties believe that they influence the ultimate outcome. To be sure, in our studies, most adults and children reported that they would act as one would expect, with adults providing help and children accepting that help. However, often, both adults and children expressed reservations that should alert us to the importance of their concerns. Adults are not automatic helpers, and children are not automatic recipients of help.

A growing body of literature highlights strategies utilized by children to meet the challenges of their everyday lives, such as how to assert themselves and their wishes in a world run by adults (Waksler 1996), how to negotiate access to public space (Punch 2000; Valentine 1997), or how to cope with danger in public space (Matthews, Limb, and Taylor 2000; Percy-Smith and Matthews 2001; Watt and Stenson 1998). Our research in Cleveland illuminates the active role children play in seeking adults' help for problems they may encounter in their neighborhoods, as well as the children's active role in the dance of negotiation. Yet the research also suggests that to understand the dance completely, the perspectives of all the dancers are necessary. In our case, the perspectives of both children and adults are needed in order to understand how social capital or collective efficacy may work to influence children's well-being.

In a broader sense, our research suggests that a multiple-perspectives approach that includes both children and adults may be needed to understand other neighborhood processes, including community building. Unfortunately, although efforts to improve communities often involve the participation of a variety of adult stakeholders (for example, representatives of local community organizations, parents, civic leaders, and school officials), children's place at the stakeholders' table should also be recognized and facilitated. Children have contributed meaningfully to a range of community concerns, such as community health issues (Morrow 2001) and the design of play spaces and other attributes of the urban environment (Francis and Lorenzo 2002; Hart 1997; McKendrick 2000). The involvement of children and youth has been fostered through the use of a variety of methods, from qualitative interviews and visual techniques such as photography (e.g., Morrow 2001) to participation in design workshops (Sutton and Kemp 2002). We suggest that without input from and participation of children and youth, adults who are working to understand and improve neighborhood conditions for children may in effect be dancing alone.

Notes

This research was supported by the Department of Health and Human Services (90CA1548) and grants from the William T. Grant Foundation, the Schubert Center for Child Development, and the Armington Research Program on Values in Children. The authors thank their colleagues who participated in the various neighborhood research projects: Claudia Coulton, Sarah Chard, Heather Lindstrom, and Marilyn Su.

1. Because the adult and child studies were not designed to be parallel, the child, but not the adult, study included in-depth questions concerning the bicycle scenario. Additionally, the adult study was aimed more at maltreatment-related possibilities (including a child neglected and thus wandering the neighborhood), while the child study included the accidental possibility of a bicycle mishap. Unfortunately, the in-depth interviews were conducted in only one of the neighborhoods where we conducted the child study. However, information obtained from parents in this one neighborhood mirrored parents' responses in the other neighborhoods where the in-depth interviews were held, and we therefore utilize information from the entire subsample of sixty-two adults participating in the in-depth interviews to illustrate the range of parents' responses to the wandering-child scenario.

2. Because participants could report more than one theme, percentages in this section do not total 100.

References

Barnett, M. A., C. S. Sinisi, and B. P. Jaet 1990. "Perceived Gender Differences in Children's Help-Seeking." *Journal of Genetic Psychology* 151 (4): 451–460.

Belle, D. 1989. "Studying Children's Social Networks and Social Support." In *Children's Social Networks and Social Supports*, edited by D. Belle. New York: Wiley.

Bryant, B. K. 1985. "The Neighborhood Walk: Sources of Support in Middle Childhood." *Monographs of the Society for Research in Child Development* 50 (3, Serial No. 210).

Coleman, J. A. 1988. "Social Capital in the Creation of Human Capital." *American Journal of Sociology* 94 (suppl.): S95–S120.

Coulton, C. J., J. E. Korbin, and M. Su. 1999. "Neighborhoods and Child Maltreatment. A Multi-level Analysis." *Child Abuse and Neglect* 23:1019–1040.

Coulton, C. J., J. E. Korbin, M. Su, and J. Chow. 1995. "Community Level Factors and Child Maltreatment Rates." *Child Development* 66:1262–1276.

Earls, F., and M. Carlson. 2001. "The Social Ecology of Child Health and Well-Being." *Annual Review of Public Health* 22:143–166.

Farley, R., and W. H. Frey. 1994. "Changes in the Segregation of Whites from Blacks during the 1980s: Small Steps towards a More Integrated Society." *American Sociological Review* 59 (1): 23–45.

Feiring, C., and M. Lewis. 1989. "The Social Networks of Girls and Boys from Early through Middle Childhood." In *Children's Social Networks and Social Supports*, edited by D. Belle. New York: Wiley.

Feiring, C., and M. Lewis. 1991a. "The Development of Social Networks from Early to Middle Childhood: Gender Differences and the Relation to School Competence." *Sex Roles* 25 (3/4): 237–253.

Feiring, C., and M. Lewis. 1991b. "The Transition from Middle Childhood to Early Adolescence: Sex Differences in the Social Network and Perceived Self Competence." *Sex Roles* 24 (7/8): 489–509.

Fine, B. 1999. "The Developmental State Is Dead—Long Live Social Capital?" *Development and Change* 30 (1): 1–19.

Francis, M., and R. Lorenzo. 2002. "Seven Realms of Children's Participation." *Journal of Environmental Psychology* 22:157–169.

Garbarino, J., F. M. Stott, and the Faculty of the Erikson Institute. 1989. *What Children Can Tell Us: Eliciting, Interpreting, and Evaluating Information from Children.* San Francisco: Jossey-Bass.

Harman, M. J., M. W. Armsworth, and D. L. Henderson. 1989. "Rural Texas: To Whom Do Children Turn with Problems." *TACD Journal,* Fall, 107–113.

Hart, R. 1997. *Children's Participation: The Theory and Practice of Involving Young Citizens in Community Development and Environmental Care.* London: Earthscan; New York: UNICEF.

Korbin, J. E., and C. J. Coulton. 1997. "Understanding the Neighborhood Context for Children and Families: Epidemiological and Ethnographic Approaches." In *Neighborhood Poverty: Context and Consequences for Children,* edited by J. Brooks-Gunn, L. Aber, and G. Duncan. New York: Russell Sage Foundation.

Lewis, C. E., M. A. Lewis, A. Lorimer, and B. B. Palmer. 1977. "Child-Initiated Care: The Use of School Nursing Services by Children in an 'Adult-Free' System." *Pediatrics* 60 (4): 499–507.

Massey, D. S., and N. A. Denton. 1993. *American Apartheid: Segregation and the Making of the Underclass.* Cambridge: Harvard University Press.

Matthews, H., M. Limb, and M. Taylor. 2000. "The 'Street as Thirdspace.'" In *Children's Geographies: Playing, Living, Learning,* edited by S. Holloway and G. Valentine. London: Routledge.

McKendrick, J. H. 2000. "The Geography of Children: An Annotated Bibliography." *Childhood* 7 (3): 359–387.

McKessar, C. J., and D. R. Thomas. 1978. "Verbal and Non-verbal Help-Seeking among Urban Maori and Pakeha Children." *New Zealand Journal of Educational Studies* 13 (1): 29–39.

Morrow, V. 1999. "Conceptualising Social Capital in Relation to the Well-Being of Children and Young People: A Critical Review." *Sociological Review* 47 (4): 744–765.

Morrow, V. 2001. "Using Qualitative Methods to Elicit Young People's Perspectives on Their Environments: Some Ideas for Community Health Initiatives." *Health Education Research* 16 (3): 255–268.

Nelson-LeGall, S. A., P. DeCooke, and E. Jones. 1989. "Children's Perceptions of Competence and Help Seeking." *Journal of Genetic Psychology* 150 (4): 457–459.

Nestmann, F., and K. Hurrelmann, eds. 1994. *Social Networks and Social Support in Childhood and Adolescence.* Berlin: Walter de Gruyter.

Percy-Smith, B., and H. Matthews. 2001. "Tyrannical Spaces: Young People, Bullying and Urban Neighbourhoods." *Local Environment* 6 (1): 49–63.

Portes, A. 1998. "Social Capital: Its Origins and Applications in Modern Sociology." *Annual Review of Sociology* 24:1–24.

Punch, S. 2000. "Children's Strategies for Creating Playspaces." In *Children's Geographies: Playing, Living, Learning,* edited by S. Holloway and G. Valentine. London: Routledge.

Rudolf, M., O. Tomanovich, J. Greenberg, and L. Friend. 1992. "Gender Differences in Infirmary Use at a Residential Summer Camp." *Developmental and Behavioral Pediatrics* 13 (4): 261–265.

Sampson, R. J., J. D. Morenoff, and F. Earls. 1999. "Beyond Social Capital: Spatial Dynamics of Collective Efficacy for Children." *American Sociological Review* 64 (5): 633–660.

Saunders, S., M. D. Resnick, H. M. Hoberman, and R. W. Blum. 1994. "Formal Help-Seeking Behavior of Adolescents Identifying Themselves as Having Mental Health Problems." *Journal of the American Academy of Child and Adolescent Psychiatry* 33 (5): 718–728.

Schuller, T., S. Baron, and J. Field. 2000. "Social Capital: A Review and Critique." In *Social Capital,* edited by S. Baron, J. Field, and T. Schuller. Oxford: Oxford University Press.

Spilsbury, J. C. 2002. "'If I Don't Know Them, I'll Get Killed Probably': How Children's Concerns about Safety Shape Help-Seeking Behavior." *Childhood* 9 (1): 101–117.

Srebnik, D., A. M. Cauce, and N. Baydar. 1996. "Help-Seeking Pathways for Children and Adolescents." *Journal of Emotional and Behavioral Disorders* 4 (4): 210–220.

Stephenson, C. 1983. "Visits by Elementary School Children to the School Nurse." *Journal of School Health* 53 (10): 594–599.

Sutton, S. E., and S. Kemp. 2002. "Children as Partners in Neighborhood Placemaking: Lessons from Intergenerational Design Charrettes." *Journal of Environmental Psychology* 22:171–189.

Townsend, M.A.R., M. Manley, and B. F. Tuck. 1991. "Academic Help Seeking in Intermediate-School Classrooms: Effects of Achievement, Ethnic Group, Sex, and Classroom Organization." *New Zealand Journal of Educational Studies* 26:35–47.

Valentine, G. 1997. "'Oh yes I can.' 'Oh no you can't': Children and Parents' Understandings of Kids' Competence to Negotiate Public Space Safely." *Antipode* 29 (1): 65–89.

Waksler, F. C. 1996. *The Little Trials of Childhood and Children's Strategies for Dealing with Them*. London: Falmer Press.

Watt, P., and K. Stenson 1998. "The Street: 'It's a Bit Dodgy around There.'" In *Cool Places*, edited by T. Skelton and G. Valentine. London: Routledge.

Westcott, H. L., and G. M. Davies. 1995. "Children's Help-Seeking Behavior." *Child Care, Health, and Development* 21 (4): 255–270.

Chapter 12   Are We Having Fun Yet?

RHONDA SINGER

*Well, having a good time is extremely important, and I bet
you the NBA players, if they didn't have a good time, they
wouldn't be up there.*

        —LeAnn, fourth grade

*I think it's just fun to play. Everything. Shooting. Just
about everything.*

        —Jerry, seventh grade

WHEN I ASKED FOURTH- through eighth-grade recreational players why they
played basketball, not a single player said, "I started playing because I wanted
to be socialized" or "because I wanted to learn the value of healthy competition
and teamwork." These are adult reasons, the kind we give at coaches' meetings,
in our talk with other adults, in our articles and pamphlets about the value of
sport, and in our well-intended speeches to players. If you ask kids why they
play, they are most likely to talk about how much fun it is.[1] And even those
kids who don't play to have fun report having fun while they play. This finding
is not surprising, given research that has found a positive correlation between
enjoyment and sports involvement of youth (Scanlan and Lewthwaite 1986;
Wankel and Berger 1990).

So, in order to ensure a satisfying, rewarding sports experience for kids, all
that must be done is to keep it fun. Sounds simple. Unfortunately, it's not. Fun
has an amorphous character, difficult to nail down to a single definition. It is
an experience that is shaped by the situation, the team culture developed by
players, the gender of the players, and the model of sport promoted by adults.
Fundamentally, fun is a result of the situation that is collectively negotiated and
created within each team.

The purpose of this chapter is to increase our understanding of kids' conceptions of fun and the potential for a lack of fit between kids' situated interests and league goals. As numerous researchers have shown, the participation rate of kids in sports begins to drop dramatically by sixth or seventh grade for both boys and girls, although the rate of decline is much greater for girls than boys (Gould and Horn 1984; Scanlan and Lewthwaite 1986; Leonard 1998). It would seem to be the case that kids drop out of sports because, among other things, they are no longer having fun. This explanation fits with Vogler and Schwartz's (1993) finding that kids stop playing sports because they are not getting playing time, feel too much pressure from adults, encounter a disproportionate amount of failure, and experience sports as overly organized and controlled by adults.

This research provides an excellent starting point for considering the relationship between definitions of fun and kids' participation in sports. Using qualitative research methods, I was able to examine in some depth the situated behavior and discourse of kids as they actively participated in defining fun. Drawing on a wide repertoire of activities that might be defined as fun—ranging from water fights and wrestling matches to winning a highly competitive game—kids made sense of their experiences and announced their identities in recreational basketball. This process involved navigating the competing demands of the prevailing sports ethic, adult interests, peer pressure, and the kids' ages and athletic and gender identities. As situated conduct, this definitional process was always dynamic and at times seemed contradictory as kids moved among social acts that emerged in their everyday practices.

The Study

This chapter is based on research I conducted in 1995 and 1996 with four teams in the Westland Youth Recreational Basketball League (WYRBL), which is located in a small college town in the northeast United States. The Westland league has two divisions: the coed division, which is open to girls but is nearly all male, and the all-girl division, which is open only to girls. Each division is divided into levels based on the players' grade in school. Teams are made up of players from two consecutive grades; the exception is the sixth/seventh/eighth-grade girls' team, which includes the eighth grade because of the low number of girls in eighth grade and above who sign up for basketball. My season-long study involved the players from four teams: one fourth/fifth-grade coed team, one fourth/fifth-grade all-girl team, one sixth/seventh-grade coed team, and the sixth/seventh/eighth-grade all-girl team. I was the head coach of the fourth/fifth-grade coed team, and I provided assistance to coaches on the other three teams. The kids ranged in age from nine to fourteen, half of them boys and half of them girls. All but one of the girls, Yvonne (fourth grade), were on all-girl teams. Although no official statistics were available on the racial group of players in the league, most would have been identified as white. Three players in this study—two fourth-grade girls (Ann and Yvonne) and one fifth-grade boy (Jason)—were African American. Two boys—one sixth grader (Paul) and one seventh grader (Robert)—were Latino.

My research involved participant observation, interviews with players, informal conversations with adult participants in the league (parents and coaches), as well as videotaping and photographing a number of games and practices. I attended all practices, games, and team events for the season. At the end of the season, I interviewed most of the players (three were unavailable) in sixty- to ninety-minute semistructured conversations, which I tape-recorded. All players, their parents, and coaches signed consent forms; the names of the participants have been changed here to ensure their privacy.

Defining Fun

I have had the occasion of attending, and hearing reports of, youth coaches' meetings for a variety of sports in which the adults all agree that the objective of the league is that kids have fun. League administrators and training videos warn that players will drop out of the league if they don't have fun. But adults in the league also feel it is their responsibility to teach players how to achieve success in sport and life through dedication, self-discipline, and practice. At these meetings coaches trade strategies for convincing kids that they can have fun learning how to play basketball better.

Two strategies are particularly popular among coaches, myself included. The first is to treat activities as investments in future fun. When players openly complain about having to run "suicides," an appropriately named drill involving running back and forth along the length of the court touching baselines, or having to do lay-up drills, coaches remind them of how much fun they will have when they become better players and can out-play their opponents. In effect, this is a lesson not only in what is really fun (being a better player) but also in deferring fun. Coaches also try to define the various drills as fun themselves. For instance, suicides and lay-up drills become contests between individuals and teams. Here adults are using notions of success, competition, competence, and effort to signify fun. Ultimately, in both strategies adults attempt to tell kids when they should be having fun and how they will know they are having fun.

On the face of it, this attempt seems counterintuitive. Why is it necessary to teach kids about fun? After all, don't kids inherently know how to enjoy themselves? In my research I found that adults expected players to be socialized into and through a league-sanctioned definition of fun in basketball. Yet, it also seemed that fun in the WYRBL as conceptualized by adults was an acquired taste—it was something that had to be learned.

To have fun, one must feel like something is fun, to experience enjoyment. The recognition of fun, then, depends on the assignment of an affective meaning to an experience. As Becker (1963) argues in reference to his study of marijuana users, while the physiological conditions for enjoyment and pleasure are present, novice participants must learn to define sensations as pleasurable. Although I do not mean to equate drug use with sports, I think the same principle applies. In organized youth sports, kids are expected to "learn to enjoy effects" (53) and to learn "to answer 'yes' to the question: 'Is it fun'"(58).

From the perspective of the WYRBL players, many of the activities associated with learning and playing the game of basketball were not necessarily experienced as fun. The league's position was that being on a basketball team involves learning and following the multiple rules of the game (some of which kids do not agree with); taking time to develop skills; engaging in repetitive, highly structured activities (otherwise known as drills); and always being told what to do by adults. Kids often resisted these efforts on the part of adults by engaging in informal play, talking instead of paying attention, making up their own rules, and in the case of one fifth-grade girl, sitting down in the middle of the court and refusing to participate. When I asked sixth grader Sam why kids didn't always seem to want to do the same things coaches wanted them to do, he replied, "I think most people just wanted to do what they wanted, like go out and do something fun."

Clearly there was often a gap between what players thought was fun and what the coaches tried to convince them was fun. In part, this gap resulted from the kids' resistance to the imposition of adult control on their play. But kids were also constructing notions of fun that drew on multiple models of play and sport, putting together situational definitions that fit their sense of themselves as kids, athletes, and gendered individuals. While adults worried about "socializing" the youth in their charge, the kids were busy creating a set of meanings and accompanying behavior that made sense given their experiences and objectives.

The Agency of Players

As Prout and James (1990) argue in their summation of the "new paradigm of childhood," kids are active in the "construction and determination" of their social worlds and are "not just the passive subjects of social structures and processes" (8). Furthermore, when we attempt to understand the social worlds of kids, we need to look at the multiple structures that shape their lives, including hierarchies of age, gender, class, race, and ethnicity. To understand fun from the perspective of kids, we need to move beyond adult interests and assumptions and attempt to view the world from the standpoint of the kids themselves.

The WYRBL players did not simply absorb the values and meanings of adults or even of the larger, prevailing culture. Rather, they redefined and transformed (Fine 1987) these elements of the league environment in their negotiation of a team culture and of individual behavior. Kids in the league drew on organizational, social, and personal understandings of sports and play as they defined, experienced, and talked about fun. Yet, although the kids were agential, they were also confronted with the constraints and opportunities imposed by the social structures that organized their everyday lives. Adults, and the institutions they represent, have real power over kids in our society. Thus, in the basketball league, kids who challenged organizational expectations of behavior risked disciplinary actions and, possibly, exclusion.

Institutionalized expectations concerning appropriate sports behavior, and therefore fun, could be found in the way that formal and informal rules in the league reflected beliefs about appropriate levels of competitiveness for players based on age and gender. For instance, at the second/third-grade level, teams were not supposed to keep score (no scoreboard was provided), and referees kept time and officiated the games rather casually. Sixth/seventh/eighth graders used electronic scoreboards and time clocks and were subjected to much more rigorous officiating. Older kids who didn't follow the "rules" were likely to be singled out by referees, coaches, and teammates as disruptive and inappropriate. I also observed instances when the sixth/seventh/eighth-grade girls' were discouraged from being too competitive and aggressive in ways that boys their age were not. In one case, a referee stopped a girls' game to tell the players they "were getting out of control" and "to calm down." His behavior implied that aggressive play was not an appropriate source of fun for these players.

Numerous scholars have commented on the close identification of sports with masculinity; both are associated with strength, aggressiveness, competitiveness, and physicality (Boutilier and SanGiovanni 1983; Messner 1994). In contrast, femininity is conventionally associated with passivity, physical restraint, cooperation, and being nice. Consequently, while boys are faced in sports with the task of living up to the mutually reinforcing ideals of masculinity and athleticism, girls must carefully negotiate the potentially conflicting ideals of femininity and athleticism, trying to find a space where they can find validation for both identities.

Conventional notions of sport and gender were present in WYRBL's institutionalized expectations, in informal adult conversations, and in the players' own talk about their basketball experiences. For instance, nearly all the players I spoke with considered boys and girls in basketball to be categorically different. In particular, girls were seen as nicer and more concerned for others than the boys were, while boys were considered physically rougher and more intense than the girls. Just the same, few players fit perfectly with these ideals of gender; some girls were pretty rough, whereas some boys were not very good at playing basketball or at being intense about the game. Thus, definitions of fun reflected players' efforts to negotiate the expectations of the league, prevailing ideals of gender and athleticism, and their own sense of athletic competence and gender identity.

Clearly, kids had to be aware of institutional, cultural, and peer expectations as they collectively and individually defined fun. Yet they had their own experiences as well as age, gender, and athletic identities to consider as well. Consequently, definitions of fun emerged in the "middle ground" between individual agency and societal constraint.

The Continuum of Fun

The WYRBL players' definitions of fun can be conceptualized as fitting along a continuum that runs between three different models of play and sport (Figure 12.1). This continuum is anchored on either side by two somewhat opposing models: the Informal Play Model and what Coakley (1994) has termed the Performance and Power Model. At the center of continuum is the Participation and Pleasure model, also described by Coakley (1994). These models were available to the kids in the league, and they drew on all three in various degrees as they constructed individual and team definitions of fun.

The Informal Play Model is characterized by unstructured play in which enjoyment is the primary objective; this model includes the nonsports notions of fun that players bring into the basketball situation. This model involves the least amount of restriction on the events or experiences that signify fun, in large part because of the relative absence of formalized rules and boundaries concerning behavior. Nevertheless, informal play is shaped and constrained by status relations among the participants and group culture. Ideally, adults do not directly interfere in activities, although adults are seen as valuable mediators of conflict.

The Participation and Pleasure Model probably best represents the official position of the youth league, and it was promoted at coaches and players' meetings, in coach and referee training sessions, and in the handbooks of the National Youth Sports Coaches Association (1997a, 1997b). This model is associated with a somewhat more limited definition of fun than that of the Informal Play Model; in this definition fun arises through structured activities that emphasize inclusive participation and enjoyment. As in the Informal Play Model, having fun is a primary motive and objective, although the Participation and Pleasure Model places greater restrictions on the kinds of activities that are considered fun. Within this model, participants are expected to conform to the organiza-

Figure 12.1. The continuum of fun.

tional objectives of the game being played. Adults play an important role in organizing and planning events, as well as in ensuring that all players have the opportunity to participate in and enjoy the activities.

The Performance and Power Model, elements of which informed league expectations for older players, especially boys, could be found in players', parents', and coaches' talk and behavior. This is the model used in media depictions of professional and college sports. It is characterized by structured activities that emphasize competition, domination, and winning (Coakley 1994). Winning is the primary motive, and activities associated with winning are associated with fun. As in the Participation and Pleasure Model, participants are expected to conform to organizational objectives. Adults play an important role in planning and implementing activities, as well as in ensuring that participants are prepared to compete and, ideally, to win.

I next examine the five types of situations that the WYRBL players described as fun and the models of sport and identities that shaped these definitions and experiences. I then look closely at how players used definitions of fun to announce their own athletic and gender identities.

Players' Definitions of Fun

Players told me about five types of situations that they defined as fun in basketball. These definitions can be positioned along the continuum of fun, reflecting the influence of each model of sport. In the players' discourse they are managing an array of desires, self-images, and identities as they describe their conceptions of fun. In particular, players' ideas about gender and athleticism can shape the relevance of each of the three models of sport for defining a situation as fun.

FREE PLAY

Kids often came to practices and games with objectives and definitions of fun that reflected an informal, unstructured form of play. For example, when I asked what they liked to do at practices, players talked about the fun they had when they played games like knock-out, had individual and mini-team contests, played and visited with friends, made jokes, had water fights at the fountain, were able to "be goofy," and did "what they wanted." Many of the players commented on how much more fun they had when coaches left them alone and did not make them do a bunch of drills and learn plays. For instance, Alex (seventh grade), echoing comments made by a number of his teammates, talked about the desirability of coaches turning over a third of every practice to the players so they could do whatever they wanted: "Yeah, wouldn't that be awesome? We would just shoot around. Just shooting around is fun. Not like playing crappy plays. I don't think we really learn anything from that because we aren't really paying attention. We would pay attention if we got a lot more time shooting and doing what we want to. It's fun to just come in and shoot."

Informal play was an important aspect of players' experiences of fun. But few players expected that this type of fun would predominate in the team's activities. In fact, being socialized into the sport of basketball involved players' recognition that informal play had a time and place. On a number of occasions, I witnessed players shift from being fully involved in informal play activities to chastising their teammates for goofing off and not paying attention. They were most likely to make this shift on the coed teams, where boys were under pressure to live up to peer and adult expectations of appropriate masculine athleticism. One minute, sixth grader Ted was pushing, shoving, and whispering with his teammates while players were supposed to be settling down for the team meeting early in practice. The next minute, he was yelling "Come on, guys," acting disturbed at the inability of his peers to take the meeting seriously. Ted seemed to be shifting between being just a kid having fun and being a serious basketball player who disdained the disruptions caused by informal play.

PARTICIPATION

Many of the players mentioned that simply participating in basketball activities was fun, a perception that fits nicely in the middle of the continuum of fun. As Sydney, a fifth-grade girl said, "You wanna play." Boys and girls were eager to participate in games, asking the coaches when they would get back into the game or resisting being subbed out. LeAnn, a fourth-grade girl who was playing on a team for the first time, told me she had fun when she had the ball and when someone passed to her. Max, a seventh grader, told me that he had more fun when all the kids were kept involved, and no one was left sitting around and waiting. Other players mentioned the fun of teamwork or full-team involvement. Ellen, a sixth grader, mentioned the fun she had being part of, and working with, a team. And Ted, a sixth grader, said he had fun when "people are playing good, when they aren't playing selfish. Pass it [the ball] around and stuff like that."

Neither age nor gender seemed to matter much in the kids' perceptions of how important participation was in experiencing basketball as fun, although the way in which the issue of participation was framed was different for the older boys than it was for the other players. The seventh-grade boys tended to couch their remarks about the fun of participation in a critique of their team experience. Tom said that his idea of fun was "the whole idea. Well, if I'm playing 'cause I'm sitting [out] most of the time." Allen explained why a game wasn't fun: "What he [the coach] ended up doing is kind of gave us less time, put more over to the younger players, like the key positions." For the older boys, participation was a matter of rights and fairness. Many of the seventh-grade boys did not think it was fair that they did not get more playing time, especially relative to the sixth graders on the team. They had put in their time as the least experienced, less-played players the previous season, and they felt they were due more playing time this year. Such concerns suggest a more competitive model of sport, in which players earn the right to play, and playing time is treated as a scarce resource to be rewarded to a deserving few.

Among the four teams that I worked with, the sixth/seventh-grade boys' team had the most visible status hierarchy. Coaches supported a hierarchy by positioning older boys above younger ones and the more athletic above the less athletic by rewarding older athletic boys with more playing time and choice positions. As Fine (1979, 1987) argues, in order for an item to be included in a group's culture, it must be appropriate—that is, it must "not undermine the group's social structure in not supporting the interpersonal network and power relations in the group" (1987, 741). The inclusive participation suggested by the Participation and Pleasure Model disrupts the construction and maintenance of status hierarchies founded on competition and exclusion and, therefore, the relations among the sixth/seventh-grade boys. Thus, it was not enough to simply participate for the situation to be fun; participation on the team also had to meet group definitions of fairness.

SUCCESS AND ACHIEVEMENT

The comments of many players focused on success and achievement as a source of fun; this definition falls on the continuum of fun somewhere between the Participation and Pleasure Model and the Performance and Power Model. Kids' comments concerning success, achievement, and fun covered a range of events, from exhibiting basketball skills to contributing to the teams' score. Kids mentioned as fun scoring, making an assist, making a "good play," making a "long shot," and "having the team make a comeback." As one sixth-grade girl put it, "Well, it makes you feel good because you did something for your team."

Sports psychologists consider these sources of fun as aspects of intrinsic motivation and a form of task-achievement orientation, distinguished from more external standards and rewards (such as winning, awards, and comparing one-self to others) (Weiss and Chaumeton 1992). Conceptualizing success and achievement as arising from intrinsic sources may lead us to associate "success as fun" with the Participation and Pleasure Model. Yet what is considered an intrinsic motivation can be understood only within a social environment that includes sports-specific skill requirements and objectives; only when a particular way of organizing sports defines and values these acts do they come to signify fun. The game of basketball, as it is organized and played by youth, is inescapably defined by the ultimate objective of the game: to be the team that scores the most points. Everything, from learning how to dribble and shoot properly to learning how to cooperate with teammates in plays to mastering sophisticated game strategy, is designed in light of this goal. Thus, fun through success and achievement falls at the middle point between the Participation and Pleasure Model and the Performance and Power Model.

However, some players specifically distinguish the fun they have playing basketball from being good at the sport. Yvonne, in the fourth grade, said, "Well, yeah. Practice makes you good at basketball, but it doesn't make you necessarily have fun. You can still be good at basketball and have fun. Even if you are bad at basketball, you can still have fun." Tiffany, in the sixth grade, said, "You don't have to be good to play it [basketball]. It's just everybody want to have fun." Success leads to fun, but success itself is a situationally defined condition. Although some players closely associated success with fun, others—especially those who were not as successful in the skills associated with the game—resisted the notion that you had to be "good" to have fun.

COMPETITION AND DOMINATION

Many players mentioned dominating the opponent on the court and intense competition as sources of fun, although, as Diana's and Ted's comments suggest, there may be differences in how some girls and boys talked about this type of fun.

> DIANA (fifth grade): 'Cause it's fun; 'cause if you don't go for the ball, the other team will automatically get it. But if you go for the jump ball, then your team could get it. So at least you let your team have a chance. It is fun trying to pull it [the ball] out of their hands.
> RHONDA: What makes it fun trying to pull it out of their hands?
> DIANA: Maybe, I'm like thinking it will put them down because they lost the ball. I don't know. I just like doing it. It's fun . . . because if someone steals the ball from you, you like start feeling like you're not any good for a little bit. And then your team scores, and you feel good again. I like stealing [the ball] 'cause maybe it feels, I don't know, it makes me feel good.

Ted, a seventh grader, also talked about the fun in dominating the opponent when he played basketball in a local three-on-three tournament: "Oh, like one game, the one that we won, we won by sort of a lot, and we were getting on these kids' nerves. They were all stumbling and everything, and we're like happy 'cause they're getting all mad and frustrated, and they showed it. And we were winning. And they were calling fouls and everything. And that's what got us mad. But it was kind of fun; we were having fun; we didn't have to worry about anything. We're just having fun."

For Diana and Ted, part of the fun they reported came from dominating their opponent, and they enjoyed knowing that they could put the other players down, shake them up, and, ultimately, leave them at a disadvantage, at least temporarily. A striking difference between Diana's and Ted's remarks was that Diana seemed to be combining elements of both the Participation and Pleasure Model and the Performance and Power Model. Dominating was not only acceptable behavior but an appropriate source of fun. But she also seemed to expect turn taking; she would dominate this time, but her opponent would get to feel good later. In this way, Diana presented herself as "nice," a trait that many of the players I talked to associated with girls but not boys. Ted, in contrast, focused on the way that his team's dominating and competitive behavior would lead to winning the game. For Ted, domination and competition as fun drew more heavily from the Performance and Power Model, and they were ways he could show himself to be appropriately tough and serious, traits that most players associated with masculinity.

Another aspect of competition that came up in discussions of fun was experiences of challenge and pressure. Samantha, a fifth grader, remembered one game in particular when a high-pressure moment resulted in fun for her: "I just really like playing during the end of the game 'cause the pressure was all on you; and it's like, I tried playing that, and it's like I played really well. Like one game, I got the basket on the buzzer, and I was really happy about that. That was really fun 'cause everybody was like, 'Good job, good job.'" After a positive experience playing under pressure and succeeding, Samantha defined these types of situations as fun. This definition of fun was most certainly influenced by the positive feedback she got after making the basket.

Fun associated with competition was elevated for some players when the competition was particularly intense, with highly skilled opponents. Allen and Tim, two boys on the sixth/seventh-grade coed team, came closer to fully embracing the Performance and Power Model than any other of the players with whom I spoke. Allen remarked, "Maybe a lot of kids don't like it; some kids like it competitive, some don't. I think it makes [it] more fun because people are trying harder and it actually means more." Tim said, "If you win by a lot, like maybe even thirty, it's not fun. It's just a blow-out; the game wasn't even worth playing. But if it's by like two, you feel really glad 'cause you pulled it off." Allen didn't have as much fun in sports when the teams were more inclusive and the "talent was more spread out." He felt that this way of making up teams reduced the competitiveness of the play. Tim preferred a more "intense" level of competition, with teams more evenly matched. In both cases, highly competitive play against opponents meant more to these players and made playing more fun.

Other players did not have such positive experiences. On the contrary, they felt that high-pressure moments left them self-conscious and possibly decreased their likelihood of succeeding. Tom, a seventh grader, told me he had more fun at practices than at games because he didn't have people watching him and therefore the pressure he felt while playing was reduced. As he put it, "I do okay in practice during scrimmage, but I couldn't make a shot in a game."

Talk about competition revealed some of the difficulties in attempting to separate sources of fun into separate categories. In reality, there was a great deal of overlap among the categories that I have created here. For instance, Tom's dislike of pressure was due in large part to the effect it had on his feelings of competence and achievement. He could not perform at the level he expected when people (other than his teammates) were watching him. Samantha, however, was able to feel particularly successful during a game because she achieved the objective of scoring during a high-pressure situation. The basket she made increased in value because of the conditions under which she shot it.

WINNING

For both boys and girls, the relationship between winning and fun was complex and, on the surface, sometimes contradictory. On the one hand, all the players seemed to agree that winning made playing more fun. On the other hand, winning was seldom viewed as the most important part of playing the game and having fun, and too much emphasis on winning was likely to be met with criticism. Fifth-grader Sydney's remarks were typical of those of most of the players I spoke with: "Well, I mean, everybody says like winning's not important and stuff. But, I mean, everybody . . . you don't go there to like lose. You know, everybody wants to win, and so . . . it's more fun to win."

The players recognized that the ultimate objective of playing basketball was winning. But most clearly didn't see winning as the only, or even the most important, way to have fun.

> RHONDA: So winning is important in terms of having fun?
> PAUL (sixth grade): It doesn't have to exactly be winning. I mean, you can lose, but as long as you have a good game and it's fun for you guys, for like the team.

A number of players made similar statements, an indication that although winning could add to the fun of a game, playing well was also important and could counter the disappointment of a loss. For instance, Marti, a fifth-grade girl, noted that even though her team lost a game, she played well, and "if you play a good game, that's [fun too]." Terry, a fifth-grade boy, felt the same way, chuckling as he told me that "it's kinda like, 'ah man, we lost,' you know. But when I play a good game, I feel perfectly fine."

Sports sociologists generally agree that winning is a dominant value in sports, "taught much more assiduously in sport than are other goals" (Theberge 1981, 285). But kids are not simply internalizing this goal at face value. Winning is important and fun, but most of the players I talked with thought that it is not the only way to have fun in basketball.

Clearly these players had no simple, single definition of fun. Their ideas of which situations were fun and which were not depended on a multitude of intersecting factors, including their sense of their own ability, the value they placed on the competitive ethic, how they performed and felt at a particular moment, and the available options for behavior. Furthermore, these intersecting factors seemed to be filtered through age and gender expectations. Consequently, the linear perspective on development that sees kids progressing naturally in sports from less competitive to more competitive is a poor fit for many kids as they move back and forth between sport models in their definition and experience of fun.

Fun and Identity

When participants construct a definition of a situation, they are also "implying roles and identities" (Hewitt 1997, 128). The WYRBL players understood that there were different ways to define the basketball situation as fun, and they combined and used these multiple definitions in unique ways to distinguish between types of basketball players and to make their own identity announcements. In our interviews, players referred to different definitions of fun as a way to make distinctions between players on the basis of gender and motivation for involvement in sports.

GIRLS' FUN AND BOYS' FUN

Some girls differentiated between the fun they had playing with boys and the fun they had playing with girls. The distinction they made is similar to the difference between the Participation and Pleasure Model and the Performance and Power Model. In general, these players saw boys as far more concerned with the outcome of the game, as more aggressive during play, and as less supportive of teammates than girls. Darbi, a sixth grader, said:

I'll have fun [playing with the boys], but it might be a different kind of
fun, and maybe I'll feel better about myself after I play with girls than
when I play with boys. . . . With the guys I play in school, so it's a more
casual thing, and there's no refs and you can joke around more[;] . . . [but
with girls] there's not gonna be the guys dissing me, saying "Oh, you
suck," and everything. And people [girls] are, they're not wrapped up in
winning the game, but they're wrapped up in playing their best, and so
they're not as conscious as to what you're doing and how you mess up
and everything. And if you mess up, they're gonna say, "That's okay; it
was a good try," or something.

Darbi contrasted two, gendered categories of fun, each of which had rewards
and setbacks for her. Playing with the boys at school meant greater freedom to
joke around, maybe engage in a little bantering. Darbi experienced this playing
as fun but saw it as enjoyment coming at a cost: mistakes and losses carried much
more weight than they did when she played with girls. In addition, when she
played with boys, her ability and value as a player might be discounted on the
grounds that she was a girl. Thus, her identity as a basketball player was vulnerable to challenges when playing with boys, whereas it was more likely to gain
support when she played with girls.

Although Linda, an eighth grader, told me that she did not want to play
basketball with the boys, she did talk about one girls' game in which she experienced a kind of fun that she associated with males: "I sort of like being like
more aggressive rather than just 'okay' . . . 'cause it was more fast paced and not
just, 'Okay, let's walk down the court.' It was more like a boy's game." Like Darbi,
Linda assumed that there are two different ways to play basketball: the way boys
play and the way girls play. Each way of playing was associated with a different
meaning of fun. Despite the labeling of these styles as boys' and girls', both
were available ways of playing. Whereas Darbi felt she had chosen one over
the other, Linda talked about the integration of elements of the "boys' game"
into her teams' performance. In both cases, the players had to resolve a tension between competing models of sport and assess the fun they had relative to those definitions.

In addition, in Linda's case, the boys' type of fun acted as a standard against
which her experiences on the girls' team were measured. Not only did boys have
different kinds of fun, but in some ways the type of fun that boys had might be
seen as being better or more highly valued. A gender-based hierarchy was evident in the differentiation of and meaning attributed to boys' and girls' basketball by players. So although girls might aspire to, or at least value aspects of,
the boys' game, not one boy talked about the desirability of playing like a girl.
Thus, the available options for models of sport, as well as for definitions of fun,
may be narrower for boys than for girls.

FUN AS MOTIVE TALK

One way that people can make announcements about their identity is through "motive talk" (Mills 1981; Hewitt 1997). Motives are "linguistic devices" that explain, correctly or not, the occurrence of behavior deemed appropriate for particular categories of people (Mills 1981). For instance, among the WYRBL players, it was often more appropriate for the girls than for the boys to say that they played basketball to be with their friends, although I found that boys were as concerned as the girls with being on teams with friends they could talk to.

Sometimes players used the motive of fun to make announcements about their athletic and gender identities. Tim, who was in the sixth grade, said, "Most girls, for them a game, it doesn't really matter whether you win or lose. It's just the fun of getting to play. To most boys, it's not the fun of getting to play; it's to win. That's why most boys play, . . . to win." Tim's use of fun as a motive enabled him to differentiate boys' basketball from girls' basketball and, simultaneously, to differentiate two models of the sport. Tim's comment suggested that fun should be distinguished from other motives for playing; that one can play for fun or for other reasons. Furthermore, Tim argued that one's motive for playing was determined by one's gender. Although Tim was the only player to explicitly state this extreme dichotomy between boys' and girls' motives for playing, his comments echoed an attitude I've come across in my research and experiences: boys play basketball because they are serious, and girls play for the fun of it. Like Darbi and Linda, he assumed girls' basketball and boys' basketball were different, and they represented at least two different ways of going about playing the sport.

Some of the girls I spoke with challenged the association between gender and fun, not by disputing that girls play for fun but by arguing that all players, regardless of gender, play to have a good time. For instance, look what fourth-grader LeAnn told me when I asked her what aspects of the game were important to her, other than winning:

> LEANN: Um, having a good time . . . and, well, now, like I guess the people who said that girls don't take basketball very seriously would say, "See, all they want to do is have a good time."
>
> RHONDA: Instead of win.
>
> LEANN: Well, having a good time is extremely important, and I bet you the NBA players, if they didn't have a good time, they wouldn't be up there.

While she imagined the responses of others and acknowledged cultural distinctions made between boys and girls, LeAnn also resisted a competitive male model of sport and the trivializing of fun as a motive. This is a great example of a kid actively involved in constructing her own understanding of the meaning and value of fun in basketball while announcing a positive identity as a basketball player.

Other players talked about the importance of fun as a motivation for playing to distinguish between types of basketball players. The following comment is representative of those made by seven male and female players, all but one (a sixth-grade girl) in the fourth or fifth grade: Dan, who was in the fifth grade, said, "I just play for fun. So how I do doesn't have too much of an effect on me. Terry, I know, takes basketball seriously." Like all the other players I spoke with, Dan had fun when he played basketball. But he also used his definition of fun to separate himself from other types of players whom he imagined exist, players who are more serious, who are concerned with how good they are, and who play for reasons other than just "for the fun of it." By establishing fun as the motive, Dan was telling me that it didn't matter whether he was good at basketball (he was one of the lower-status players on the team) because he didn't embrace many elements of the Performance and Power Model. Perhaps by downplaying the importance of success and achievement, Dan was protecting his positive sense of self from challenges to his athletic and gender identities.

Although a number of players made an effort to distance themselves from a competitive, serious model of sport by emphasizing the motive of fun, other players leaned toward a competitive model in which fun as a motive diminished the legitimacy of their athletic identity. Consider my conversation with Tim, the only player to tell me that winning was the most important thing in basketball. Tim began by saying, "Winning is like the most important thing. No need to play if you're not going to win. People say that just playing is fun, but I feel like there is no need to play if you're not going to win. You shouldn't play if, if you know you can't win, you shouldn't even play." As our interview progressed though, Tim talked about the kinds of things he really had fun doing while playing basketball on the team: "When I grab a good rebound, like a really hard one, or if I grab it over somebody who is taller than me. I guess that. Or when I play defense on somebody who is really good. Like Paul's really good, and I score 'cause I played good defense on him. And he gets so mad."

Even though Tim begins by stating that the desire to win should be the motivating force behind playing basketball, as opposed to playing just to have fun, it is clear that having fun is part of his basketball experience. Yet as an "older" boy who has embraced many elements of the Performance and Power Model, Tim believes that playing for fun is inappropriate and trivializes the more important elements of sports like winning, competing, and dominating. Tim concedes that he has fun winning, competing, and dominating, but he treats this definition of the situation as an inevitable outcome of his serious participation as opposed to a motive for playing. Tim not only has learned the appropriate vocabulary of motives (Mills 1981) for a serious player but has also learned to experience as fun those activities and outcomes associated with the Performance and Power Model of sport.

Conclusion

A better understanding of what players define as fun in sports is essential if adults are truly interested in keeping kids in sports. As Scanlan and Lewthwaite (1986) noted, we need to ask why sports seem to be a more enjoyable experience for younger kids than for older kids. Psychological research has clearly demonstrated that kids' perceptions of competence in sports and of the value of sports and participation in them all decline during childhood and through adolescence (see Jacobs et al. 2002 for a review of this literature and additional data). Perhaps, as kids get older, they face increasing pressure to conform to the organizational and peer definitions of appropriate behavior and of fun. Those who are unable, or unwilling, to narrow their definitions of fun find it more difficult to find positive support or opportunities for fun. There may also be less flexibility in the types of player a kid could be and in the types of motive talk she or he could engage in.

This research suggests that adults may not comprehend the range of situations that kids define as fun or the intersecting factors that influence players' definitions of fun. Kids bring numerous concerns and experiences with them to sports, and their goals may not neatly coincide with league and coach objectives. Although adults assume that players will eventually come around, grow up, and adapt to institutionalized goals of youth sport, it seems more likely that many kids either drop out or are cut from teams when their own interests can no longer be reconciled with the demands of the league. Closing the gap between adult and kids' conceptions of fun may be the best way to stem the tide of player attrition in youth sport.

Contemporary scholars studying childhood have criticized the assumption that children are "incomplete adults" or "adults-in-the-making" (Thorne 1993, 3; see also Corsaro 1997; Prout and James 1990; Waksler 1991) as being an adult-centered and biased perception of children's experiences. We could make the same criticism about the way adults often perceive the "function" of sports in socialization. We have a tendency to talk about how sports will teach our children self-discipline and the value of hard work, teamwork, competition, and an array of other traits we believe that "good" and successful adults should have.

I have shown above, however, that players do not march happily along the institutionalized path to athleticism and maturity. As Thorne pointed out in regard to the students in her research, kids "don't necessarily see themselves as 'being socialized' or 'developing'" (1993, 13). On the contrary, kids have numerous concerns and interests that go beyond what adults have in mind for them, including their own hopes for future achievement, peer acceptance, gender and athletic identity, competence and maturity, status among their peers, and feeling good about themselves in general (see also Brustad 1988). So although adult interests may have affected the structures and expectations of the WYRBL, the players navigated these constraints in light of their immediate goals and concerns.

In addition to acknowledging the variety of kids' interests in sports by making room for varied definitions of fun, adults might also examine the ways that gender and other social identities continue to be institutionalized in sports. Even with increasing numbers of women athletes, "excellence in sports is equated with masculinity," and "the phrase 'woman athlete' is almost an oxymoron" (McKay, Messner, and Sabo 2000, xiii). Focusing on growing opportunities in sports allows the differences between girls' and boys' participation rates to emerge. It also allows sports performance and experience to be seen as equitable and fair. It deflects our attention from the competitive male hierarchy that dominates boys' sports and that raises the stakes in boys' negotiation of identities on their youth teams.

Additional qualitative research is needed to further our appreciation for the complexity of kids' lives and experiences in sports. Further, a child-centered approach is essential if we truly want to understand why kids play sports and how best to support their efforts when they do.

Note

1. I began using the term *kids* instead of *children* in my own research after reading Thorne's (1993) argument that "kids" better reflects how young people think of themselves. In the interest of presenting these data as closely as possible from the perspective of the players, I use "kids" in the hope of stepping away from the "adult-ideological viewpoint" evoked by "the word 'children'" (9).

References

Becker, H. 1963. *Outsiders*. New York: Free Press.

Boutilier, M. A., and L. SanGiovanni. 1983. *The Sporting Woman*. Champaign, Ill.: Human Kinetics.

Brustad, R. 1988. "Affective Outcomes in Competitive Youth Sport: The Influence of Intrapersonal and Socialization Factors." *Journal of Sport and Exercise Psychology* 10:307–321.

Coakley, J. 1994. *Sports in Society: Issues and Controversies*. 5th ed. St. Louis, Mo.: Mosby.

Corsaro, W. A. 1997. *The Sociology of Childhood*. Thousand Oaks, Calif.: Pine Forge Press.

Fine, G. A. 1979. "Small Groups and Culture Creation: The Idioculture of Little League Baseball Teams." *American Sociological Review* 44:733–745.

Fine, G. A. 1987. *With the Boys: Little League Baseball and Preadolescent Culture*. Chicago: University of Chicago Press.

Gould, D., and T. Horn. 1984. "Participation Motivation in Young Athletes." In *Psychological Foundations of Sport*, edited by J. M. Silva III and R. S. Weinberg. Champaign, Ill.: Human Kinetics.

Hewitt, J. 1997. *Self and Society*. 7th ed. Boston: Allyn & Bacon.

Jacobs, J. E., S. Lanza, D. W. Osgood, J. S. Eccles, and A. Wigfield. 2002. "Changes in Children's Self-Competence and Values: Gender and Domain Differences across Grades One through Twelve." *Child Development* 73:509–527.

Leonard, W. M., II. 1998. *A Sociological Perspective of Sport*. 5th ed. Boston: Allyn & Bacon.

McKay, J., M. Messner, and D. Sabo. 2000. *Masculinities, Gender Relations, and Sport*. Thousand Oaks: Sage.

Messner, M. 1994. "Sports and Male Domination: The Female Athlete as Contested Ideological Terrain." In *Women, Sport and Culture*, edited by S. Birrell and C. L. Cole. Champaign, Ill.: Human Kinetics.

Mills, C. W. 1981. "Situated Actions and Vocabularies of Motive." In *Social Psychology through Symbolic Interaction*, edited by G. Stone and H. A. Faberman. New York: Wiley.

National Youth Sports Coaches Association. 1997a. *NYSCA: Basic Level Handbook*. West Palm Beach, Fla.: National Youth Sports Coaches Association.

National Youth Sports Coaches Association. 1997b. *NYSCA: 2nd Level Member's Handbook*. West Palm Beach, Fla.: National Youth Sports Coaches Association.

Prout, A., and A. James 1990. "A New Paradigm for the Sociology of Childhood? Provenance, Promise and Problems." In *Constructing and Reconstructing Childhood: Contemporary Issues in the Sociological Study of Childhood*, edited by A. James and A. Prout. Basingstoke, U.K.: Falmer Press.

Scanlan, T., and R. Lewthwaite. 1986. "Social Psychological Aspects of Competition for Male Youth Sport Participants: IV. Predictors of Enjoyment." *Journal of Sport Psychology* 8:25–35.

Theberge, N. 1981. "Sex Differences in Orientations towards Games: Tests of the Sports Involvement Hypothesis." In *Studies in the Sociology of Sport*, edited by A. O. Dunleavy, A. W. Miracle, and C. R. Rees. Fort Worth, Tex.: Texas Christian University Press.

Thorne, B. 1993. *Gender Play: Girls and Boys in School*. New Brunswick, N.J.: Rutgers University Press.

Vogler, C. C., and S. E. Schwartz. 1993. *The Sociology of Sport*. Englewood Cliffs, N.J.: Prentice-Hall.

Waksler, F. C. 1991. "Beyond Socialization." In *Studying the Social Worlds of Children: Sociological Readings*, edited by F. C. Waksler. New York: Falmer Press.

Wankel, L. M., and B. G. Berger. 1990. "The Psychological and Social Benefits of Sport and Physical Activity." *Journal of Leisure Research* 22:167–182.

Weiss, M. R., and N. Chaumeton. 1992. "Motivational Orientations in Sport." In *Advances in Sport Psychology*, edited by T. S. Horn. Champaign, Ill.: Human Kinetics.

Part V

Voice and Agency as Legal Rights

Chapter 13

Re-Visioning Rights for Children

BARBARA BENNETT WOODHOUSE

THE TERM CHILDREN'S RIGHTS presents a paradox. In the U.S. system, rights usually belong to an autonomous party capable of exercising an informed and independent choice. But children are not fully autonomous. The infant's dependence is a fact of nature. Adding to children's essential dependence, Americans have created a layer of cultural dependence that masks children's actual abilities. We have constructed the life stage called childhood as a special time during which the young must be protected from their own immaturity and sheltered from adult experiences and adult responsibilities. Legal concepts like minority status and the age of majority reflect our cultural beliefs about children's lack of capacity to act rationally in their own interests and their need to be under some responsible adult's control.

In describing rights for adults, the law has traditionally divided them into categories that seem distinct and separate but that often overlap in practice. Legal scholars speak of "positive" and "negative" rights (Berlin 1958; Waldron 1984). A negative right is the right to be free from state intervention, a right to be left alone by the government. A positive right is a right requiring active state intervention, such as the right of an individual to receive a positive good or benefit. It is easy to see how these categories are interdependent. For example, protecting citizens' negative right to be free from unlawful deprivations of liberty may involve conferring a positive right on poor defendants to be provided with an attorney at public expense.

International human rights law now generally accepts that these categories are inevitably interrelated—positive rights may be necessary for the exercise of negative rights, and such economic and welfare rights as education and income security may be necessary ingredients in the realization of values of equality and dignity (*Indivisibility and Interdependence* 1989; Stark 1992). Whether negative or positive, rights typically involve choices by the rights holder, who must decide whether and when to invoke them. Rights holders are tacitly assumed to be capable of administering the right or entitlement for themselves. Negative rights, especially, presuppose a zone of personal privacy and a state of independence that do not fit with children's reality. Are children's rights therefore simply an oxymoron?

If history teaches us anything, it teaches us to question such categorical exclusions. Too many other groups have been classified as lacking the capacity to function as full-fledged "persons" in our system of justice. Our shared certainty about the inferiority or disability of these excluded groups—Africans, women, the Irish, Jews, Native Americans, Asians—rested on universally accepted stereotypes that were later exposed as fallacies. But the fact remains—children are different. Articulating a theory of children's rights requires thoughtful people, in the United States and internationally, to stretch for a more nuanced rights discourse and a more child-centered perspective. While recognizing the tension between traditional theories of rights and the reality of children's dependence, advocates for children contend that children are persons and thus equally entitled with all others to be treated justly by the law, even if they are treated differently (Federle 1995).[1] Justice for children requires that we revise rights to fit children's unique situation. Justice for children requires that we probe the empirical bases for some of our judgments about children's lack of capacity and that we discard imagined differences without ignoring real differences (Kandel 1994; Margulies 1996; Melton 1987; Ross 1996; Woodhouse 1993).

Children in the U.S. Legal System

A brief history of children in the U.S. legal system shows how poorly our traditional concept of rights has served our youngest citizens. The law traditionally treated children more like the property of parents than like persons (Grossberg 1985; Mason 1994). Parents "owned" the child by virtue of procreation, had a duty to educate and nurture the child, and could claim the child's labor and obedience in return. Under law, children lacked independent status, and rules applying to children, contained in laws on custody, apprenticeship, and indenture, reflected children's economic value more than their personhood. Well into the nineteenth century, a vagrant child or one whose parents were too poor to meet their duty of support would be involuntarily removed from the home by the local poverty authorities and placed in indentured servitude, usually until age twenty-one (Dolgin 1997). The duty to care for the child and the right to exploit the child's labor would then shift from the parents to the new master.

Traditionally, state laws have attempted to mark a clear line between dependence and independence. Most states adopted a specific age (previously twenty-one but now usually eighteen) that divided minors, whose affairs were entrusted to adults, from all other citizens, who might speak and act for themselves unless shown to be legally incompetent. Highly intelligent and capable minors were precluded from signing a binding contract, filing a lawsuit on their own behalf, or serving as witnesses in a trial. In all legal interactions with other persons and with the state, parents or guardians exercised authority and control.

The primary source of rights in the U.S. legal system is the Constitution. Although it never specifically mentions "family" or "children," the Constitution has been interpreted as creating a zone of privacy that keeps the state out of family life. In addition, the first ten amendments to the United States Constitution, the Bill of Rights, establish limits on the powers of government in dealing with individuals. Ironically, although children's dependence would seem to suggest a need for positive rights, like rights to nurture and shelter, U.S. law has focused on children's negative rights.

Judge Richard Posner has remarked, "The Constitution is a charter of negative rather than positive liberties. . . . The men who wrote the Bill of Rights were not concerned that government might do too little for the people but that it might do too much to them."[2] The Bill of Rights tells us that government may not establish a state religion, force a person to testify against himself, or force him to forswear his God; police may not seize a person's body without a warrant; and courts may not convict a defendant of a serious crime without a trial by jury.

The Bill of Rights and other constitutional provisions have been important to children, but much of the story is written not in the Constitution itself but in the decisions of the Supreme Court. In Chief Justice John Marshall's words, the province of the judiciary is to "say what the law is."[3] As the highest court in the land, the Supreme Court has the duty to construe and interpret constitutional language to resolve specific cases and controversies. Few Americans fully appreciate that our most cherished rights rest on the nine justices' powers of interpretation. The Court has had to read between the lines of the Constitution to find protections of children's rights and family rights in the document's general statements about the values of life, liberty, property, and equality and in the historical events that motivated the drafting of the Constitution and its amendments. The Court looks to deeply rooted traditions to determine which rights are fundamental. Because our traditions have sanctioned the subjugation and unequal treatment of children, the Court has been slow to respond to their claim to constitutional protection.

Perhaps the single most important children's rights case is also the best known Supreme Court case of the twentieth century. In the 1954 decision in *Brown v. Board of Education* (347 U.S. 483), children played a pivotal role in shaping the law and in expanding the public perception of the role of law. In *Brown*, the Court placed children's right to equality under the law ahead of the states' right to follow longstanding practices of segregated education. *Brown* also had an enormous cultural impact. Television viewers saw the bravery of children on the front lines in the battle for racial equality. During the sixties and seventies, a wave of rulings expanded adults' constitutional rights of privacy, equality, and due process. These decisions affected all areas of life, including marriage, family, and reproductive choice. They also extended a measure of protection to children, albeit more limited in scope than those protections afforded adults (Mezey 1996). Even though the Court often managed to avoid addressing directly children's rights-based arguments and opted in favor of deciding cases on more traditional grounds, these cases provide the foundation on which we must build our jurisprudence of children's constitutional rights.[4]

In the past half century, children, who had been all but invisible as persons under the Constitution, came to play a significant role in constitutional law. The Supreme Court decided more than fifty children's rights cases grounded on constitutional principles during the period from 1953 to 1993. *In re Gault* (387 U.S. 1) established a minor's right to a lawyer in a delinquency trial. *Goss v. Lopez* (419 U.S. 565) and *Tinker v. Des Moines Independent School District* (393 U.S. 503) acknowledged the due process and first amendment rights of children. *Planned Parenthood v. Danforth* (428 U.S. 52) extended a right to reproductive privacy to teens as well as adults. Each of these cases provided a precedent establishing that the Constitution and its protections are not for adults alone.

We have also seen a relaxation of the bars to children's participation as witnesses in court cases and a growing recognition of children's rights to a voice and often a choice in custody and adoption cases (Green and Dohrn 1966). Nevertheless, the Supreme Court's decisions betray the Court's and our culture's ambivalence about children. As one student of the Supreme Court has observed, the Court's decisions have "yielded incoherent results at times: with the Court protecting children from the dangers of inappropriate speech, yet failing to protect them from abusive parents; allowing states to limit the reproductive decision-making of minors on the grounds of immaturity, yet, at the same time, permitting states to subject minors to the death penalty" (Mezey 1996, 26).

Compared with other nations, the United States has a unique approach to children, one that reflects its peculiar culture and history. Far more than most other systems, it tends to localize responsibility for children, concentrating family law making at the state and local level. It tends to privatize the raising of children through policies that concentrate responsibility in the nuclear family and deemphasize the roles of wider communities (as Alice Hearst shows in Chapter 14). The United States is a nation of isolationists who lavish resources on their children while disclaiming responsibility for other people's children. The U.S.

system of law, except in criminal cases, tends to treat children as objects of law making rather than as participants, speaking of children's "interests" rather than their "rights." In the legal system, children, again with the exception of child criminals, have figured primarily as passive observers in the tussle between parents and the state (or between parent and parent) over who will have the power to articulate and defend the child's "interests."

Although children in the United States lack positive rights to social support, they do have various entitlements under a range of local, state, and federal laws that provide food, shelter, medical care, education, and protection. A child's parents and child advocates can assert the child's constitutional rights to fairness and equality in the distribution of benefits created by these government programs. But the entitlements themselves are not guaranteed by any system of positive constitutional rights, and they can be taken away as the political mood of the country changes.

Youths in the United States also enjoy a fairly highly developed scheme of negative rights and certain positive procedural rights that derive from these negative rights, such as the right to counsel in a juvenile proceeding, modified rights of speech and religion, the right to a disciplinary hearing at school. But the rules developed for measuring and implementing children's rights often seem to fit children poorly. Children's rights hang loosely on their small shoulders when they are treated like autonomous adults or pinch paternalistically when mature children attempt to flex their muscles in defiance of unwanted adult control. Although the Supreme Court has opened the door to recognition of the constitutional underpinnings of rights for children, it has remained highly deferential to state authorities. It has stopped far short of giving children the right to full-blown autonomy and has consistently failed to provide children with an effective right to protection from harm.[5]

Needs-Based Rights and Dignity-Based Rights

The ad hoc approach described above has failed children, their parents, and society. It does not provide the protection and nurturing children need when they are small, nor does it honor their emerging autonomy as they mature. A scheme of rights designed for adults must be carefully tailored to fit the needs of children and youth. It is time to redesign rights for children in a way that integrates and honors both their essential dependence and their capacity for autonomy. I have proposed that we reframe our thinking to recognize two new categories of rights especially for children—needs-based rights and dignity-based rights (Woodhouse 1994, 2001).

Children's needs-based rights would include the positive rights to nurture, education, food, medical care, shelter, and other goods without which children cannot survive let alone develop into autonomous adults and productive citizens. Children's needs-based rights would also reflect their need to grow and to test the wings of their increasing autonomy.

The notion of children's dignity-based rights acts as a necessary complement to the notion of needs-based rights because it acknowledges that children are individual persons with the same claim to dignity as autonomous adults. As infants, they rely on others to articulate and protect their rights. As they mature, they gain the capacity necessary to act autonomously. This is not a novel concept. A patient in a hospital has what we usually think of as a negative right to refuse a medical procedure. Should that patient fall into a coma and be unable to object or consent to medical procedures, she does not lose her right to protection from state intrusion. Instead, her rights are exercised on her behalf by a family member or a court-appointed guardian. As the patient regains consciousness, her family members and doctors involve her as much as possible in decision making until she regains full capacity.

Similarly, children's ability to reason and understand evolves over time, but their dignity-based rights are fully present at birth. Dignity-based rights remind us that children, despite their lack of capacity, do have rights based on their present humanity as well as on their potential for autonomy. The law must reflect children's dependence but also their emerging capacity for participation and, ultimately, control. Thinking realistically about children's rights involves integrating children's needs with their capacities and acknowledging that dependence and autonomy are two sides of the same coin. A scheme of rights that focuses exclusively on one or the other will be incomplete, whether applied to adults or to children.

Sometimes children's rights will come into conflict with the rights of parents and the authority of government. No right is absolute, and children's rights must be weighed in the balance with other competing claims of rights and authority. However, because children are persons not things, the power adults exercise over children—as parents, as legislators, and as judges—must be justified as furthering children's interests and meeting their special needs.

This scheme for analyzing family relationships and for thinking about children's relationships with adult authority shifts the focus from adult rights to adult responsibilities. Scholars have adopted the metaphor of trusteeship or guardianship to describe this relationship. Society gives parents the fiduciary powers of a guardian or a trustee, with special authority to make decisions about the needs and interests of the beneficiary, their child. We entrust parents with the guidance and support of children in their journey to autonomous adulthood (Scott and Scott 1995; Woodhouse 1995). In Chapter 14 Hearst offers a less child-centered interpretation of the motives of society in granting trusteeship to parents. She sees the federal authority transferring the financial responsibility for protecting children's rights to the family with the expectation that families will act to create good citizens—that is, those who act consistently within the laws and values of the nation.

Representatives of the state—judges, teachers, police—also exercise sweeping authority over children. Sometimes the state and parent are allied (as when a police officer returns a runaway child to her parents' home). Sometimes the state supersedes parental authority (as when a police officer removes an abused or neglected child from his parents' home). The state often acts in a way that is openly "paternalistic"—for example, regulations limiting access to books, films, alcohol, or cigarettes, which would be highly inappropriate in the state's relationship with adult citizens, are routinely applied to minors. However, the model for state intervention in children's lives should not be one of absolute power justified by children's lack of power. In a nutshell, children's rights include not only the right to have their essential needs met but also the right to have their dignity respected by the community as well as by their families.

Five Unifying Human Rights Principles

I have identified five unifying principles that should guide the development of rights for children as they have guided the development of human rights generally (Woodhouse 2001). Sometimes these values or principles collide with each other, but, rather than being an obstructive force, the friction created can be an energizing and motivating force for building a balanced system of rights. These principles are equality, individualism, empowerment, protection, and privacy. Each is a basic value that ordinary people as well as judges would agree ought to be reflected in any scheme of human rights. These principles have developed in an adult-centric world. The task of advocates for children is to reexamine them through a child-centered lens that dissolves the paradox of children's rights by seeing clearly both children's dependence and their capacities—honoring both their needs-based rights and their dignity-based rights. The challenge will be to integrate these principles into a coherent scheme as we reconceptualize them to fit children's unique situation.

THE EQUALITY PRINCIPLE: THE RIGHT TO EQUAL OPPORTUNITY

At the core of the equality principle is the conviction that people should not be treated differently. Real differences may call for differential treatment. But discrimination based on factors such as race, gender, and illegitimacy reflects socially imposed inequalities that have no factual support.[6] The Constitution, as interpreted by the current Supreme Court, virtually prohibits classifications of persons according to their race or color and permits little latitude for classifications based on illegitimacy or supposed differences between the sexes. But

children, everyone acknowledges, are different, and age does bear some bona
fide relationship to the capacity for equality or right to equal treatment. Few
would argue against the proposition that persons under, say, five years of age, as
a class, are incapable of taking care of themselves. If we abandoned children to
absolutely equal rights, they would have to fend for themselves, unprotected by
special rights to care and supervision. The tension between children's claims to
"equal justice under law" and the fact of children's dependence calls for a more
nuanced concept of equality. This motto, "equal justice under law," carved in
the pediment of the Supreme Court building in Washington, D.C., does not call
for equal treatment, but it does call for equal justice.

Equality for children must mean both more and less than the formal equality provided by rules that treat all persons the same. One facet that makes up a
more complex idea of equality is the notion of equality of opportunity. This principle seems especially important for children, who inherit as their unequal legacy
the inequalities that shaped their parents' lives. We must develop an equality
norm that "promotes the equal regard in which we need to hold every child and
the energy we ought to invest in each child's future productive worth" (Cohen
1995, 2272). Applying the twin measures of children's needs and their capacity
for autonomy to the notion of equality would suggest an emphasis on creating
an environment for the individual child, and for children as a class, that supports their capacity for growth. Equality for children in society, as in family life,
begins with meeting their basic needs and continues by recognizing and supporting their individual capacities.

THE INDIVIDUALISM PRINCIPLE: THE RIGHT TO BE TREATED
AS A PERSON, NOT AN OBJECT

This principle requires government to treat all persons as individuals with claims
to human dignity and not as objects or mere means to some governmental end.
This principle has been systemically violated when it comes to children. In fact,
our family policy has historically been built on the backs of children—for centuries the stigma of bastardy, which punished children for the sins of their parents, was used to promote marriage and chastity. We now reject, as a matter of
constitutional law, the idea that punishment for an adult's violation of sexual
norms can be visited on an innocent child.

The individualism principle is at the heart of the modern standard for deciding child-custody disputes. Traditionally, fathers had an absolute right to custody in all but the most outrageous cases. In the mid-nineteenth century, mothers
began to prevail in cases involving young children by arguing that children
needed their mother's tender care. This "tender-years" doctrine, with its focus
on children's needs, evolved into the gender-neutral "best-interest" standard that
we use today. Although the standard has been criticized as too open-ended, few

now question the underlying assumption that decisions about children ought to take into account the well-being of the individual child whose case is under adjudication (Grossberg 1996; Peters 1996). The child's best interest remains the ultimate legal standard governing most children's cases, and so it is incumbent on lawyers to develop a sophisticated and nuanced understanding of how to evaluate children's interests in a variety of contexts (Peters 2001).

Examining the individualism principle through the lens of children's needs-based rights and dignity-based rights suggests that children's individuality must be honored, separate and apart from their capacity for autonomy. Treating children with the dignity owed to individual persons requires an individualized assessment of the child's specific needs. It also calls on us to approach the issues from the child's perspective even if the child is too young to express that perspective in words and to evaluate the child's best interest not by imposing generic external norms but as illuminated by this specific child's reality (Garbarino, Stott, and the Faculty of the Erikson Institute 1989). In the abstract, it may be in children's best interest to be raised in affluent homes by educated parents. But children who are separated from the less-than-perfect adults to whom they are bonded experience a subjective suffering that belies this abstract generalization (Scarnecchia 1995).

THE EMPOWERMENT PRINCIPLE: THE RIGHT TO A VOICE
AND, SOMETIMES, A CHOICE

Most of us would agree that members of a society have a basic right to participate in collective decision making and to have a voice in critical decisions affecting their own lives. The framers of the Constitution certainly embraced this concept, but they did not apply it to women, people of color, or minors. Women and slaves, so the argument went, needed no rights of their own because they were under the benevolent protection of the head of household. Although we now flatly reject such paternalism in the context of gender and race, it still makes sense when thinking about children. From a child's perspective, the world is a place populated by large strangers whose ways are both frightening and mystifying. Empowering parents as their children's protectors is obviously the most effective way to empower children. In relations with the state and its agents, whom children encounter in schools, hospitals, and in the justice and social welfare systems, parents are usually the best advocates for their children's rights. The law has empowered children, in relations with the state, by conferring special authority on parents to act and speak on their behalf and to make decisions about their welfare that children lack the knowledge and maturity to make.

When a fundamental right is at stake, however, the Constitution sometimes honors the minor's right to a choice. The Supreme Court has held that mature minors have the same constitutional rights to make decisions about reproduction and abortion as adults. But these cases are the exceptions and not the rule. State laws and judges routinely deny children standing in custody, juvenile-detention, foster-care, and adoption cases, despite the magnitude of the interests at stake (Ross 1996). Is it unjust to deny a voice to individual children based solely on their chronological age rather than on their developmental stage or the nature of the interests at stake? Sometimes, for the sake of efficiency and predictability, even a just system of laws will classify persons by generalizations such as date of birth (minimum ages for driving, for leaving school, or for collecting Social Security). But a just system should not deprive individual citizens of a voice in decisions that affect them based on group stereotypes of inferiority or disability, especially when a court is already engaged in a judicial proceeding calling for individualized adjudication of other issues. We may decide, for example, that efficiency requires an age-based rule to determine eligibility for a driver's license. But should we use chronological age to deprive a child of a voice in court when that child is developmentally capable of contributing to the fact-finding process—especially if the child's prospects or relationships may be forever stunted by choices involving health care, education, or the creation or severing of legal relationships?

THE PROTECTION PRINCIPLE: THE RIGHT OF THE WEAK
TO BE PROTECTED FROM THE STRONG

The protection principle is perhaps the most fundamental of all human rights principles—not only for children but for all of us. The very essence of law and order is the right of the weak to be protected from the strong. Traditionally, one person's liberty stopped at the point where his fist connected with another person's nose—unless the actor was a husband or a father and the body was that of his wife or child. Husbands and parents enjoyed a "privilege" allowing them to beat their wives and children into submission. In the previous century, we saw the extension of the protection principle to the family. We now believe that family members should be protected by the state from harms inflicted not only by strangers but also by other family members. Child-protective laws have been enacted requiring reporting and intervention to prevent violence toward children. Intrafamily crimes of violence are grounds for arrest and incarceration, and domestic violence, whether against spouses, elders, or children, is no longer considered a private matter. Sex crimes and crimes of violence against children that were once closely guarded family secrets are now prosecuted, thus bringing children into court as victims and witnesses (Petit and Curtis 1997). Applying the protection principle to children in light of their needs and their emerging capacities means that force may be used only as necessary to protect them from harm. We should not accept claims by religious fundamentalists that parents have a protected "right" to whip their children into submission (Woodhouse 1996).

THE PRIVACY PRINCIPLE: THE RIGHT TO PROTECTION
OF INTIMATE RELATIONSHIPS

Finally, the privacy principle protects an individual's most intimate activities from state regulation and intrusion. The Supreme Court, in its abortion and procreation cases, describes privacy rights primarily as an individual's right to be left alone to make one's own choices. But other precedents treat privacy as a value that may be shared, mutual, or collective. A zone of privacy is essential to the functioning of family systems, not just to the rights of individual family members. Once again, children present special challenges that force us to articulate the privacy principle in more nuanced ways. Privacy, understood as a right to be left alone, is of little value to young children who depend on interaction for their very survival. Left entirely alone, an infant will perish.

This enigma dissolves when we redraw the circle of privacy not around the child's self but around the child's intimate relationships. Nurturing relationships provide the environments within which bonded adults make choices (a source of empowerment) for children and ultimately teach children how to make choices for themselves. Placing a high value on children's right to family privacy suggests a preference for assigning the power to make choices for children to adults who are attached to them by bonds of intimacy. We trust families to make the most painful and conflicted of intimate decisions precisely because they are not neutral. Like the preference for family systems of decision making at the end of life, trusting families with decisions at the beginning of life maintains that crucial buffer zone between the individual and the cold and impersonal state. Family privacy, however, must be balanced against other core values. Privacy holds serious risks for less powerful members of the family system—children, elders, and women—even as it protects important values for individuals and society.

Integrating Rights for Children into Human Rights

Clearly, there are inherent tensions between principles of protection and privacy, equality and dignity. When does the protection principle favoring an obligation on the part of the state to intervene on behalf of at-risk children outweigh the privacy principle, which favors wide latitude in intimate decision making and child rearing? When does the equality principle behind equal treatment of men and women in custody disputes collide with the child's claim, based on dignity, to be treated like an individual and not parceled out fifty-fifty between competing claimants? Children are inevitably caught in the middle, and our usual fallbacks, personal choice and individual autonomy, which are the default settings for adult rights, provide no easy escape from the task of articulating a scheme of children's rights that reflects their dependence as well as their capacity. One of the critical challenges for U.S. law and policy in this century will be articulating a more delicate balance between the principles of equality, protection, privacy, empowerment, and dignity—one that avoids giving any one value primacy over all the others, acknowledges the importance of each to the other, and examines the special interplay of these values in the context of children's rights.

Fortunately, a growing body of international law points the way to integrating children's rights into the larger scheme of human rights. The most rapidly and universally accepted document in human rights history is the 1989 United Nations Convention on the Rights of the Child, popularly known as the Children's Rights Convention, or CRC. I have drawn heavily on its principles in my theory of children's rights. Unfortunately, few Americans appreciate the importance of the CRC. Although the CRC has been ratified by every other nation in the world community, as of this writing, like the Convention on the Rights of Women, the CRC still awaits action by Congress (*Report of the 3rd Committee* 1989). The United States is generally reluctant to be bound by international law and is especially skeptical of the CRC. Conservative Americans appear to distrust the very notion of rights for children as an assault on the fundamental rights of parents, and they fear that ratification of the CRC will lead to outside interference in both the family and national policy (Woodhouse 2001).

The CRC draws on a wide spectrum of international human rights traditions to focus on the special situation of children. It reflects the importance of what I call children's needs-based rights as well as their dignity-based rights. It does not impose a specific system of laws on the countries that sign it. Rather, it establishes basic norms of justice to guide those engaged in developing laws and social policies. By defining an underlying theory of adult power over children and of limitations on that power, it creates benchmarks by which adults, who act on the behalf of children, can assess the rightness of their behavior. The CRC combines recognition of children's essential dependence and recognition of their capacity for autonomy; it treats children as interdependent members of families and communities and also as individuals with unique personalities. Children are seen as persons with emerging moral and social lives that parents and government are explicitly charged with respecting.

Under the CRC, children have the capacity for growth to autonomy and deserve the right to be treated in a manner consistent with that capacity. The CRC identifies the right of children who are capable of forming their own views to express their views in matters affecting them, either directly or through a representative. Although children have rights to freedom of thought and religion, the parents (not the state) have the duty to guide their children's development in these spheres in a manner consistent with the child's evolving capacity. Entitlement to support and guidance from both parents, who will make the child's interest "their basic concern," is articulated as a child's right, not as the parent's right. Children also have the right to know and to be cared for by their parents and not to be separated from them except in the child's best interest. Children share in the same basic human rights as their elders, including rights against racial, religious, and gender discrimination and against arbitrary state intrusion in the form of attacks on their privacy, family, home, ethnicity, or religion. The CRC also recognizes certain rights that are specially important to children, such as the right to recreation, to protection from physical abuse and sexual or economic exploitation, to care within a family, and to a family identity. Finally, the CRC makes explicit the obligation of states to meet the basic economic needs of the young. It includes the right to an adequate standard of living, to education, to health care, and to social insurance. Government entities must seek to meet these economic obligations "to the maximum extent of their available resources."

The success of the CRC proves that basic concepts of human rights can be tailored to fit the special needs of children. U.S. constitutional law, which once played a leading role in shaping concepts of rights in emerging democracies, is beginning to decline in influence because we have refused to join in the process of universalizing human rights. Whether we like it or not the notion that children have rights, as articulated in the CRC, is rapidly becoming the new world standard. As South Africans learned, it is impossible to remain the lone dissenter in the human rights community. The laws of the United States will have to evolve to meet this new standard if we are to maintain our standing in the world community. It is no longer possible to ignore children's rights. Although these rights may be tailored to fit children's special needs and be held in trust until they are capable of exercising them, children's rights must be far more than mere interests, and these rights are no less than children, as members of the human community, deserve.

Notes

1. In addition to Federle, see Fitzgerald 1994; Freeman and Veerman 1992; Minow 1986; Roberts 1996; Teitelbaum 1980; Woodhouse 1994, 2001.
2. *Jackson v. City of Joliet*, 715 F.2d 1200, 1204 (7th Cir. 1983).
3. *Marbury v. Madison*, 5 U.S. 137, 177 (1803).
4. See, for example, *In re Gault*, 387 U.S. 1 (1967); *Levy v. Louisiana*, 391 U.S. 68 (1968); *Tinker v. Des Moines Independent County School. District*, 393 U.S. 503 (1969); *Wisconsin v. Yoder*, 406 U.S. 205 (1972); *Goss v. Lopez*, 419 U.S. 565 (1975); *Planned Parenthood of Central Missouri v. Danforth*, 428 U.S. 52 (1976); *Ingraham v. Wright*, 430 U.S. 651 (1977); *Moore v. City of East Cleveland*, 431 U.S. 494 (1977); *Smith v. Organization of Foster Families*, 431 U.S. 816 (1977); *Parham v. J.R.*, 442 U.S. 584 (1979); *Santosky v. Kramer*, 455 U.S. 745 (1982).
5. *Deshaney v. Winnebago County Department of Social Services*, 109 Sup. Ct. 998 (1989).
6. *United States v. Virginia*, 518 U.S. 515 (1996).

References

Berlin, I. 1958. *Two Concepts of Liberty, Inaugural Lecture as Chichele Professor of Social and Political Theory before the University of Oxford.* Oxford: Clarendon Press.

Cohen, J. M. 1995. "Competitive and Cooperative Dependencies: The Case for Children." *Virginia Law Review* 81:2217–2274.

Dolgin, J. L. 1997. "Transforming Childhood: Apprenticeship in American Law." *New England Law Review* 31:1113–1191.

Federle, K. H. 1995. "Looking Ahead: An Empowerment Perspective on the Rights of Children." *Temple Law Review* 68:1585–1605.

Fitzgerald, W. A. 1994. "Maturity, Difference, and Mystery: Children's Perspectives and the Law." *Arizona Law Review* 36:11–74.

Freeman, M., and P. Veerman, eds. 1992. *The Ideologies of Children's Rights.* Dordrecht: Martinus Nijhoff.

Garbarino, J., F. M. Stott, and the Faculty of the Erikson Institute. 1989. *What Children Can Tell Us: Eliciting, Interpreting, and Evaluating Information from Children.* San Francisco: Jossey-Bass.

Green, B. A., and B. Dohrn. 1966. "Forward: Children and Ethical Practice of Law." *Fordham Law Review* 64:1281–1298.

Grossberg, M. 1985. *Governing the Hearth: Law and Family in Nineteenth-Century America.* Chapel Hill: University of North Carolina Press.

Grossberg, M. 1996. *A Judgment for Solomon: The d'Hauteville Case and Legal Experience in Antebellum America.* Cambridge: Cambridge University Press.

Indivisibility and Interdependence of Economic, Social, Cultural, Civil and Political Rights. 1989. G.A. Res. 44/130, U.N. GAOR, 44th Sess., Supp. no. 49, at 209, U.N. Doc. A/Res/44/130 (adopted Dec. 15).

Kandel, R. F. 1994. "Just Ask the Kid! Towards a Rule of Children's Choice in Custody Determinations." *University of Miami Law Review* 49:299–376.

Margulies, P. 1996. "The Lawyer as Caregiver: Child Clients' Competence in Context." *Fordham Law Review* 64:1473–1504.

Mason, M. A. 1994. *From Father's Property to Children's Rights: A History of Child Custody in the United States.* Cambridge: Cambridge University Press.

Melton, G. B., ed. 1987. *Reforming the Law: The Impact of Child Development Research.* New York: Guilford Press.

Mezey, S. G. 1996. *Children in Court: Public Policymaking and Federal Court Decisions.* Albany: State University of New York Press.

Minow, M. 1986. "Rights for the Next Generation: A Feminist Approach to Children's Rights." *Harvard Women's Law Journal* 9:1–24.

Peters, J. K. 1996. "The Roles and Content of Best Interests in Client-Directed Lawyering for Children in Child Protective Proceedings." *Fordham Law Review* 64:1505–1570.

Peters, J. K. 2001. *Representing Children in Child Protective Proceedings: Ethical and Practical Dimensions.* Newark, N.J.: Lexis Law Publishing.

Petit, M. R., and P. A. Curtis. 1997. *Child Abuse and Neglect: A Look at the States–1999 Stat Book.* Washington, D.C.: Child Welfare League of America.

Report of the 3rd Committee. 1989. U.N. Convention on the Rights of the Child, G.A. Res. 44/25, U.N. GAOR, 44th Sess., Supp. no. 49, U.N. Doc. A/44/736.

Roberts, M. A. 1996. "Parent and Child Conflict: Between Liberty and Responsibility." *North Dakota Journal of Legal Ethics and Public Policy* 10:485.

Ross, C. J. 1996. "From Vulnerability to Voice: Appointing Counsel for Children in Civil Litigation." *Fordham Law Review* 64:1571–1620.

Scarnecchia, S. 1995. "A Child's Right to Protection from Transfer Trauma in a Contested Adoption Case." *Duke Journal of Gender Law and Policy* 2:41–61.

Scott, E. S. and R. E. Scott. 1995. "Parents as Fiduciaries." *Virginia Law Review* 81:2401–2475.

Stark, B. 1992. "Economic Rights in the United States and International Human Rights Law: Toward an 'Entirely New Strategy.'" *Hasting Law Journal* 44:79–130.

Teitelbaum, L. E. 1980. "Foreword: The Meaning of Rights of Children." *New Mexico Law Review* 10:235–253.

Waldron, J., ed. 1984. Introduction to *Theories of Rights*. Oxford: Oxford University Press.

Woodhouse, B. B. 1993. "Hatching the Egg: A Child-Centered Perspective on Parents' Rights." *Cardozo Law Review* 14:1747–1865.

Woodhouse, B. B. 1994. "Out of Children's Needs, Children's Rights: The Child's Voice in Defining the Family." *Brigham Young University Journal of Public Law* 8: 321–341.

Woodhouse, B. B. 1995. "Of Babies, Bonding, and Burning Buildings: Discerning Parenthood in Irrational Action." *Virginia Law Review* 81: 2493–2521.

Woodhouse, B. B. 1996. "A Public Role in the Private Family: The Parental Rights and Responsibilities Act and the Politics of Child Protection and Education." *Ohio State Law Journal.* 57:393–423.

Woodhouse, B. B. 2001. "Children's Rights." In *Handbook on Youth and Justice*, edited by S. O. White. New York: Plenum.

Chapter 14

ALICE HEARST

Recognizing the Roots

Children's Identity Rights

As "IDENTITY" HAS EMERGED as a significant category of meaning in modern life, the idea has also emerged that it should be protected by a variety of legally articulated "identity rights." Both groups and individuals have mobilized to assert rights to recognition of and protection for identity. Indeed, a significant number of international human rights documents now specifically endorse a variety of as yet undefined identity rights, urging signatory states to take steps to protect different facets of personal, national, and cultural or communal identity. This drive to establish identity rights as a distinct legal and political category has emerged hand-in-hand with the recognition of identity itself as fluid and fragmentary. In a world of increasingly porous social, political, and cultural boundaries, questions of identity have tremendous political importance. Yet working out the concept of identity is difficult; as Jack Meacham notes in Chapter 4, the ways in which identity can be discovered are multiple.

At one level, the law has always been intimately concerned with questions of identity: the recognition conferred or withheld by the law has a significant impact on how individuals are recognized in the social world. By categorizing human actions, laws create and re-create identities at both a local and a global level, differentiating between tortfeasors and victims, property owners and trespassers, citizens and aliens. In the United States, in fact, the protection of individual identity has a long legal history that stretches from common-law protection of personal reputation to contemporary articulations of autonomy interests in the form of constitutionally guaranteed privacy rights.

Through legal categories that define the relations among individuals, families, communities, and nations, the boundaries of belonging itself are delineated.

Typically, the relationships defined by those categories reinforce generally shared normative values in local and national communities, as in the general presumption in the United States that biological parents should be the primary caretakers for their children and thus should provide stability in a social order. Given the complex social relations that mark modern life, however, the values reflected in law may be contradictory; the law may create categories and assign roles that lead to intractable conflict or incompatible identities.

Conceptualizing Children's Identity Rights

Although identity rights per se have not been substantively articulated for children in the United States, debates over the recognition of such rights loom on the horizon. Article 8 of the United Nations Convention on the Rights of the Child, for example, expressly notes that every child has a right to "preserve his or her identity." One commentator has pointed out that the provision might be interpreted to refer to any of at least four forms of identity: familial, communal, biological, or political (Stewart 1992). Although the United States has not yet signed the Convention and has not been particularly responsive to pressure from the international human rights community to recognize domestically all the rights articulated in international documents, such international rights discourses could affect the recognition and development of a variety of identity rights for children in the United States in the future. And conceptualizing identity rights for children requires envisioning children not simply as passive objects of legal categorization but as individuals taking an active role in shaping their identities.

Children are defined by legal categories just as fully as adults are, and children may indeed be more susceptible than adults to such assignments on a day-to-day basis. By recognizing some relationships and not others—privileging one caregiver over another, for example—the law often defines the context within which a child develops his or her identity. Laws bind the child into the intimate context of the family and caregivers as well as into a multitude of outside relationships in the community and nation. How, then, does the law imagine children's identities, and how do such imagined identities overlap and interact? Answering this question requires understanding both the levels at which the law operates to stabilize or destabilize children's identities as well as how the law is invoked to mediate among those different levels of belonging.

Many of the knottiest problems in family law over the last several decades have involved children's identities at the most local level, although they have not been labeled as identity-rights issues,. Historically in the United States, the law has mapped children into relationships of dependence and caregiving with a specific preference for those family forms that presumptively can privatize the costs of dependence. Since the early 1970s, however, those traditional presumptions have been tested. The challenges have ranged broadly, from the debate over opening adoption records to the demand for recognizing adoptions by gay or lesbian partners, and from abolishing bastardy as a legal category to determining the status of surrogates unrelated genetically to the fetuses they bear. In all these areas and more, the law of domestic relations has been reconceptualizing identity issues at the most basic levels of belonging. In the context of custody decisions upon divorce, for example, as Jan Pryor and Robert Emery point out in Chapter 10, the traditional assumption that the care of young children should be accorded to the mother has implied that fathers need play little role in developing a young child's identity. In the first part of this chapter I briefly recast those developments as problems of identity to provide an understanding of how the law functions to determine ties of intimate belonging.

Moving away from the law's role in fixing relationships at the microcosmic level, I then look at how family law has created national identities. Legal rules governing the family in the United States traditionally have been as much concerned with preparing children for eventual citizenship as with attaching them to intimate caregivers and thus have been undergirded by an imperative to ensure that children are appropriately socialized for life in a liberal, democratic republic. As might be expected, this imperative has sometimes pushed the state to intervene in family life in ways that conflict with the assumption that the intimate relationship between children and their caregivers should be immune from regulation unless the child is being harmed. The second part of this chapter discusses some of the ways in which family laws have been imbued with the politics of nation building and reflects on how such impulses resound with concerns about identity.

Finally, the chapter focuses on the emergence of claims to protection of cultural or communal identity. It argues that the recognition of such rights could have a significant effect both on how the law envisions the communal webs in which children are embedded and on how children are imagined as agents in creating their own identities. These claims, currently emerging at the international level of human rights discourse, have been articulated in two forms, as both an individual right and as a right asserted by a group to strengthen the child's ties to a particular cultural community. These are difficult rights to conceptualize; they raise myriad questions about how to define culture, how to identify cultural groups, and how to articulate the scope of identity rights in general. This class of rights has yet to be articulated in concrete contexts, but a number of interesting possibilities flow from contemplating their recognition. On the positive side, recognizing such rights could enhance a child's ability to connect to a community and to shape his or her identity; alternately, such rights could simply subject a child to conflict by imposing yet another control in addition to that already exercised by parents and the state.

Recognizing identity rights for children is certainly worth extended consideration. The chapters in this book all call for recognizing children as active participants in constructing their worlds. This chapter concludes that recognizing some form of identity rights for children, although not unproblematic, could fundamentally change the way children are imagined in the law because such rights provide a mechanism for acknowledging children as at least partial authors of their own lives.[1]

Before examining specific forms of identity rights for children, however, we need to note how such rights would mesh with traditional concepts of the rights of children. At both a local and a global level, legal regimes affecting children are infused with an obligation to protect the child's best interests. Indeed, Article 3 of the Convention on the Rights of the Child states, among other things, that "the best interest of the child shall be a primary consideration" in all actions taken on behalf of children by any public entity. Given that the best-interest standard guides all actions relating to children, it might be argued that there is no need to introduce a new category of rights for children.

But it is precisely in the area of identity that the best-interest standard falls short. When courts or legislatures or public and private social welfare institutions make decisions about what the child's best interests are, they act within particular social and cultural boundaries. As discussed in greater detail below, decisions about where to place children or whom to privilege as a caretaker will, in part, fix the child's identity. The question of identity often needs to precede a best-interest determination. A child's best interest can vary considerably depending on the social or cultural group making the decision. To allow an administrative, judicial, or legislative body to move directly to a best-interest determination without first looking at the issue of identity can elide the foundational determination of who exactly will articulate the child's best interests. For this reason, it may be important to look at identity issues prior to moving to a best-interest analysis.

Identity Rights and Day-to-Day Belonging

How the law creates, confirms, and categorizes identity presents a set of problems that resound uniquely in children's lives because their identities develop largely within contexts prescribed by law. As Woodhouse has argued, "Law is both an active agent in prescribing, proscribing and attributing identity, and a public medium for choosing and enacting it" (1995, 111). Although Woodhouse reminds us that children are certainly not passive actors in the complicated process of identity formation, their options for moving among a variety of relationships—

and in and out of legal categories—are limited. Unlike adults, children have virtually no ability to leave the relationships of dependence in which they are fixed by law.

Laws defining a child's relationships of dependence take effect immediately at birth and continue to place the child in relation to various adults throughout the child's dependence; these laws outline custody rules and assign responsibility in circumstances ranging from parental remarriage to emancipation. In fact, from conception, legal assumptions operate to identify a child's parents and thereby assign responsibility for the child's welfare: the woman carrying a fetus is assumed to be the child's mother, while the husband of a woman bearing a child is assumed to be the child's father.

But determining parenthood has become a complicated business. First, new reproductive technologies have created a bewildering number of people with various degrees of biological connection to a child: a woman may have a gestational but not a genetic link to a child or a genetic but not a gestational link, for example, while a man may be an anonymous or nonanonymous sperm donor. Second, an increasing number of adults historically disabled by the law from asserting parental interests in children, such as gay and lesbian partners of biological or adoptive parents, are demanding legal recognition as parents. Third, courts and lawmakers have seen a host of other parties seeking rights to develop or maintain connections to children with whom they are or have been associated as grandparents, siblings, caregivers, stepparents, or in other ways. Finally, courts and legislatures have had to grapple with cases that attempt to disengage the relationship between child and adults, as in proceedings to terminate parental rights or to emancipate minors from relations of dependence.

Characterizing these claims as identity-rights issues is cumbersome because they typically arise in the context of determining who has a right or duty to care for a child rather than as an assertion of identity rights on behalf of the child. But they are fundamentally identity claims. Every claim to establish—or nullify—legal connections to a child involves wrapping the child within a specific set of intimate relationships that will profoundly affect the formation of the child's identity. When the law designates an adult or a set of adults as responsible for a child's welfare, it is instrumental in defining the environment with which the child will interact as he or she develops a sense of self and belonging.

In most cases in the United States, the legal regime regulating children's lives tracks the general societal norm that biological parents should care for their children and that parents should be left relatively free of direct state intervention in determining how to rear their children. The justifications for recognizing both parental rights and imposing duties of care range from arguments that biological parents should be responsible for the consequences of their presumptively voluntary actions in initiating the child's existence to arguments that the right to rear children is implicit in the recognition of adults as autonomous individuals entitled to make their own decisions about what constitutes a good life. These arguments are striking to the extent that they are typically framed wholly in terms of the rights and interests of adults, although the tacit assumption in each is that biological parents are likely to be the best guarantors of a child's well-being and healthy development.

Thus, the law is careful to delineate a private sphere within which the child's identity will be formed under the influence of caregivers presumptively tied to the child through natural bonds of love and affection. In repeated affirmations of parental rights to rear children as they see fit, for example, the Supreme Court has noted that parents and guardians have the liberty "to direct the upbringing and education of children under their control" and that "the custody, care, and nurture of the child reside first in the parents, whose primary function and freedom include preparation for obligations the state can neither supply nor hinder."[2]

In 1965, the Supreme Court's recognition of the right to privacy in marital relationships provided the impetus for a rapid expansion of rights relating to the family, autonomy, and intimacy.[3] In the next thirty-five years a number of constitutional pronouncements affected the rights and legal status of children and parents; these rulings ranged from acknowledging that unmarried fathers should be presumed to be fit caregivers to refusing to override a mother's decision to limit visitation with grandparents in the absence of a showing that the mother was unfit. In most of the cases the Supreme Court has considered since the early 1970s, it has underlined the primacy of biological bonds in determining who should have access to a child. Thus, in effect, laws governing a child's relationships will continue to privilege, for the most part, the child's biological ties, with the result that those connections will form the environment within which the child grows up.

In numerous instances, however, tracing biological bonds provides no satisfactory answer to who shall have the right to direct a child's upbringing. Identifying parenthood in cases involving new reproductive technologies has proved particularly difficult. In these cases, courts and legislatures have found that biological ties provide only an entry point for deciding who should be assigned legal rights and responsibilities for rearing a child. In *Johnson v. Calvert*, for example, the California Supreme Court declined to recognize a woman who had gestated a child as the mother because the woman was not genetically related to the child.[4] The majority of the court found that the law should respect the "intentional" parents who provided the genetic material with the aim of raising the child who resulted.

Cases such as *Johnson v. Calvert*, and the earlier case of Baby M., which first tested the legality of surrogacy agreements, put a child's identity squarely in question, as the parties to those cases argue over who the child's "real" parents are.[5] The legal assignment of parenthood is often the single most important factor in determining how a child's identity develops. In cases where the biological connection is not determinative in itself, statutes typically direct courts to consider the best interests of the child in determining where a child should be placed; these cases range from adoption in all its forms to child-custody determinations to requests for visitation rights by third parties. But few of these cases give any real consideration to what a right to identity might look like in such a context, especially when the child might assert interests in maintaining ties to persons not ordinarily recognized by law. In both constitutional and statutory law, courts and legislatures have exhibited a marked reluctance to protect the multiple affective ties a child might develop.[6]

Expanding the law governing these primary connections to recognize the independent right of a child to identity might allow fuller consideration of the child's interests in making and maintaining intimate connections. An identity right could be invoked to reflect children's interests in establishing and maintaining bonds of affection with a variety of actors; such a right could be framed as a cognizable interest in securing affective bonds because they are essential to the formation of a stable self. It could alter the way in which various factors are weighted in determining who should care for a child. Thus, children in long-term foster care might have, at the least, a hearing before they are moved from that home.[7] Adopted children who have formed bonds with adoptive parents might not be wholly removed from their custody should the legality of the adoption prove flawed.[8] A child who has developed a familial relationship with a man she believes to be her father might be able to assert a right to maintain that relationship independent of the alleged father's rights.[9] Likewise, a child who has lived with her mother's same-sex partner could be enabled to continue contact after the breakup of the adults' relationship.[10]

On some fronts, the conceptualization of children's interests in maintaining nontraditional ties has shifted. Courts and legislatures are increasingly willing to recognize a multiplicity of relationships between children and care providers. Trends toward open adoption, for example, reflect a responsiveness to the idea that a child may be embedded in more than one set of family relationships. So also do judicial and statutory pronouncements recognizing lesbian and gay partners as "second parents" in a growing minority of jurisdictions.[11] But unless and until such rights to connect with intimate caregivers are recognized as residing in the child, these claims will continue to be evaluated primarily on the basis of the rights of interested adults, and the courts are unlikely to be fully sensitive to the independent needs of the child or to the role that the child plays in forming such relationships.

As well as attaching children to caretakers, the law may be used to detach children from relationships, as in proceedings to terminate parental rights because of abuse or neglect. Such proceedings often occasion additional trauma for children already uniquely vulnerable, as they may result in a complete legal severance of the parent/child bond. Although statutes typically require state social service agencies to make reasonable efforts to rehabilitate family relationships before initiating such proceedings, the ultimate legal response is typically rigid; it generates an either-or situation in which the child remains attached to the parent/guardian or responsibility is transferred to the state or caregivers selected by the state. This approach is a disservice to children who may continue to feel bonds of connection to intimate caregivers, even when their care has been inadequate or abusive.[12] The legal regime is framed to perceive only two options—terminating or not terminating parental rights. Although the child's identity is shifted legally, there may be no corresponding shift in the way the child understands his or her relationships of belonging. Under such circumstances, the failure to recognize a more flexible continuum of rights of connection can result in a child's permanent alienation from an intimate relationship that could have had a significant effect on the child's development. Recognizing an identity right on the part of the child might provide an avenue for allowing some form of continued contact between a child and a person perceived by the child as important.

The law may improvidently alter children's identities in another circumstance. All states in the United States make emancipation a possibility for certain classes of minors. Such statutes are, on their face, designed to accommodate the needs of mature minors who for a variety of reasons may need to exercise greater legal authority over their own lives. Because most state statutes require that a petition for emancipation be initiated by the minor, courts enforcing such statutes often assume that the emancipation proceeding reflects the child's wishes; the majority of such petitions are passed through courts with few, if any, objections being raised. However, one research project suggests that minors often find themselves pressured to file such petitions by adults—stepparents or parents who for their own reasons want to disengage the child or disavow responsibility for the child's actions (Sanger and Willemsen 1992). In such circumstances, recognizing a right to identity might provide a needed degree of protection for children whose legal ties to significant adults might otherwise be abruptly dismantled.

Identity Rights and Citizenship

The "local laws of belonging" contained in statutory and constitutional principles that articulate a child's relationship to a particular set of caregivers are typically underpinned by larger concerns about where and how the child is likely to fit into society as that child matures into an adult. In other words, the law of family relations is often as much about nation building as it is about attaching the child to a particular set of caregivers. Thus, while the legal regime affecting the child is concerned with ensuring that the majority of the costs of dependence are borne privately, it is also driven by the concern that the child be adequately socialized to become a responsible member of a particular national community. The imperatives to privatize dependence on the one hand and to ensure adequate socialization on the other may, and often do, conflict. The tensions generated in that conflict raise fascinating problems in regard to the appropriate scope and limits of state intervention in the life of the family. For purposes here, however, the important issue is how the law creates a layered identity for the child.

The body of U.S. family law that took shape from the end of the nineteenth century through the first half of the twentieth century was organized around a remarkably consistent understanding of the national identity, despite the fact that the legal regimes were embodied in distinct state codes. The laws governing the family in various states privileged a specific family form as ordained by nature and therefore truly "American": the partners were heterosexual, married, and financially self-sufficient, and they shared racial or ethnic characteristics. Families that did not fit that mold were often viewed as unnatural and subject to greater surveillance and regulation, for such families could not be relied on to produce fit citizens (Lindsay 1998). In one of its earliest pronouncements on the family, in *Reynolds v. United States* (1878), the Supreme Court affirmed the criminal conviction of a Mormon polygamist, denouncing plural marriage as "abhorred" by civilized peoples, being "almost exclusively a feature of the life of Asiatic and African people," and "odious among the Northern and Western Nations of Europe."[13] This expression of a "deep [public] interest in a particular form of marriage as 'the foundation of the family and of society, without which there would be neither civilization nor progress,'"[14] was a permanent fixture in family law throughout the United States.

The legal regime governing the family began to shift dramatically in the mid–1960s, as noted earlier, with the recognition of the constitutionally protected right to privacy in matters of family and intimacy. In the three decades following the 1965 decision in *Griswold*, many of the traditional justifications advanced to support the system of rules regulating the family were undercut, both by decisions of the Supreme Court and by revisions to the legal codes governing the family. These developments—including, but not limited to, recognizing interracial marriages,[15] easing restrictions on divorce,[16] and allowing women to obtain an abortion without spousal consent[17]—upset conventional understandings of the ways the family functioned to support a national community. Over time, these changes, together with other developments in the national social consciousness, altered the terms on which individuals could participate in both the public and the private spheres by dispensing with traditional notions of appropriate race and gender roles.

But concerns about how nontraditional families raised their children and inculcated them with the values of citizenship did not drop easily out of family-law pronouncements. In 1972, the Supreme Court's opinion in *Wisconsin v. Yoder* reflected how deep the association between particular family forms and good citizenship was presumed to be.[18] Upholding the right of Amish parents to terminate their children's schooling at the age of fourteen, the majority opinion for the Supreme Court drew an interesting picture of civic identity. While admitting that Wisconsin had an interest in "prepar[ing] citizens to participate effectively and intelligently in [an] open political system"[19] through compulsory education, the Court went on to sing a paean to the Amish way of life as emblematic of good citizenship. As a community, the Amish were self-reliant, law-abiding, and productive; the majority opinion noted particularly that the Amish "reject public welfare in any of its usual modern forms."[20] Over the objections voiced in dissent—that the independent interests of Amish children in being prepared for a life outside the Amish community were being ignored in the ruling—the Court responded that Amish children were adequately educated for life in the Amish community and, by extension, in the nation itself.

Since the 1972 decision in *Yoder*, family law has become increasingly complicated and more open to respecting a variety of family forms, but tensions have continued between using the law to create solid familial ties for children at an individual level and using it to define which families are or are not worthy of protection. In *Bowen v. Gilliard* for example, the Supreme Court upheld a portion of the Deficit Reduction Act in ways that reflected a continued devaluation of poor families and the needs of children within such families.[21] The Deficit Reduction Act required parents applying for federal welfare benefits to report income received as support for one child in the family as "family income" available for all children in the family. In other words, a woman who had children by different fathers had to use income contributed by one of the fathers for the support of all the children in the family. Not surprisingly, many fathers objected to this change, with the net effect being that they discontinued payments altogether on learning that their money was used to support children who were not their own. The new requirements disrupted the family lives of several of the plaintiffs, and children in some of the families lost contact with their fathers as a result: the custodial parent in each family had the option of forgoing benefits altogether, accepting reduced benefits, or surrendering custody of the child receiving support to the noncustodial parent. All these outcomes had the potential for significantly disrupting the affective ties of children in needy families, with both their custodial and noncustodial parents, but the Court found that the statute did not "'directly and substantially' interfere with family living arrangements and thereby burden a fundamental right [to family life]."[22]

The correlation between the identity effects that local rules of belonging have on children's development, discussed above, and the identity effects of these more amorphous concerns with proper socialization may seem attenuated, but in fact the link is clear—and important for understanding the ways in which children are imagined in the law. Children are at the same time made subject to the control of their immediate caregivers and made the object of intense public scrutiny as the state looks into the family to ensure that children are being raised to be proper citizens. The cases discussing children's potential as future citizens—often cases involving various disputes over education—might be somewhat easier to resolve if identity rights for children were recognized. If such a right were to emerge, discussions about which family forms are and are not worthy of recognition might be less rigidly defined by reference to traditional values and more attentive to how the recognition of particular family forms and affective ties contributes to the development of stable and responsible citizens. The degree to which particular family forms are seen as worthy or unworthy of recognition in the public sphere affects the security and well-being of children growing up in such families. As children's identity comes to be understood in law, identity rights could contribute to understanding children both in their particular environments and in relation to the communities they will eventually join as political actors.

Identity Rights and Cultural/Communal Belonging

Even though the tensions between securing local and national identities in the regime of family law promise to raise enough thorny issues to occupy legal and political scholars for some time, that picture must now be complicated by introducing the concept of rights to cultural and communal identity. Debates about the nature and scope of rights to the protection of culture for both groups and individuals have dominated much of the conversation over identity rights since the early 1990s, particularly in international human rights discourses.[23] The advent of such a set of rights multiplies the sites for conflict. The challenge will be to coordinate rights to belonging and identity for children on a number of different levels. Recognizing rights to identity in the context of belonging to cultural communities could in fact lend considerable coherence to the problem of locating children under the law. Rights to cultural identity try to ensure some protection for cultural groups in ways that stabilize and foster the development of strong communal ties at a level intermediate between family and the national state. These communities have the potential to provide networks of support for individual children and their families, and it is therefore worth exploring the ways in which such rights might evolve.

A number of international human rights documents are designed to protect the cultural integrity of groups and the rights of individuals to participate in the cultural lives of their distinct communities. The Declaration of the Rights of Persons Belonging to National or Ethnic, Religious or Linguistic Minorities, Article 1, asserts that "States shall protect the existence and the national or ethnic, cultural, religious and linguistic identity of minorities within their respective territories and shall encourage conditions for the promotion of that identity." Similarly, the Draft Declaration on the Rights of Indigenous Peoples declares that indigenous populations have the right to maintain and strengthen the group's distinct political, economic, social, and cultural characteristics. Finally, the Convention on the Rights of the Child states unequivocally that every child has the right to "preservation of his or her identity," with concomitant rights to grow securely within a culture. (The full text of each of these documents is reprinted in Brownlie and Goodwin-Gill 2002.)

The push for recognition of cultures directly entails identity concerns. The claims arise in part as a reaction against modern nation-building strategies centered on the sometimes brutal assimilation of aboriginal and minority cultural groups. Not all the effort to generate national communities has been illegitimate, but attention is increasingly being focused on what was lost in the process of modern nation building: What cultural communities were dismantled or erased in the effort to bind national states together? And what were the deep human costs involved in that process of assimilation and erasure?

Increased attentiveness to the problems of cultural identity has not simplified the problem of determining belonging and of articulating rights however. Recognizing cultural rights raises a host of extremely complicated questions. Articulating rights to cultural belonging or identity requires, for example, defining culture itself. That task is beyond the scope of this chapter; here it suffices to note that as the pressure to recognize such rights continues, the status of children in this debate becomes central.

A cultural community imparts a set of historically contingent systems of meaning and significance that are reflected in a particular group's social, political, and economic institutions. Cultural or communal belonging is critical to understanding identity: cultural systems provide a way of understanding the world itself (Kymlicka 2001; Parekh 2000). Although individuals may stake out different positions with respect to particular cultural understandings, cultural norms provide the setting within which those positions make sense. Cultural belonging, then, is part of the very fabric of identity or of what Wade Boykin and Brenda Allen refer to in Chapter 6 as integrity—the bits and pieces of everyday life that are the threads in the social fabric that imparts meaning in people's lives.

The demand for recognition, protection, accommodation, and, often, affirmation of different cultural communities has grown at both national and international levels since the early 1980s. Without evaluating the whole debate over the legitimacy of recognizing cultural communities (Kymlicka 2001; Parekh 2001; Barry 2001), it is sufficient to say that there are compelling reasons to fully air the arguments for recognizing some forms of cultural rights. Given the extent to which the debate over cultural identity rights of national minorities, aboriginal groups, and others has dominated political conversations, however, it is surprising that relatively little of that debate has touched on what the recognition of such rights might mean for children. Of course, many of the rights sought will redound to the benefit of—or at least substantially affect—children. Language rights, for example, which recognize the right of a group to use its language in public business or to provide education in an indigenous language, will significantly affect children. Demands for accommodation of cultural practices will enable groups to pass on cultural understandings and to bind children to the ways of thinking of their particular cultural milieu. But with one or two exceptions (Stewart 1992; Harris-Short 2001), most scholars engaged in this debate have not yet addressed children's cultural identity rights in and of themselves.

Children loom as a large but unseen presence in the conversations about cultural identity, recognition, and integrity because cultural rights, for all their ambiguity, are fundamentally about maintaining community over generations. Claims for cultural recognition and respect for cultural forms are about preserving and, more critically, passing on modes of understanding and being in the world. Children are thus essential to the conversation. And children, as Boykin and Allen point out in Chapter 6, are active agents in both renewing and revising cultural understanding.

Cultures are by nature dynamic and porous; members of a cultural group may position themselves at dramatically different points within that group and may change their positions over time. Understanding how a right to cultural identity should be interpreted for children becomes exponentially complicated. If culture consists in a way of life, children's cultures can be difficult to locate. Indeed, the very notion of culture can dissolve into incoherence when applied to children, whose identities are in flux and will be mediated by their social environment. Formulating the idea of cultural belonging and articulating cultural rights are complicated by transnationalism and the mobility inherent in modern life in general. Moreover, cultural groups may assert interests that differ from the interests of both immediate caregivers and national communities. Parents may or may not wish to rear children in accordance with the dictates of a group of which they are identified as a member, for example, and cultural groups may object to raising children in accordance with the norms of a mainstream national community.

For purposes of illustration, this chapter examines adoption to understand of how cultural rights might affect the law's understanding of children's identities. But the issues raised in this illustration are not so confined. The recognition of rights to cultural identity arise as often in custody debates between natural parents, in disagreements between parents and cultural groups over the extent to which particular cultural values will be included in public education, and in a host of other arenas. Questions surrounding transracial/transcultural adoption, however, provide a manageable lens through which to explore the issues.

In the United States, issues of cultural belonging for adopted children have been resolved in two directly contradictory fashions, neither of which has proven satisfactory for dealing with the multiplicity of issues involved. The first approach is illustrated by the statutes currently governing the general practice of transracial adoption. In 1972, the National Association of Black Social Workers (NABSW) issued a position paper condemning the placement of black children with white families.[24] Although the resolution was criticized by many commentators, the NABSW had compelling reasons for its position. Members of the NABSW pointed out that, despite a rhetoric of color-blindness, U.S. society was pervasively racist and that African American children placed with white families were not being adequately prepared to live in such a society, even when white parents were well intentioned. Moreover, the NABSW pointed out, African American families were systematically disqualified in adoption and foster-care proceedings because of the racist biases of white social workers who screened them out in disproportionate numbers or failed to solicit their participation in the first place. In 1994, the NABSW amended its position somewhat, arguing that transracial adoptions might be a last resort: they might be considered, for example, if the adopting parents made and maintained contact with an African American community group.

This debate, which moved onto the public scene concurrently with an increased demand for "adoptable" infants in the early 1970s, touched off a controversy over transracial adoption that continues to generate considerable discussion. In 1996, Congress passed the Inter-Ethnic Placement Act,[25] which prohibited race matching in adoption and foster-care proceedings. The enactment of that legislation appeared to foreclose the idea of asserting identity or cultural rights for African American children, at least to the extent that such rights might be grounded in race alone.

Foreclosing consideration of the interplay of race and culture does a disservice to everyone concerned; the Inter-Ethnic Placement Act has done little to resolve the fundamental tensions that arise in transracial/transcultural adoption.

As Woodhouse (1995) and, more recently, Fogg-Davis (2002) have pointed out, children are often acutely aware of difference and need some avenue for understanding its nature and effect. Indeed, children are continually engaged in "racial navigation," in Fogg-Davis's words, and are quite active in forming their own identities in such situations. In this context, recognizing a child's identity right and construing it broadly as the child's right to gain access to a cultural community could go a long way toward facilitating a child's healthy development in a number of interrelated and overlapping communities of meaning.

A wholly different statute governs the adoption and foster-care placement of American Indian children; this statute is specifically attentive to issues of cultural belonging. The adoption and foster-care placement of American Indian children is governed by the Indian Child Welfare Act, which recognizes tribal authority over children who are, or are eligible to become, tribal members.[26] The act grants distinct legal authority to the tribe to determine the adoptive and foster-care placement of Indian children and thus places the interests of the tribe in a child's adoption or foster-care placement on a par with the interest of the parents. Cultural belonging and cultural protection are central to the operation of the act, which attempts to recognize, protect, and accommodate children's American Indian identities, as well as being central to the interests of a tribe, qua tribe, in nurturing children and raising them within its cultural community.

The distinct political status of American Indian tribes explains the difference between the statutory treatment of Indian children and the treatment of children of other racial and ethnic backgrounds, but it does not necessarily clarify the basic issues. The boundaries of cultural belonging are not necessarily clearer for Native Americans than they are for African Americans, Latinos, or any other distinct cultural group, despite the significant difference in political history and status. This approach is directly at odds with the position asserted in the Inter-Ethnic Placement Act in its sensitivity to the issue of cultural belonging, but it is no more attentive to the issue of fluid cultural boundaries, dynamic identities, and the needs of children embedded in multiple cultural communities.

Neither the Indian Child Welfare Act nor the Inter-Ethnic Placement Act provides a tidy solution, then, to the issue of cultural belonging. But the shortcomings of both acts suggest the importance of recognizing rights to identity: such rights can, as noted earlier, help to create access for children to a variety of communities of meaning. Understanding the specifics of how such a right to identity might be articulated in particular contexts is a discussion that is barely begun with respect to children, but the very concept of such rights suggests interesting possibilities for providing children not only with secure familial bonds but with secure communal bonds. Moreover, the recognition of such rights may create a space within which children can act to bring their own understandings of belonging to the table.

Identity Rights and Children's Lives

The law operates at many levels to shape children's identities, and those who make and interpret the laws that affect children's lives need to be attentive to the myriad ways in which it does so. Under the current system, the law fixes children into both local and national environments but pays scant attention to what the day-to-day impact on children's lives might be and even less to how children participate in creating their own identities. In an ideal world, the law would operate on a local level to provide children with stable and secure immediate relationships of dependence within which they could develop a healthy sense of self-esteem. At another level, the legal regime has a legitimate interest in assuring that children develop into adults who identify sufficiently with their national culture to be able to function successfully as citizens. It should also reflect an understanding that children are embedded in cultural communities of meaning that deserve recognition as well. Framing identity rights as being held by children on their own calls attention to the interests of children in creating their own identities and should assist in opening dialogues about how belonging and identity can be supported and extended in the law.

Notes

1. All the chapters in this book urge attention to the ways in which children participate in shaping their own lives. Chapter 4, by Meacham, and Chapter 6 by Wade Boykin and Brenda Allen, are particularly instructive in the attention each gives to understanding how children themselves shape their identities. Meacham calls for broadening the ways in which we assess children's development by moving away from a developmental model locked into a nature/nurture paradigm and looking at how the individual contexts of children's lives and their own actions contribute to their identities. Boykin and Allen remind readers that, far from assessing children's backgrounds along a hierarchy from enriched to deprived, adults interested in fostering children's development should be attentive to the vibrant cultural understandings all children bring to the table—and learn how to invoke those strengths to further children's growth. Both these chapters suggest the need to be attentive to the myriad factors affecting children's identity development.
2. *Pierce v. Society of Sisters*, 268 U.S. 510, 534–535 (1925); *Prince v. Massachusetts*, 321 U.S. 158, 166 (1944).
3. *Griswold v. Connecticut*, 381 U.S. 479 (1965).
4. 851 P.2d 776 (Calif., 1993).
5. *In re Baby M.*, 537 A.2d 1227 (N.J., 1988).
6. In *Michael H. v. Gerald D.*, 491 U.S. 110 (1989), for example, a child asserted a claim to maintain a connection to a man seeking to establish his paternity with whom she had lived off and on for the first three years of her life. After finding that claim to

be barred by California's rules of evidence, the Supreme Court dismissed the child's claim out of hand, observing that "we have never had occasion to decide whether a child has a liberty interest, symmetrical with that of her parent, in maintaining her filial relationship. . . . Victoria's due process challenge is, if anything, weaker than Michael's [the man seeking to establish paternity]. [Victoria] claims a due process right to maintain filial relationships with both Michael and Gerald [the putative father]. This assertion merits little discussion, for whatever the merits of the guardian ad litem's belief that such an arrangement can be of great psychological benefit to a child, the claim that a State must recognize multiple fatherhood has no support in the history or traditions of this country" (130–131).

7. Compare *Smith v. OFFER*, 431 U.S. 816 (1977) (ruling that foster parents are not entitled to a hearing to contest the removal of a child in their care because the foster-parent contract outlined the expectations and entitlements of the parties, and recognition of such a right on behalf of foster parents might interfere with the rights of biological parents).

8. Two well-known cases in the early 1990s, popularly known as the Baby Jessica and Baby Boy Richard cases, involved faulty adoptions that resulted in the removal of children from adoptive homes after the children had spent their earliest years with the adoptive families. *In re B.G.C.*, 496 N.W.2d 181 (Iowa, 1994), *cert. denied Deboer v. Deboer*, 114 S. Ct. 1 (1993), and *In re Doe*, 638 N.E.2d 181 (Ill., 1994), *cert. denied Baby Richard v. Kirchner*, 115 S. Ct. 499 (1994). In neither case did the courts recognize an independent interest of the child in maintaining some kind of tie to the affective parents.

9. Compare *Michael H. v. Gerald D.*, discussed in note 8.

10. Compare *Alison D. v. Virginia M.*, 572 N.E.2d 651 (N.Y., 1991) (ruling that a former lesbian partner of a biological parent cannot compel a fit parent to allow visitation over the parent's objection even though the former partner has a relationship with the child). State laws vary in the extent to which they recognize adoption by same-sex partners of biological or adoptive parents.

11. See *Adoption of Tammy*, 619 N.E.2d 315 (Mass., 1993) (recognizing second-parent adoption by a lesbian partner); compare *In re Adoption of Luke*, 640 N.W.2d 374 (Neb., 2002) (ruling that the nonmarried partner of a biological parent cannot adopt the parent's minor son).

12. This is not to suggest that children should remain tied to parents who have been abusive or neglectful, but simply to urge that consideration be given to protecting some form of continued connection when it would be in the child's best interest.

13. 98 U.S. 145, 164 (1878).

14. *Maynard v. Hill*, 125 U.S. 190, 211 (1888).

15. *Loving v. Virginia*, 388 U.S. 1 (1967).

16. See, for example, Uniform Marriage and Divorce Act, sec. 302.

17. *Planned Parenthood of Central Missouri v. Danforth*, 428 U.S. 52 (1976).

18. 406 U.S. 205 (1972).

19. *Id.* at 221.

20. *Id.* at 222.

21. 483 U.S. 587 (1987).

22. *Id.* at 603.

23. See note 1.

24. The NABSW resolution is quoted in Simon, Altstein, and Melli 1994, 50.

25. Amended as the Multiethnic Placement Act, 42 U.S.C.A. sec. 5115(a), in 1998.

26. 25 U.S.C.A. sec. 1901 et seq. (1998).

References

Barry, B. 2001. *Culture and Equality.* Cambridge: Polity Press.

Brownlie, I., and G. S. Goodwin-Gill, eds. 2002. *Basic Documents in Human Rights*, 4th ed. Oxford: Oxford University Press.

Fogg-Davis, H. 2002. *The Ethics of Transracial Adoption.* Ithaca, N.Y.: Cornell University Press.

Harris-Short, S. 2001. "Listening to 'the Other'? The Convention on the Rights of the Child." *Melbourne Journal of International Law* 2:304–361.

Kymlicka, W. 2001. *Politics in the Vernacular: Nationalism, Multiculturalism, and Citizenship.* Oxford: Oxford University Press.

Lindsay, M. J. 1998. "Reproducing a Fit Citizenry: Dependency, Eugenics and the Law of Marriage in the United States, 1860–1920." *Law and Social Inquiry* 23:541.

National Association of Black Social Workers. 1994. "Position Statement: Preserving African American Families." Unpublished manuscript, Detroit.

Parekh, B. 2000. *Rethinking Multiculturalism: Cultural Diversity and Political Theory.* New York: Palgrave.

Sanger, C., and E. Willemsen. 1992. "Minor Changes: Emancipating Children in Modern Times." *University of Michigan Journal of Law Reform* 25 (winter): 239.

Simon, R. J., H. Altstein, and M. S. Melli. 1994. *The Case for Transracial Adoption.* Washington, D.C.: American University Press.

Stewart, G. A.1992. "Interpreting the Child's Right to Identity in the U.N. Convention on the Rights of the Child." *Family Law Quarterly* 26 (no. 3): 221–223.

Woodhouse, B. B. 1995. "'Are You My Mother?': Conceptualizing Children's Identity Rights in Transracial Adoptions." *Duke Journal of Gender Law and Policy* 2:107–129.

Resources for Further Research

RAYMOND A. DUCHARME

A Road Map for Surfing the Internet

THIS LISTING OF INTERNET sites is intended to provide readers with a convenient and organized means of accessing Internet resources useful for further study of the ideas, issues, themes, and perspectives in this book. The relative ease with which the vast quantity of material available on the web can be obtained is a powerful invitation. The Internet supplements library research and is a valuable resource for those without access to a research library. At the least, Internet sites conveniently provide immediate information about recent developments and texts of studies, reports, and reviews. One caveat should be kept in mind: the life span of Internet sites varies considerably. Some disappear; others have considerable longevity. New sites appear regularly, often unannounced. The best sites are well maintained and are updated frequently.

A few tips for using this listing:

- The sites are grouped into sections according to their principal emphases. These sections are not meant to be mutually exclusive; there are many overlaps.
- In each section the listed sites serve as a starting place. Many of them are sources for links to other directly or tangentially related sites.
- This listing is deliberately selective and attempts to address concerns about the unreliability of unedited information available on the web.
- Although each listing is not "certified," each is what it claims to be, and many provide reliable guidance or suggestions for using the Internet as a tool for further exploration of childhood issues.

Search engines are where many Internet users begin to locate sites useful for their research. The more commonly used engines (AltaVista, Yahoo, Excite) frequently require a good deal of digging to get to pertinent sites. Northernlight.com is a more efficient engine. However, the most useful search engine for research and scholarly work is www.google.com. Two specialized search engines are www.teoma.com and www.wisenut.com.

It is at times important to exercise some imagination or flexibility when identifying key words for a search. One should attempt to narrow down the search as much as possible. For example, "children's lives" will lead to thousands of sites; "children and the law" will screen out many sites.

Not all web users are cognizant of portals and how they can be used. There does not seem to be a hard and fast definition. Some consider all search engines to be portals. But they can be viewed more narrowly. They can be thought of as pages that allow one entry to a reservoir of resources and references for a specific area or topic. For example, useful portals for education issues are:

> Copernicus Education Gateway: www.edgate.com
> www.gradebook.org/educationsites.html
> Education Portal: www.theeducationportal.com (contains links to additional useful portals for educators)

Another example of a portal is www.saferinternet.org, which contains links to "safe sites" for use by children.

Although there has never been a time when so much information and so many ideas were so readily available to so many people, critics of the Internet cite two problems with its use. A frequent charge is that there is just too much information; this information is often unorganized and hence it is overwhelming. The listings that follow provide the reader with a way to overcome this weakness. They allow one to bypass some of the frustration and confusion frequently generated by the web. At the least, they should facilitate a reader's effort to seek out more and newer information.

A second charge is that much of what is available on the Internet is not reliable, and it can be difficult to affirm the validity of the content on some sites. In some instances identifying the sponsor or bias or posture of a site is problematic. However, with increasing familiarity of the Internet, one can apply a critical, questioning approach. By exercising some caution, the user should be able to make sound judgments about the validity and reliability of information.

Foundations and Grants

A comprehensive list of grant-making institutions can be found at www.foundations.org/grantmakers.html.

The following six foundations support promising work and research of interest to practitioners, policymakers, and the public.

Annie E. Casey Foundation

www.aecf.org

Provides grants and funded demonstrations to foster the support of children and families.

Carnegie Corporation of New York

www.carnegie.org

Provides grants for education with a focus on early childhood education, urban school reform, and higher education. Reports available: *Learning in the Primary Grades*, *Meeting the Needs of Young Children*, and others.

Bill and Melinda Gates Foundation

www.gatesfoundation.org

Provides grants for research and other work supporting innovations in the areas of health and education.

Charles Stewart Mott Foundation

www.mott.org

Provides grants for programs in the areas of civil society, "pathways out of poverty," the environment.

Ford Foundation

www.fordfound.org

Provides grants and supports operations in the United States, Africa, Middle East, Latin America, and Russia.

Spencer Foundation

www.spencer.org

Supports research focused on the improvement of education.

Research

Collectively these sites provide access to a broad range of research studies and reports, some from an interdisciplinary perspective.

The Brookings Institution

www.brookings.org

Lists research studies on academic achievement.

Cato

www.cato.org

Provides links to research and educational institutes, including a number of conservative organizations.

Center for Children and Childhood Studies
http://children.camden.rutgers.edu
Supports collaborative research projects, coordinates service and outreach projects, and sponsors the development of new, multidisciplinary educational and publication projects. The Center is the publisher of this book.

Center for Research on Child Wellbeing (Princeton University)
http://www.crcw.princeton.edu
Sponsors interdisciplinary research on "children's health, education, income and family structure." A long list of working papers is provided on the site.

Center for Research into Parenting and Children (Oxford University)
www.apsoc.ox.uk/Parenting/main/htm
Lists research focused on families and children.

Centre for the Social Study of Childhood
www.hull.ac.uk/cssc
Lists interdisciplinary research focused "on the everyday lives of children in the home, the school, and the community, and the mediation of children's agency through the policy context and the discourses of childhood."

Childwatch International Research Network (University of Oslo, Norway)
www.childwatch.uio.no
An international network of a number of key institutions engaged in child research "representing all continents and a variety of disciplines."

The Children's Foundation
www.childrensfoundation.net
Provides research, information, and training on child-related issues and problems.

Dana Foundation
www.dana.org
Lists brain research.

Early Childhood Longitudinal Study
http://nces.ed.gov/ecls/
A potentially powerful research study with a focus on two overlapping age cohorts: from birth through first grade and from kindergarten through grade five.

William T. Grant Foundation
www.wtgrantfoundation.org
Through research and grants supports the foundation's plans to "help the nation value youth as a resource."

GSE-UCB: Graduate School of Education, University of California, Berkeley
www.gse.Berkeley.edu/research.html
Lists research centers and projects.

IPR Research: Child, Adolescent, and Family Studies Program (Northwestern University)
www.nwu.edu/IPRresearch/reschild.html
Conducts interdisciplinary "research on the ways in which social programs, policies, and context affect the lives of young children from birth to adulthood and the impact of these outcomes on their families."

Learning Research and Development Center (University of Pittsburgh)
www.lrdc.pitt.edu
Emphasizes multidisciplinary research on processes of learning, learning in schools and museums, policy, and technology.

CREL: Mid-Continent Research for Education and Learning
www.mcrel.org

National Library of Education
www.ed.gov/NLE
Main U.S. resource center for education information.

Project Zero Research Projects
www.pz.harvard.edu/Research/Research.htm
Sponsors research programs "to understand and enhance learning, thinking, and creativity in the arts, as well as the humanistic and scientific disciplines, at individual and institutional levels." Lists current research projects.

Rand
www.rand.org
Sponsors research and publications on a broad range of issues and topics.

Search Institute
www.search-institute.org
"Conducts *applied scientific research* on positive child and adolescent development."

Society for Research in Child Development
www.srcd.org
Publishes *Child Development*, *Monographs of the Society for Research in Child Development*, and *Child Development Abstracts and Bibliography*.

The Spencer Foundation
www.spencer.org
Lists research on improving education.

University of Pittsburgh: Research and Development Center
www.lrdc.pitt.edu
Lists brain research.

U.S. Department of Education
www.ed.gov/index.jsp

Policy

This is a selective listing of institutes, centers, councils, and foundations with a central interest in public and social policy and its impact on children, family, schooling, and educational programs. Certain sites have a stated interest in promoting specific policies.

American Enterprise Institute for Public Policy Research
www.aei.org
Provides information on culture and society, education, social issues, and
   government programs and policy evaluations.

Brown Center on Educational Policy
www.brook.edu/gs/brown/brown_hp.htm
Provides transcripts of Brookings papers on education policy and descriptions of recent research studies by the Center.

Bush Center in Child Development and Social Policy (Yale University)
www.yale.edu/bushcenter/
Goal "to bring research-based knowledge of child development to the
   federal and state policy arenas, . . . to improve social policy affecting the
   lives of children and families in the United States."

Center for Child and Family Policy (Duke University)
www-pps.aas.duke.edu/centers/child
Goal is to "bridge the gap between basic research and policy and practice."
   Provides links to current and previous research projects of the Center.

Center for the Study of Teaching and Policy
http://depts.washington.edu/ctpmail
Lists research program investigating the following topics: policy, leadership, and the quality of teaching; school-based instructional improvement and intervention; and strengthening teacher development and
   careers.

Century Foundation
www.tcf.org
Lists studies of the interface of education ideas and policy.

Council for Basic Education
www.c-b-e.org
Provides reports and comments on recent and current developments and issues in education.

The David and Lucile Packard Foundation
www.futureofchildren.org
Provides "research and analysis to promote effective policies and programs for children."

Georgetown University Child Development Center
www.gucde.georgetown.edu
Provides information on child health and mental health.

The Heritage Foundation
www.heritage.org
Promotes conservative public policies. Offers a wide range of studies, research, and resources.

National Center for Infants, Toddlers, & Families
www.zerotothree.org
"Dedicated to advancing current knowledge; promoting beneficial policies and practices; communicating research and best practices."

Public Agenda Online
www.publicagenda.org
Source for public opinion and policy analysis. See recent surveys in conjunction with *Education Week*.

Poverty and Welfare

These sites provide access to studies and resources useful in the study and analysis of the impact of poverty and welfare on children and families.

Annie E. Casey Foundation: Publications and Reports
www.aecf.org/publications

Child Welfare
www.childwelfare.com
A rich site with links to *Child Welfare Review, Children and Youth Services Review,* and organizations.

Child Welfare Library
www.childwelfare.com/kids/library.htm

Child Welfare League of America
www.cwla.org
Lists child-welfare databases.

Foundation for Child Development
www.ffcd.org
Emphasizes early-childhood issues and the effects of poverty on children.

National Center for Children in Poverty (Mailman School of Public Health, Columbia University)
http://cpmcnet.columbia.edu/dept/nccp
Mission: "to identify and promote strategies that prevent child poverty in
   the United States." Provides statistics and fact sheets.

Children and Divorce

A search for children and divorce using www.wisenut.com brings up pages of
links to a wide variety of sites. The following site listed is probably the most
useful for readers of this book.

American Academy of Child and Adolescent Psychiatry (AACAP)
www.familymanagement.com
Family-resources page provides links to "Facts for Families."

Children, the Law, and the Courts

In addition to the sites listed below, states, a number of universities and law
schools, law firms, and private attorneys have sites that, depending on one's needs
and interests, can be useful.

American Bar Association: Center on Children and the Law
www.abanet.org/child
Goal is to improve the lives of children "through advances in law, justice,
   knowledge, practice, and public policy." Provides links to a number of
   issues: child custody, child protection, children, families and the law.

American Academy of Child and Adolescent Psychiatry
www.aacap.org
Advocate for juvenile-justice reform. Provides a listing of many publications under the heading "Facts for Families."

Child Rights Information Network
www.crin.org
Useful site for links to a range of topics, children's rights organizations,

international information on children's rights, and the Convention on the Rights of Children.

Child Welfare League of America
www.cwla.org
Promotes the "well-being of children, youth, and their families, and protecting every child from harm." Includes *Making Children a National Priority.*

GE Fund
www.ge.com/community/fund/index.html
Funds studies on educational quality and access.

Harvard Center for Law and Education
www.cleweb.org
Advocates for the rights of students to effective education. Provides assistance to parents and attorneys on students' rights and other issues: standards-based reform, high school restructuring, rights of students with disabilities, and parent and community involvement.

Human Rights Watch
www.hrw.org/children
Lists children's rights around the world with links to related organizations.

Children, Media, and Technology

For those interested in and concerned about the place of the mass media and technology in the lives of children and their impact on children as consumers, this is a useful listing of sites that provide research findings, studies, reports, resources, and links to additional sites.

Alliance for Childhood
www.allianceforchildhood.net/projects/childhood/reports
Includes *Ending the Commercialization of Children*. Lists studies and reports on children and computers.

AT&T Foundation
www.att.com/foundation
Lists education programs with an emphasis on technology and life-long learning.

Center for Media Education
www.cme.org
A rich site with links to a variety of resources on children and the media: research studies, book chapters, articles, and Center for Media Education press releases.

Childnet International
www.childnet-int.org/links/index.html
Provides links to Internet organizations, hot lines, international bodies.

Children and the Media (Children Now)
www.childrennow/org
Research and action organization with the aim of "helping America to build a sustained commitment to putting children first." Resource for race and gender studies and interactive media. Includes links to many useful sites.

Connect for Kids
www.connectforkids.org
Provides links to many sites including those of organizations with a focus on children and the media.

ERIC/ECE
www.ericece.org/pubs/digests/haugland00.html
Provides information on computers and young children.

Fair Play 2001 (Children Now)
www.childrennow.org/media/index.html
Describes a video-game study.

Media Literacy Review
http://interact.uoregon.edu/MediaLit/mlr?VO2NO1/index.html
Describes a media-literacy online project supported by the University of Oregon. A most useful site for work with children and media with annotated links to children and teen web directories, search engines for kids and teens, educational resources about the Internet, library resources, evaluating information on the Internet, kids publishing on the Internet.

Child-Advocacy Organizations

Most of these sites contain links to organizations and groups committed to the rights and the well-being of children. This commitment manifests itself in a variety of advocacy efforts.

Action Alliance for Children
www.4children.org
Provides links to useful sites in English and Spanish.

Advocates for Youth
www.advocatesforyouth.org

Provides lists of publications and information on rights, respect, responsibility.

Alliance for Childhood
www.allianceforchildhood.net
Advocates for children's right "to a healthy, developmentally appropriate childhood."

Child Advocacy Resource Links
www.rollanet.org/~childlaw/gallnk.htm
Provides links to many child-advocacy and child-abuse sites.

Children's Defense Fund
www.childrensdefense.org
A voice for children with the mission to "leave no child behind." Provides extensive links to other resources and organizations, including data resources and government sites.

Connect for Kids
www.connectforkids.org/resources3139/resources.htm
Provides many links to advocacy organizations.

Save the Children
www.savethechildren.org
Sponsors change in the lives of children.

Children's Voices
www.sozialarbeit.de/europa/newslett/news/nee09.htm/
Includes an electronic newsletter: Euronet. Encourages children to become active participants in society and shares best practices "in implementing children's rights."

Children Now: Youth Voices
www.youthvoices.org

Child Welfare League of America
www.cwla.org/articles
Provides links to featured articles in *Children's Voices*.

Youth Link
www.youthlink.org
Forum for the "voice, ideas, and solutions of youth."

Voices for Children
www.voicesforchildren.ca
Canadian nonprofit with a focus on the healthy development of children.

Professional Associations, Organizations, and Other Resources

Links to the home pages of professional and education associations are provided at http://www.ed.gov/Programs/EROD. In addition the website for *Education Week* (www.edweek.com), the paper of record for education in the United States, with an emphasis on preschool through secondary school, describes recent and current developments and issues and provides a link to *Teacher Magazine*, a monthly publication. It also publishes occasional reports on the condition of education, and its archives link is useful.

Contributors

ENOLA G. AIRD received her J.D. from Yale University. She is currently an affiliate scholar at the Institute for American Values, where she directs the Motherhood Project. She is an advisor to the National Parenting Association's Task Force on Revitalizing Parenting for the 21st Century and a network affiliate of Future Focus 2020. She has served on the Institute's Council on Civil Society and contributed to the Council's 1998 report, *A Call to Civil Society*; she was the lead author and chief Institute spokesperson for the 1999 consensus statement, *Turning the Corner on Father Absence in Black America*.

BRENDA A. ALLEN received her Ph.D. from Howard University and is currently an associate professor of psychology and the director of institutional diversity at Smith College. She has published research and written theoretical articles on the relationship between culture and learning, memory and cognitive processing.

A. WADE BOYKIN is currently professor of psychology and director of the Center for Research on the Education of Students at Risk at Howard University. His publications include *Talent Development, Cultural Deep Structure, and School Reform; Schooling Students Placed at Risk*; and, forthcoming, *The Psychology of African American Experience* (with B. Allen and R. Jagers).

JUSTINE CASSELL holds a master's in literature from the Université de Besançon (France), a master's in linguistics from the University of Edinburgh (Scotland), and a double Ph.D. (in psychology and linguistics) from the University of Chicago. She is an associate professor at MIT's Media Laboratory, where she directs the Gesture and Narrative Language Research Group. She is currently investigating the role that technologies play in children's lives. She is the co-editor of *From Barbie to Mortal Kombat* (with Henry Jenkins) and the author of *Embodied Conversational Agents*.

RAYMOND A. DUCHARME received his M.A. and Ph.D. from Teachers College, Columbia University. He is professor emeritus of education and child study at

Smith College and is the past director of the Smith College Campus School. His scholarship has focused on education in the United States.

ROBERT E. EMERY received his Ph.D. in psychology from the State University of New York at Stony Brook. He is currently the director of the Center for Children, Families, and the Law at the University of Virginia, a professor of psychology, and the director of the department's clinical-training program. His research focuses on family conflict, violence, divorce, and child-custody disputes. Included among his many publications are *Marriage, Divorce, and Children's Readjustment* and *Renegotiating Family Relationships*.

SUSAN ETHEREDGE received her Ed.D. from the University of Massachusetts and is currently an assistant professor of education and child studies at Smith College. Her research focuses on the teaching-learning process within primary and preschool classrooms, the classroom as a discourse community, and teachers' use of story and inquiry. She has published *Introducing Students to Scientific Inquiry* with Al Rudnitsky.

KAREN A. GRAY received her M.A. from the University of Kansas and her Ph.D. from the University of Texas at Austin. She is currently an instructor in the College for Social Work at the University of South Carolina. Her current research focuses on poverty, welfare reform, community organization and development, as well as child abuse and neglect. She is a Southeast Region board member of the Association for Community Organization and Social Administration.

ALICE HEARST received a J.D. from the University of Washington and a Ph.D. in American politics and political theory from Cornell University. She is currently an associate professor of government at Smith College and has been a research fellow at the Queen's University in Belfast, Ireland, where she continued her research on children's rights.

ALLISON JAMES is a professor of sociology at Sheffield University (United Kingdom) and researches children's identity, especially in relation to disability and food. She is deputy head of the School of Comparative and Applied Social Sciences and director of the Centre for the Social Study of Childhood. Her publications include *Childhood Identities*, *Growing Up and Growing Old*, and *Constructing and Reconstructing Childhood*.

JILL E. KORBIN received her Ph.D. from the University of California, Los Angeles. She is a professor of anthropology at Case Western Reserve University, where she also serves as associate dean of arts and sciences, director of childhood studies, and codirector of the Schubert Center for Child Development. Her published research focuses on cultural and medical anthropology, cross-cultural child rearing and family studies, child abuse and neglect, family violence, adult and children's perceptions of neighborhood within the United States, and specifically on Old Order Amish.

EILEEN W. LINDNER is a Presbyterian minister holding a Ph.D. in U.S. church history. She is currently the deputy general secretary for research and planning at the National Council of the Churches of Christ of the United States. She is the author of numerous books and articles on a variety of child-advocacy subjects, most notably *When Churches Mind the Children*. She has also served on national and international commissions dealing with topics related to children and to families.

GARETH B. MATTHEWS received his Ph.D. in philosophy from Harvard University and is currently a professor of philosophy at the University of Massachusetts at Amherst. His research interests include ancient, medieval, and early-modern philosophy, the philosophy of religion, and the philosophy of childhood. He is currently working on a project, with S. Marc Cohen, on Aristotle's *Metaphysics*. His published books include *Socratic Perplexity and the Nature of Philosophy*, *The Augustinian Tradition*, *The Philosophy of Childhood*, and *Thoughts' Ego in Augustine and Descartes*.

JACK A. MEACHAM received his Ph.D. from the University of Michigan and is currently a distinguished teaching professor at the State University of New York at Buffalo and chair of the department of psychology. He has published widely in areas of human development. His current research interests include the influence of student diversity on teaching and learning, pedagogy for and assessment of undergraduate teaching and learning, and general issues of diversity and multicultural education in higher education.

JAN PRYOR is a professor of psychology at Victoria University in New Zealand and director of the Roy McKenzie Centre for the Study of Families. Her research centers on children and their families, family change, and the ways in which children experience and cope with family transitions such as parental separation and stepfamily living. Her research is reported in her book *Children in Changing Families*.

PETER B. PUFALL received his Ph.D. in psychology from Catholic University, Washington, D.C., and is emeritus professor of psychology and senior fellow of the Kahn Institute for Liberal Studies at Smith College. He has published research on cognitive development and the development of art as communication and has coedited two books: *Constructivism in the Computer Age* (with G. Forman) and *Piaget's Theory* (with H. Beilin). His current research is on artistic development and children's conceptualization of the United States following September 11, 2001.

RHONDA SINGER received her Ph.D. from the University of Massachusetts and is currently professor of sociology at Rollins College in Florida. Her areas of specialization include gender, family, and childhood. She is presently involved in research that examines gender on college campuses and the transformative possibilities of collegewide discourse and programming on gender issues.

JAMES C. SPILSBURY received his Ph.D. in anthropology from Case Western Reserve University. He is currently a postdoctoral fellow in the Division of Behavioral Pediatrics & Psychology, Rainbow Babies' and Children's Hospital in Cleveland, Ohio. His research interests focus on the effects of neighborhood conditions on children's health and well-being. He is currently conducting research on neighborhoods, violence, and children's sleep habits.

RICHARD P. UNSWORTH is senior fellow at the Kahn Institute for Liberal Studies and a retired professor of religion and dean of the chapel at Smith College. He holds a B.D. from Yale Divinity School and a Th.M. from Harvard University Divinity School. He has also served as dean of the William Jewett Tucker Foundation and professor of religion at Dartmouth College, president and headmaster of Northfield Mount Hermon School, headmaster of Berkshire School, trustee of Mount Holyoke College, and member of the Harvard University Overseers Committee to Visit the Divinity School.

BARBARA BENNETT WOODHOUSE received a Diploma Superiore from the Universita per Stranieri (Perugia, Italy) and her J.D. from Columbia University. She holds the David H. Levin Chair in Family Law and is the director of the Center on Children and the Law at Levin College of Law and a codirector of the Child Policy Research Institute at the University of Florida. She is a cofounder of the Center for Children's Policy Practice and Research at the University of Pennsylvania. She currently is a member of the Executive Council of the International Society of Family Law and the vice-chair of the American Bar Association Sub-Committee on Children's Rights, and is an editor of the *Family Court Review* and the *Journal of Law, Psychology and Public Policy*.

Index

Abrahams, R., 105, 109

action(s): agendas for, 77; behaving, 73, 76; children's, 69–72; consequences of, 77; describing, 78; development and, 69–72; emergence of capacity for, 72; importance of, 81; interpretation, 73, 77; in Junior Summit Program, 132–134; metaphors for, 72–78; neglect of, 70; self-organization, 73, 75; self-reflection, 73; understanding, 78

activism, 98, 99

adults: patronization of children by, 3; perspectives on providing help to children, 196–198; power over children, 211; responsibilities toward children, 40; social capital perspectives, 191–204

advertising and marketing: aggressive strategies in, 150; authoritarianism in, 143; behavior and, 149; education and, 149–150; effect on children, 3; effect on health, 148–149; focused on children, 2, 141–151; implications for voice and agency, 150–151; KGOY (kids getting older younger) phenomenon, 145; low-income children and, 158; pervasiveness of, 144–147; playing to children's vulnerabilities, 152; resistance to,

150, 151; role of behavioral science/psychology in, 147–148; in schools, 147; targeting preschoolers, 145–146; targeting "tweens," 146; values and, 149

African American children: cultural exclusion and, 106; educational process and, 14; poverty and, 104–116; preference for communal learning style, 15, 110–115; resilient schools and, 10; schooling outcomes for, 104–116; social domains of, 109–110; task performance of, 112–115; triple quandary of, 109

age, importance in granting agency, 57

ageism, effects on lives of children, 33

agency: advertising and marketing and, 150–151; changing quality of, 16; children's capacity for, 9, 10, 64; consumerism and, 142–143; defining, 9; erosion of perception of children as having, 57; exercising, 9; importance of age in granting, 57; reconstruction of, 15; religious, 62; spirituality and, 56; of sports players, 210–212; voice as expression of, 9

Aidman, A., 136

Albury, A., 113

Alderson, P., 35

Allatt, P., 174